The Professional
Practitioner
In Probation

The Professional Practitioner In Probation

By

CLAUDE T. MANGRUM, Jr., M.A., M.P.A.

San Bernardino County Probation Department
San Bernardino, California

CHARLES C THOMAS · PUBLISHER
Springfield · Illinois · U.S.A.

Published and Distributed Throughout the World by

CHARLES C THOMAS • PUBLISHER

Bannerstone House

301-327 East Lawrence Avenue, Springfield, Illinois, U.S.A.

© *1975, by* CHARLES C THOMAS • PUBLISHER

ISBN 0-398-03396-x

Library of Congress Catalog Card Number: 74-32090

*With THOMAS Books careful attention is given to all details of
manufacturing and design. It is the Publisher's desire to present books that are
satisfactory as to their physical qualities and artistic possibilities and
appropriate for their particular use. THOMAS BOOKS will be true to those
laws of quality that assure a good name and good will.*

Printed in the United States of America

C-1

Library of Congress Cataloging in Publication Data

Mangrum, Claude T.
  The Professional practitioner in probation.

  Bibliography: p.
  1. Probation officers. 2. Probation. 3. Corrections. I. Title.
HV9278.M35   364.6'3   74-32090
ISBN 0-398-03396-X

Law

PREFACE

THE PURPOSE of this book is to provide practical guidelines for the effective application of the philosophy and principles which underlie the concept of probation. The main emphasis is on the practical rather than the theoretical. This is not to belittle the importance of theory, which is necessary to organize and bind together the discrete principles. Rather, it is to more precisely focus attention on the everyday aspects of probation work.

The realization of this purpose requires a clear and realistic delineation of the functions and responsibilities of the practitioner in probation. Hopefully, this will dispel some of the aura of mystique about the work, which is meaningless, and will spotlight the practical day-to-day activities, which are quite real and all-important.

This is not a textbook designed to be used in formal training courses, although it is hoped that it will provide some practical assistance and guidance to newcomers to probation work and will be a source of stimulation to those practitioners already in the field. No attempt has been made to be scholarly in any research or philosophical sense. The thoughts expressed are simple and practical, but very important to effective probation practice. However, part of the practical approach, as well as an impetus for further development, is the selected bibliography found at the end of the text. It is hoped that the reader of this volume will be stimulated enough to follow through and study more fully at least some of the material suggested.

The philosophy of probation expressed here is that of the author. It has developed from two major sources: on-the-job experience as a probation officer, line supervisor, and administrator; and preparation for teaching various courses in the field. There is no claim that all the thoughts in this book are original. Like most people's thoughts, those of this book represent ideas gleaned from formal courses in college, wide reading in the field, informal conversation and interaction with other practitioners, and a variety of personal experiences. In such a situation, it is impossible to give credit to everyone who may have directly or indirectly contributed to the planting, germination, growth and flowering of these thoughts. The author gladly and gratefully acknowledges many such contributions, especially those which have come from my colleagues in the field and from the Chapman College and Pepperdine University students who have been in my classes.

Very special thanks are due my wife, Elaine, for typing and proofreading, and without whose dedicated efforts this work would have been far more difficult.

C.T.M.

CONTENTS

Page

Preface   v

Part One
Philosophy

Chapter

One   A PHILOSOPHY OF PROBATION   5

Two   PROBATION AND RISK-TAKING   14

Three PROBATION AND PROBLEM SOLVING   23

Four   PROBATION OFFICERS AS PACESETTERS   35

Part Two
Professionalism

Five   THE PROBATION OFFICER'S PROFESSIONAL IDENTITY .   48

Six   THE PROBATION OFFICER'S PROFESSIONAL RELATION-
       SHIPS   62

Seven DESIRABLE CHARACTERISTICS OF PROBATION OFFI-
       CERS   79

Eight THE EXERCISE OF GOOD JUDGMENT   99

Part Three
Performance

Nine   THE PROBATION INVESTIGATION   110

Ten   THE PROBATION REPORT   125

Eleven WHAT SHALL I RECOMMEND?   139

Twelve CONSISTENCY IN PERFORMANCE   150

Thirteen CASELOAD MANAGEMENT   161

Fourteen COMMITMENT TO EXCELLENCE   177

Part Four
Treatment

Fifteen   THE CONCEPT OF TREATMENT   186

Sixteen   DEVELOPMENT OF A TREATMENT PLAN   198

Seventeen THE HUMANITY OF PROBATION OFFICERS . . .   208

Eighteen   THE FUNCTION OF COERCIVE CASEWORK IN PRO-
           BATION   216
Nineteen   THE PROBLEM OF NONCOMPLIANCE   222
Twenty   SHORT-TERM TREATMENT IN PROBATION   .   .   .   231
Twenty-One   HOW TO EXTEND YOURSELF   252

Conclusion   264
Bibliography   266

The Professional
Practitioner
In Probation

Part One

PHILOSOPHY

Chapter One

A PHILOSOPHY
OF PROBATION

MODERN CONCEPTS and practices of probation have their historical and philosophical roots in earlier efforts to humanize the administration of criminal justice in a time when penalties were excessively harsh and social consciousness was awakening to the plight of individuals caught up in the worst aspects of the general social scene as well as of the criminal justice processes.

Early social reformers felt that the dignity of man as a worthwhile being in his own right demanded more personalized and humane treatment. They believed that then current methods, particularly the more harsh punishments, were more degrading and deteriorating to the individual than they were a deterrent on his own behavior or that of others. At first, concern grew that the processes of criminal justice were ineffective and changes were needed. This was followed by conscious, but not always well thought out, efforts to mitigate the harshness and inhumanity of the systems of punishment. Subsequently, legislative actions resulted in some specific procedures designed to correct some of the problems identified. Then came such things as laws providing for suspension of sentences, creation of probation and parole officers, indeterminate sentences, Juvenile Court and other methods for implementing a rehabilitative philosophy.

Through the years of practice, there have developed various techniques for dealing with offenders within the framework of the philosophy of rehabilitation by legal constraints. These have included the use of social casework practices and methods, general and occupational education, psychological and psychiatric services and other procedures taken from various disciplines and applied in the correctional setting. Specifically developed in corrections have been such processes as classification systems for determining offender needs in both field and institutional settings, parole performance predictive devices and pre-release preparation programs, among other techniques.

Today, probation is an integral and generally accepted part of the criminal justice continuum which includes law enforcement agencies, court systems, prosecution and defense personnel, probation departments, local, state and federal institutions and parole agencies. As such, and like the other components of the continuum, probation is rooted in the laws of the jurisdiction in which it functions.

The union of the legal and social basis for present day probation practice constitutes the appropriate framework for discussion of the philosophy of probation as a method for both the control and treatment of the criminal offender. It is from these two reference points that the remainder of this chapter will be developed.

CONTROL

Of the two facets of the probation officer's responsibility, the protection of community welfare must take priority. This is done through the medium of control of the offender's behavior, by which we mean setting limits of behavior and enforcing those limits.

Obviously, all behavior cannot be controlled. No matter how close supervision or surveillance may be, there will be occasions when the probation officer is not present or is not able to enforce the limits. But, in the main, clearly and firmly structuring the probationer as to what behavior will not be tolerated and following through on promised action when the limits are breached, will serve to keep most offender behavior within acceptable bounds.

The success of this activity will largely depend on the kinds of limits which are set, the manner in which they are established and the degree to which they are enforced.

Kinds of Limits

These limits are more legal than social in their definition. The client may be quite obnoxious in his interpersonal relations; but that is not against the laws of the land. While the probation officer may legitimately and wisely try to help the client develop more pleasing and acceptable personal traits and social relations because the end result might be more gratifying and beneficial to the client, he cannot require the client to be "a perfect gentleman"; he can only require him not to violate the law or the conditions of probation laid down by the Court.

A corollary of this thought is that the probation officer must not try to impose his own personal values or standards of conduct upon the client. His task is to help teach and enforce the behavioral standards of the law, and those of the community, which will help the client learn to cope with his life's situation. In every society there are behavioral requirements which, though not strictly legal, are necessary for the orderly functioning of the group. The more complex the society, the more formal are the restraints used to insure the desired conduct. The individual is not strong enough to do battle against community standards and win; the group will always outlast him. Consequently, one must learn to conduct his affairs in such a way as to minimize the potential for conflict with his fellows if he expects to survive without constant strain and tension. If the probation officer can help his client to learn this lesson, he can contribute immeasurably to the client's contentment with living, even though he may have many other problems with which to cope. In this framework, the probation officer may insist, for the client's own benefit, that he conform his daily behavior to community social expectations.

Underlying all legal and social requirements imposed on the client is a requirement imposed on the probation officer; that all attempts to set behavioral limits be realistic. Realistic in the legal and social senses discussed above and realistic in the sense that the limits are feasible, attainable and appropriate to the circumstances. Any form of control which requires more of an individual than he can do, will, sooner or later, break down. Controls which break down are no controls at all.

Manner in Which Limits Are Expressed

In many legal relations, expectations of behavior must be precisely set forth in order to be binding. We have a multitude of laws in this regard dealing with contracts of all kinds, marital relations, property concerns and others. In criminal law the defendant must be told precisely the charges against him. In correctional law most states require a probationer or parolee be given a written set of conditions under which he is expected to live. The very sound legal basis for these requirements is simply that it is unfair to require one to behave in a certain way without clearly informing him of what is expected of him.

There is also a social/psychological factor operating here. If one is continually frustrated in his efforts to conform because he does not know what is required, he will soon give up his effort and drift with the current or strike out against what he perceives as the cause of his frustration. Under these circumstances there is no possibility of successful adjustment of behavior because there is no known standard by which to judge adjustment and there is no motivation to attain a particular level; rather, there is an aimless wandering without direction or purpose.

Thus, it is imperative that limits be precisely established and clearly expressed to the client so there is no doubt in his mind, or in the mind of the probation officer, as to what is expected of the client. Of course, the Court sets many of these limits, but usually upon recommendation of the probation officer; and it is the probation officer who must explain the requirements to the client. It is also the probation officer, not the Court, to whom the client looks for direction. Additionally, the probation officer is usually the one who initiates action if the client violates the limits imposed on him. So one of the first steps in providing control is to clearly establish and explain what sort of behavior is expected of the client. This must be done firmly and authoritatively.

The setting of limits of behavior, in no uncertain terms and in a firm manner, puts the probation officer in the best position to assist the client in learning to cope with his life situation while complying with reasonable demands on him. He knows where he stands, what is expected of him, what he can and cannot do. He may not agree with the requirements and it may take intense effort on the part of the probation officer to convince him that, agree or not, he must comply for his own best interests. However, the establishment of a firm and clearly understood foundation of expectations will allow the probation officer to begin to help the client to adjust his behavior to the expectations because there is a known standard by which to judge deviation and conformity.

Degree to Which Limits Are Enforced

This same process also establishes the probation officer's position to enforce the limits of behavior and to act decisively when the limits are breached. Two aspects of such action are sureness and swiftness; it is nearly impossible to discuss one without bringing in the other.

There will inevitably be some conscious or unconscious testing of limits in the beginning. Even law-abiding people do this and many of the probation officer's clients have had a lifetime of experience in the process. Do not despair at these attempts; rather one should expect them and be prepared to deal with them. Ready and certain action will establish the ground rules of the probation officer-client relationship and demonstrate to the client that the probation officer means business.

Here again, this does not mean harsh or vindictive reaction to attempts to test the limits of behavior. Rather, it means a reiteration of the limits, not through verbal explanation, but through action. Depending on the situation and the seriousness of the testing attempt, the action may range along a continuum from mild additional restriction all the way to incarceration. But the very vital point is that decisive and appropriate action is taken, thus reinforcing what has already been established as required behavior. In this way, the probation officer is saying to the client, "I'm here to help you learn to more effectively handle your life situation, but we cannot tolerate illegal or antisocial behavior; so, cut out the game-playing and let's get down to the business of learning how to live with less conflict in your life." The client can understand this kind of communication and is far more likely to respond positively than he is where he does not know what is expected of him nor what might happen if he does not live up to expectations.

This kind of control, setting and enforcing limits on client behavior, establishes the framework within which positive treatment efforts can be made. It is to treatment that we now turn our attention.

TREATMENT

This is a favorite term of writers and practitioners in corrections. Somehow, it seems that when we talk about treatment we feel that our work is more worthwhile. The problem is that often the talk is nothing more than talk, because we are not even sure what is meant by the term which we use so freely. We are using the term here to refer to any activity which is designed to modify the behavior of the offender. This would, of course, encompass any number of activities from support of self-efforts already begun on the part of some clients to psychotherapy for the more disturbed.

The definition of this extensive range of treatment activities is not to imply that the probation officer must be adept in all of them. It is important for him to be reasonably adept in determining on which end of the continuum the client may fall; but he must also know which treatment activities fall within his defined job function and his abilities to carry out. For those needs on the psychotherapy end of the range, the probation officer must be very careful not to try to go beyond his own area of demonstrated expertise, and must be prepared to pass these treatment activities to those who have been specially trained in their application.

The other end of the continuum, however, offers more than enough opportunity to keep the probation officer busy with most of his clients. Supportive assistance, firm direction, authoritative counsel, enforcement of limits and positive problem-solving are the treatment approaches needed by a large proportion of the probation officer's clients. These are the areas in which probation officers have generally been trained, not the intensive psychotherapy techniques. If he expects to be more helpful than harmful, he must know and stay within his own abilities.

Corrections has too long been hung up on processes of restructuring personality as though everyone who violates the law is at least emotionally disturbed, if not worse. There are, of course, many correctional clients who are deeply disturbed psychologically and there are many correctional practitioners who have the expertise to deal with such offenders. But the vast majority of offenders are psychologically reasonably well-balanced and most probation officers are not properly and adequately equipped to deal with those who are not.

It is a serious and potentially disastrous error to assume that all criminal behavior is caused by sinister unknowns or deeply-imbedded psychological disturbances. We cannot explain crime merely through personality defects. More likely the offender is rather normal psychologically and his illegal act was more of an "it seemed like the best thing at the time" action. Most criminal acts are not matters of uncontrollable behavior but of circumstances which provided the opportunity at the time the offender was willing to make the choice because it seemed to him to be a pretty good choice to make; usually because he believed he had something to gain from it, either in material goods or psychic satisfaction.

We do not see the probation officer's job as that of restructuring unbalanced personalities. And even if it were his job, he generally lacks the training, experience and time, under present conditions, to do it. Rather, the probation officer's main mission is to deal practically and realistically with client behavior and with those more situational problems which led or may have led to his illegal conduct.

Most of the clients with whom the probation officer deals have many practical problems of employment, housing, finances, family relationships and others. He may also have psychological problems which to one degree or another impair his optimum functioning. But he is also most often very practically oriented; and to him, the resolution of some of his practical here-and-now problems is all he understands or really cares about for the moment. It is very difficult, if not impossible, to deal with him about some personality defect if he believes his most pressing need is to find a job in order to care for his family.

The probation officer must start with the client where he is and provide assistance in his efforts to resolve some of his most immediately pressing problems. This will serve to relieve him of some of the many pressures which he feels impinging on him. Relief from these pressures will allow the client additional energies and other resources from within himself which he can then direct toward more effectively coping with the remainder of his problems. Sometimes, this sort of practical help is all the client needs to enable him to regain his social balance and begin to adjust his life and behavior to legal and social demands.

A PRACTICAL APPROACH

We began this discussion of a philosophy of probation by observing that probation is a two-pronged effort to deal with criminal offenders through control and treatment. We have now come back to this point and must comment on the necessary balance between control and treatment. Either, to the exclusion of the other, would be lacking a needed offsetting balance.

To focus entirely on control ignores the many problems which hinder the effective social functioning of most probation clients. To think solely of treatment ignores the fact of public violation of legal standards of conduct which so often represents a long history of legal and social conflict. The illegal behavior which brings the client to public attention and the problem areas which quite likely contributed to it are both integral parts of the individual offender's situation. In trying to carry out his mission the probation officer must be able to deal with both of these elements in a realistically balanced manner.

This balance may be expressed by the phrase someone else has used, "freedom within limits." Even in setting up controls, the client is not deprived of all choices and decisions. He still has great leeway in action so long as he stays within the established boundaries of acceptable behavior. As we will discuss in more detail later, the ability to face a situation and make legally and socially acceptable choices is crucial to anyone being able to adequately cope with life. The probation client is no exception to this; he, too, must be able to so order his choices and decisions as to avoid legal and social conflict. One can learn to make proper choices only through the exercise of choices. The probation officer must work with the client in this regard, encouraging him to make his own decisions, pointing out where they may have been proper or improper decisions and helping him to understand the consequences of those decisions. Freedom of action and choice within the limits imposed by law and social demands should be the balanced approach for which the probation officer strives.

There are many elements of both control and treatment which have not been discussed here, but which will be developed in subsequent chapters. The thrust of this book is to help the probation officer to understand his mission and its requirements and to offer some suggestions which may help him to carry out this mission. The approach will be practical, dealing with the daily functions of the probation officer in a down-to-earth fashion; all within the frame of reference established in this first chapter.

Chapter Two

PROBATION AND RISK-TAKING

MANY ORDINARY ACTIVITIES of our daily lives involve risk-taking; some calculated, some unwitting, some foolish. Financial investments, crossing a busy city street, driving the freeway without seat belts fastened, heavy smoking, routine housework, constant overeating; all are examples of activity involving some kind of risk. They also illustrate the inconsistency with which we act in considering the risks in some instances, ignoring the risks in others and being unaware of the risks in still other cases.

In some respects this inconsistency is based on logic. If the consequences are not too great, one seldom gives further thought to the risks involved. On the other hand, a careful consideration of the consequences may lead one to conclude that the potential positive results are worth the risk involved.

Somehow, many people view probation as involving too much risk-taking because of the possible serious consequences of the offender's future actions. Here again, we are often inconsistent because we know little about the risks involved when we try to predict further human behavior. Or we assume the presence of risks based on emotional states rather than a careful estimate of the potential consequences.

This approach has often resulted in failure to fulfill the basic philosophy of probation; because we do not know the results of the risks we do take in terms of accurate measurement of probation performance; because we have been "burned" by some dramatic failures of probationers; because of these factors we have become risk averters and have tended to accept a lower expected value of probation program accomplishment in exchange for a smaller proportion of "mistakes." In other words, we feel much safer when we take no risks. But whatever is worthwhile in terms of human dignity and contribution is worth taking risks to achieve and to protect.

Perhaps it is time that all those involved in the administration of criminal justice take another look at the concept of probation within the framework of risk-taking. To do so leads us to ask some important questions: When should an offender get probation? Is prison rehabilitation realistic? What are the real advantages of probation? What do we do about the answers to these questions?

WHEN SHOULD AN OFFENDER GET PROBATION?

One of the most concise yet comprehensive answers to this question comes from the American Bar Association's *Standards Relating to Probationers* (p. 10):

Criteria for granting probation.

(a) The probation decision should not turn upon generalizations about types of offenses or the existence of a prior criminal record, but should be rooted in the facts and circumstances of each case. The court should consider the nature and circumstances of the crime, the history and character of the offender, and available institutional and community resources. Probation should be the sentence unless the sentencing court finds that: (i) confinement is necessary to protect the public from further criminal activity by the offender; or (ii) the offender is in need of correctional treatment which can most effectively be provided if he is confined; or (iii) it would unduly depreciate the seriousness of the offense if a sentence of probation were imposed.

(b) Whether the defendant pleads guilty, pleads not guilty or intends to appeal is not relevant to the issue of whether probation is an appropriate sentence.

The ABA criteria outlines an individualized approach to sentence decision-making which considers the needs of the community, the needs of the offender and available correctional resources in institutions and in the community. One may not fully agree with all the wording of the criteria, but it would be difficult to argue with these three considerations.

This gets to the heart of the theme of this chapter—risk-taking. Unless the offender is a threat to the welfare of the community (violent, aggressive, dangerous); or his needs cannot be met without confinement; or the impact of the sentence would tend to dilute the dignity and thrust of justice (the enormity of the offense in terms of loss, public outrage, need for deterrence);

unless these criteria are true, the defendant should be tried on probation. Indeed, he may become something of a nuisance and even may become a recidivist; but this is part of the risk we are discussing and, as will be shown, is a risk worth taking when one considers the alternatives.

IS PRISON REHABILITATION REALISTIC?

The answer to this question involves an analysis of the types of offenders in prison, the kinds of programs which operate there and the negative and positive results of the programs.

For the most part, prisons have never succeeded in rehabilitating those persons committed to them. There are many reasons for this record of failure throughout the history of penology. Among the major reasons are the changing but always uncertain and confused philosophy of punishment and incarceration, the historical fact that society has most often sent to prison vast numbers who really don't need to be there, the prevalent but unrealistic fear we have of convicted offenders and prisoners which results in overemphasis on mere custody, and programs in the prison which are not aligned with the often articulated goals of "rehabilitation."

A few general comments about these reasons for lack of success should suffice. A review of the history of penology will quickly reveal the confusion with which society has most often approached the question of incarceration. Many writers have called for a rationally based and clearly articulated philosophy to undergird our correctional efforts. Yet we still operate our prisons in an irrational manner, sending offenders there "for their own good" when what we really want to do is get revenge for their daring to break our laws and getting caught at it. There is really nothing wrong with disciplinary punishment rationally designed to rehabilitate. But there is something dishonest about all the dehumanizing things we do to people in our prisons under the guise of "treating him for his own good."

What type of offenders are in prison? This is relatively easy to answer in terms of offense categories; all one need do is to check the statistics of any state's prisons and determine how many commitments are for various offense categories. They range from murder to drunken driving, and everything in between.

It is not easy, however, to determine if all those people really needed to be sent to prison in terms of the ABA criteria because one could not know the circumstance of each case. Even so, one can legitimately and rationally question whether prison is the best way to handle such a wide variety of offenses.

Public attitudes and expectations toward both the offender and the correctional process are very important factors in the rehabilitation of offenders. In the practical areas which really count, these attitudes are frequently negative. Nationwide surveys show that less than half the respondents feel that rehabilitation is the major focus of prisons today, but most feel this *should be* the main emphasis. While a few feel the main emphasis in prisons today is protection of society, even fewer say protecting society is what the emphasis should be in the future. Almost no one believes that corrections has been very successful in rehabilitating criminals and one in five believes that time in prison will often turn someone who is not really bad into a hardened criminal. Given this lack of public confidence in the effectiveness of the prison system, it is no wonder that although most approved the idea of the halfway house, less than half favored one being located in their neighborhoods and two thirds felt their neighbors would be against it.

The public's lack of confidence in the prison system is not without solid foundation. Writers have long decried the ineffective operation of prisons, so there is no need to belabor the point here; a few comments are sufficient. Prison experience has a hardening impact on human behavior, attitudes and styles of life. No matter how good the programs are, this impact is difficult to offset. The focus of prison programs typically is not on the hope for self-fulfillment which is essential to rehabilitation. Rather, the emphasis is on custody, security, order and peace. It should be on building hope through educational opportunities, vocational training, physical and mental well-being, meaningful human relationships and a sense of worthwhile accomplishment.

It is very difficult to thoroughly understand the dehumanizing effects of the prison experience; it is easier to grasp recidivism rates. Accurately depicting success/failure rates is an impossible task in our present state of knowledge. What is success? What is failure? How can they be measured even if they can be defined? To get even a hazy picture, we must select some measurable criterion. Consider rearrests after release: as part of its Careers in Crime Program, since 1963 the FBI has kept track of offenders released from the Federal criminal justice system. As much as six years later, 65 percent had been rearrested.

This is not to say we should do away with prisons. They are needed in some cases, but not on the present scale or of the present type and emphasis. Neither are we implying that all is a failure. We are saying that prisons have not been successful enough to be counted on for rehabilitation. We must try other ways, and the judicial use of probation with an accompanying willingness to take the risk is one of these ways.

WHAT ARE THE ADVANTAGES OF PROBATION?

No matter how good the prison programs nor how low its recidivism rates may be, probation offers some advantages that the prison system by its very nature and function cannot provide. There are numerous such advantages both to the community and to the probationer. They will be briefly sketched here.

To the Community

Probation offers the best potential for a positive contribution. Society has a definite stake in well-adjusted people who are carrying on a constructive life plan. Probationers in the community who can be helped to make positive contributions to the general welfare are assets, even if they have previously violated the law.

Probation offers the best prospects for complete resocialization. The offender's problems began in the community, so it is proper that community resources be utilized to work through those problems. This is being more fully recognized in efforts to redirect emphasis to the local level, even in location and types of institutions.

Probation offers a better test of the offender's ability to function within the demands of a free society. The unnatural and isolated setting of prison often serves to damage, if not destroy, the positive influences of the local community. Removing the individual from the community for long periods of time creates problems of readjustment upon his return which are frequently so frustrating as to prohibit constructive behavior change.

Probation offers the most effective control over an individual's behavior. A vital component of the concept of probation is social control. However, control which is artificial because the offender has no way to exercise choice, is not conducive to the constructive use of control. Certainly, probation supervision that is effective provides a quicker knowledge of potentially dangerous behavior than does a release from jail or prison if it is without parole supervision.

Probation offers the best, and frequently only, means for a victim to be recompensed for material loss or personal injury. If he goes to prison the offender cannot repay, whereas a probation program under which he works can be a useful means of recompense for the victim as well as a practical lesson in responsibility for the offender.

Probation offers a far more economical program of rehabilitation. Probation supervision is probably about eight times less costly than maintenance in a prison. In addition, if the offender is working and supporting his family, the community saves on welfare expenditures as well as gains from the circulation of more wage earnings.

To the Offender

Probation offers a meaningful "second chance." It shows him that society has confidence in him and is willing to take a chance on his positive contribution to the overall welfare of the community. Many times he really wants to "make good" but feels frustrated and isolated from society, especially after a period of incarceration. This evidence of trust is often just the helpful boost he needs to succeed.

Probation offers the opportunity to avoid the stigma of being labeled an "ex-con." Such stigma causes almost insurmountable problems of securing employment, finding acceptance by others, being trusted by others; things necessary to the feeling of self-worth and dignity which any man must have if he is to be a positive factor in the community.

Probation offers more protection for his family. Frequently the innocent family suffers most from the stigma of a "jailbird" father. Many children have become rebellious and delinquent themselves after facing community ridicule and hostility as a result of a father sent to prison.

Probation offers a more constructive exercise of individual initiative. It does not foster dependence, as does imprisonment, but permits opportunity for assuming responsibility for himself, his family and his community.

Probation offers the opportunity for more positive social relationships. Thereby he is able to avoid such close association with more sophisticated criminals in prison where any weaknesses or criminal tendencies he may have will only be reinforced and intensified.

WHAT TO DO?

Probation is by no means a perfect panacea nor a magic potion to cure all the ills of the correctional system. It has, however, had some success where staff and resources have been even reasonably adequate to the task. The FBI follow-up study noted earlier revealed that probation and probation with a fine had far fewer rearrests in the six-year period than did any of the dispositions.

For many years correctional authorities have been pointing out that as many as four out of five of the people committed to prison could have quite safely remained in the community without threat to the community. Apparently, we have not been taking very many risks! Could it be that there is a correlation between our failure to take more risks and the generally recognized lack of success of the criminal justice system to rehabilitate offenders?

Chief Justice Warren E. Burger has noted that the correctional process is the payoff stage in the administration of criminal justice. Obviously, we should be doing all we can to maximize this payoff; but what can we do?

We can begin by supporting legislative efforts to remove eligibility for probation restrictions from the laws. As a matter of rehabilitative principle, all except the most serious offenses should be eligible for probation at the discretion of the sentencing court based on an individual, as opposed to a categorical, approach to justice.

With most eligibility restrictions removed, we should be willing to take more risks. The idea of having a presentence investigation and report by the probation officer is to provide the court with sufficient information about the offender to permit an enlightened and appropriate sentence; to give the court some idea of the risks involved, but not to preclude risk-taking! Assuming that probation is effective, we can greatly improve our rates of success if we are willing to give more offenders an opportunity on probation.

Of course, we cannot simply assume that probation is automatically effective. It will work to the extent we work at it! This means that people placed on probation cannot be left to go their own ways. We must provide for them individualized service designed to meet the probationer's needs and to enable him to function in the community without resorting to illegal and/or antisocial behavior. Without the sort of assistance the probation officer can provide many probationers will revert to old behavior patterns; then the whole process becomes a farce.

Probation, of course, is not without its shortcomings. These are partially due to our being in the rut of doing things in the same old way simply because that's the way it has been done before. It is time for us to break out of this rut and try some new approaches. Many probation departments are doing just this, and with considerable success. Witness the use of volunteers and paraprofessionals. Note the stress on community based programs, some subsidized by the State, rather than the traditional penal system. Look at recent emphasis on the *over reach* of criminal law and efforts to repeal statutes designed to legislate morality. Now let's look around for other innovative approaches. Let's focus on practical problem identification and goal-directed treatment instead of trying to restructure personalities. Let's involve in ways of keeping people out of the criminal justice system instead of trying to pick up the pieces after they are shattered by it.

Probation is risk-taking! But the results are worth it!

Chapter Three

PROBATION AND PROBLEM SOLVING

A LARGE PROPORTION of the clients a probation officer sees are very likely to be nearly overwhelmed by various personal and social problems. These include financial, employment, housing, transportation, marital, familial, legal, physical, emotional, psychological and many other problems which disrupt orderly living. Many of these problems are, of course, interrelated; influencing and being influenced by one another. It is virtually impossible to separate them, unravel each thread and follow it to its ultimate source. Sometimes, looking at a situation like this, the probation officer himself may feel overwhelmed by the magnitude of the client's needs.

Neither the probation officer nor the client can afford to just give up and not try merely because of the size of the task. The problems will not go away all by themselves; something must be done about them. It is part of the probation officer's job, in conjunction with the client, to identify as nearly as possible what the problems are and what can be done about them. This is, obviously, no easy task and may not offer great reward. But a beginning must be made somewhere and if the probation officer does not start, there is a great probability that no one else will.

The crucial question then arises as to where and how to begin. Obviously, neither the probation officer nor anyone else is going to quickly and permanently resolve all the problems every client has, especially the many-faceted situations which characterize most of his clients. The decision as to where and how to begin is crucial, because it establishes the framework for so much which will follow.

Here, as in many decision-making situations, one's choices reflect to a large degree his basic philosophy and beliefs about the various factors involved in the situation.

In the probation setting, the way the probation officer chooses to begin to work for the resolution of the client's problems will, among other things, be the result of how he views his basic mission and what he sees as the scope of his job. Perhaps it will help to clarify some of these points if we give some time to a discussion of what the probation officer can and cannot expect to accomplish as part of his job.

WHAT THE PROBATION OFFICER CANNOT DO

We begin our discussion with what the probation officer cannot expect to accomplish in order to consider the limitations under which he must work. We can then more properly and profitably establish the parameters of the positive issue of what he can expect to do.

As a general consideration we can say that the probation officer can seldom, if ever, meet all the needs of his clients. On an even more limited scope he can probably not do all the things he would like to accomplish with and on behalf of the client. Drawing the limits even tighter, the probation officer will seldom accomplish all those things he may set out to do as he begins his work with the client. All this is not to imply that the probation officer's job is overly restricted, nor that he cannot expect some success in what he does. It does, however, point up the importance of being realistic in his expectations; of knowing the limitations involved in trying to meet client needs; of being aware of the many variables that can interfere with his best efforts; and of understanding the fundamental validity of the social casework principle of setting limited and attainable goals. In one context or another we will get at all of these issues as we go along. At this point, it will suffice to think in more general terms of some of the very real, and often quite frustrating, limitations within which the probation officer may be forced to work.

Legal and Political Constraints

The probation officer may not be able to respond to some of the needs of the client due to legal considerations, including orders of the court. It is his responsibility to enforce the law and the conditions of probation. He does not have the authority or right to ignore or circumvent these, even if he feels they stifle his response to client needs. The probation officer may work to change the law or try to convince a judge to modify a term of probation; but until the condition is altered, he must uphold the legal requirements and the orders of the court. An example of such a situation would be mandatory jail time or fine, even when probation is granted, and the client might suffer financially or his family may suffer because he must go to jail. The probation officer cannot void such orders, as he is sometimes asked to do and may wish he could do, because they are beyond the scope of his authority. Such orders, however, may very well be detrimental to a treatment program. In such a circumstance the probation officer's efforts to implement an appropriate treatment plan could be stymied, or at least curtailed.

Sometimes the probation officer may not be able to accomplish certain things due to public concern or political pressures. He may not like this situation but he must recognize that it is a fact of life and that it might seriously hinder the implementation of a needed treatment plan. This is not to imply that the probation officer meekly surrenders to pressure to the detriment of treatment efforts. It is merely to point out one of the realities of our society with which the probation officer may be forced to contend. Unfortunately, there are influential persons and groups who, because of their own interests, desires, or biases, are able to exert pressures on and/or against others to their own ends. Usually the probation officer's client is on the receiving end of such pressures and may thereby be the victim of a failure by the probation officer or other community agencies to respond to his identified needs.

If, for whatever reasons, the probation officer is not permitted to implement what he believes to be the most appropriate treatment plan, he must recognize this, fall back to his *second line of defense* and do the best he can under the given circumstances. It is rather futile to fret over what cannot be done as the fretting will dissipate the time and energies and, perhaps, other valuable resources of both the probation officer and the client.

Lack of Public Commitment

This is somewhat related to the preceding consideration as it concerns the limitations placed on the probation officer due to lack of general community support for rehabilitative efforts. The prevailing attitudes of the community can and do have a very forceful impact on the probation officer's work. His is a public agency supported by local taxation. If the taxsetters and taxpayers do not believe in rehabilitation for criminal offenders or believe it is not worth the high costs, there will be little financial support allocated to the agency and its work. Obviously, this will severely curtail what can be done on behalf of probationers, as well as hinder the potential effectiveness of what is done. On the other hand, firm public financial support will open doors to effort and achievement which can make the probation officer's task much easier, more enjoyable and more effective.

Financial support is not the only important form of community commitment. Also of importance is a general atmosphere of at least enough superficial understanding of the *crime* and *criminal* problem to create a willingness to give the offender a *second chance*. This positive community attitude is very crucial to the effectiveness of so much of the probation officer's work because acceptance or lack of acceptance in the community has a lot to do with positive attitudes on the part of the client. It is the members of the community who provide, or deny, employment opportunities which are so important to the stability of the client. It is out of the general community that various groups develop which are specifically interested in working for offender rehabilitation. The existence of such positive forces in the community can add immeasurably to the overall effect of the probation officer's work with the client. The lack of such forces can greatly hinder, and quite often almost completely negate, his best efforts.

Lack of Resources

Perhaps, this is the most serious limitation placed on the probation officer's activities. It may well be that there are no legal or political barriers to the implementation of an ideal treatment plan. There may be full support for such efforts by the court and no persons or groups may exist who try to put pressure on the probation officer to do or not do certain things in behalf of the client's needs. It is certainly often the case that the general public is frequently unaware of or uninterested in local rehabilitative processes. Even if legal, political or public limitations do not exist, the lack of agency, client, or probation officer resources can seriously hamper, if not negate, treatment efforts.

The lack of agency resources may be the result of the lack of community commitment to and support of the rehabilitative philosophy. It may be due to lack of financial resources in a limited tax-base community, even if public attitudes are positive and supportive. It may be a problem of optimum allocation of available resources on the part of the agency head or the lack of dynamic activity on the part of its leadership. The probation officer can generally do little, if anything, about the lack of agency resources as this very important responsibility belongs to others. This is not to say he has no responsibility whatsoever, as we will see when we discuss this point later in Chapter Four. Often, however, the probation officer will have to learn to live with such limitations and do what he can personally to increase his effectiveness in working with clients, recognizing that he will never attain his potential if he is hindered by lack of agency resources.

Another very important limitation to the probation officer's implementation of treatment plans is the lack of client resources. We do not refer here to financial resources; the typical probation client seldom has much to rely on, even though quite modest means could allow him to purchase needed services which neither the agency nor the community provide without costs. One of the given limitations under which the probation officer must work is the scarcity of client finances. However, more importantly, the lack of other less tangible client resources also places severe limitations on what the probation officer might hope to accomplish. A history of failure and being put down; the resultant sense of defeat and loss; lack of opportunity to participate in and benefit from culturally enriching experiences; a *what's-the-use* attitude due to constant social rejection; health problems resulting from long neglect or lack of money to pay for care; setbacks in acceptance or employment opportunity because of his *record;* lack of meaningful but necessary support from family; one could go on and on enumerating the background and attitudinal areas which may be present with many probationers and which demonstrate the lack of positive resources on his part. When the probation officer is faced with this sort of situation, what he can hope to accomplish with the client is limited. Of course, the probation officer must work with whatever resources are available, trying to find latent reserves which are not apparent at first examination and developing these and the more obvious resources possessed by the client to their highest potential. But he must always be aware that lack of client resources may be a serious hindrance to the achievements outlined in his treatment plan and that there may be very little he can do to overcome these limitations of the client.

The lack of personal resources on the part of the probation officer can also place severe limitations on what he can do. This is an area which is, for the most part, totally his own responsibility and one about which he can do a great deal to overcome the limitations. Although the probation officer may be genuinely concerned for the needs of his clients and may be highly motivated to respond to those needs, the effectiveness of his response can be aborted if he lacks the essential expertise to meet some client needs. The lack may be due to not having the knowledge, training, or experience required for the situation at hand. It could be due to personal characteristics or problems which restrict the development of expertise. Whatever the case, this is a personal thing with the probation officer and one for which he is responsible to act. He can seek the assistance of others to resolve personal problems; he can improve the state of his knowledge through study, either formally or informally; and he can expand his training in both conventional and unconventional ways. It is his responsibility as a professional to be aware of and work to overcome the gaps in his expertise which may hinder his work with his clients. This is not a quick or easy thing to do; it takes time to learn and develop. Meantime, the probation officer must recognize his personal limitations and how they may hamper the implementation of plans to meet client needs.

The probation officer who is not aware of these factors which can and do limit what he can hope to accomplish, and who does not learn to adjust his planning and actions accordingly, will continually be frustrated. A useful beginning step in working with a new client is for the probation officer to determine as clearly as possible what are the limiting factors operating in the case. This helps him to define the areas where he can most effectively expend his time and energies and the areas to avoid because they would be an unnecessary waste of time and energy. The situation described above is obviously not the ideal for responding to client needs, but it is the reality of the probation officer's milieu. Seldom does life provide one with the ideal setting in which to pursue his desires. The setting in which the probation officer works is even less ideal because of the limitations we have mentioned as well as the very nature of the illegal and anti-social behavior of the clients with whom he works.

WHAT THE PROBATION OFFICER CAN DO

At this point, one might be tempted to respond, "with all these potential limitations facing the probation officer, why should he bother? It seems as though he can expect to accomplish very, very little under the circumstances." The answer, of course, has to be, "Because it needs to be done. Because it is the probation officer's job and if he does not do it, no one else is likely to. Because, despite all the potential limitations, there are some things he can do." Many of these have already been hinted at in the discussion above; we now must look at them in more detail.

Limit the Scope of Activity

One of the first things the probation officer can do is to analyze the situation to determine what outside variables operate to limit the potential for action. This helps to delineate the arena in which he can act. Although the limitations may be confining and frustrating, at least he knows where to focus his attention and action. A psychological advantage to this is that it forces those involved to more realistically and effectively use the available resources. The more limited field of action helps one to give undivided attention to a few concerns rather than spread himself too thin in his anxiety to cover every possible area of need. Trying to attack a large number of variables with limited choices and resources dissipates time and energy to the disadvantage of everyone. On the other hand, giving careful attention to how to best attack a few of the most important variables will enhance the potential for successful resolution of those problem areas.

The probation officer who is not realistic in estimating the most advantageous course of action is setting himself and his client up for failure, and perhaps recriminations. We have already taken the position that it is not the probation officer's job to restructure an unbalanced or unintegrated personality. In the first place, it is a mistake to assume such action is required, or even appropriate, in many cases. Most often the probation officer is not trained for the kind of probing psychotherapy needed when the client does manifest such personality problems. Neither does the probation officer have the time to devote to such a long-term process. Generally, his best and only course of action in this situation is to refer the client to those who have the expertise to follow through on such personality needs.

One of the greatest problems in corrections has been to measure success. It is difficult, if not almost impossible, to establish external criteria to measure personality changes, insight gained, or new psychic awareness. However, whether practical problems are solved can be more objectively determined and does not need to wait for the *long-term results;* they can be seen immediately.

This consideration and the other limitations discussed above are all the more reason for the probation officer to be aware of and practice the basic treatment principle of setting reasonably limited and attainable goals. We will come back to this principle several times in the pages ahead. It is sufficient for our purposes here to simply note that one of the basic professional responsibilities of the probation officer is to always deal with his client in the way which offers the best potential for practical success, rather than the pursuit of high-sounding and often unreachable goals somewhere in the future.

Concentrate on Practical Problem-Solving

This thought is a natural consequence of limiting the scope of activity; but is not to imply that the probation officer has no concern for emotional, attitudinal, or personality problems of the client. It is merely to emphasize that there must be a realistic evaluation of what he and the client can most effectively do to meet the client's immediate needs.

Most of the probation officer's clients have a basic here-and-now orientation. This has generally been the history of criminal offenders as they struggle with the basics of living. The poverty, cultural deprivation, setbacks and failures which characterize so many probation clients have left them little time to be concerned with their personality or psychological shortcomings. It has usually been a real accomplishment for many of them to "keep their heads above water" in trying to secure the basic necessities of life. This underscores an important advantage of this practical problem-solving approach: the client can readily understand and respond to such basic efforts because they are really extensions of his previous experience and represent gratifying success if he can work out some of the solutions.

The problems which beset many probationers remind one of the juggler who is having to juggle more balls than his abilities will allow him to effectively handle. The result is that he becomes confused, perhaps tired of trying, and he begins to drop a few balls or even lets them all fall. If the number of balls is reduced so that the remaining ones are within his ability to handle, he can comfortably and reasonably well keep juggling for a long time. He may not, even yet, do a perfect act, but certainly he can perform much better than before.

When the probation officer concentrates on assisting the client to resolve some of his practical problems, he is setting the stage where the client can much more effectively handle those which remain. The first step, of course, is to clearly identify just what are those problems. Again, we need to look at the here-and-now and focus on such things as: lack of a job to provide at least minimum support for himself and his family; lack of transportation to get to jobs available within his skills; how to have a suspended driver's license reinstated for employment purposes, or how to get a driver's license if he never possessed one; how to get a basic set of tools needed to carry out the job he can secure; how to conduct himself in the job interview; and the importance of punctuality and dependability if he gets the job. These and many other seemingly small but significant areas are among those with which the probation officer can immediately deal and begin to demonstrate to the client that someone cares and will work hard to assist him, and that he does have potential for functioning successfully.

The detail with which we have here examined one possible problem area, employment, can be repeated with many other areas that interfere with the client's satisfactory living; areas such as housing, marital relationships, parent-child relationships, finances, education for the children and the adults, neighborhood conflicts, conflicts with legal authorities, problems with community social agencies which may be involved with the client's family, health problems, and many other everyday-living problem areas. There is usually no lack of practical things on which to concentrate if the probation officer will get down to basics and make optimum use of available resources.

Direct Behavior Toward a Goal

We have previously noted that the task of the probation officer is to deal with behavior, especially the behavior which led to the client's conflict with legal authorities. Another aspect of dealing with behavior is focused on client action in his efforts to resolve his problems. The probation officer must be constantly alert to insure goal-directed behavior on the part of the client, and in his own actions as well.

Once the problem areas have been identified, the probation officer and the client together must answer some other questions: Can the problem be resolved, or is it the sort of thing which is beyond the time or ability of those involved? What is needed to bring the problem to a satisfactory resolution; that is, what goals do we set, the attainment of which will signal a resolution of the problem? How do we go about reaching the goal?

It is here, in the specific steps toward the goal, that both probation officer and client must be alert to anything which would distract them from the goal and from their actions to gain it. There are many, many pressures and desires which could force or lure one from the path, and some detours might be interesting to follow. But those involved must remember that, given the limited time and resources with which they have to work, any detour is potentially disastrous. Therefore, they must focus on the business at hand, if they hope to reach the goal they have set.

Plan for the Future

Thus far, our discussion has centered on the immediate response to the here-and-now problems of the client. Lest we be misunderstood and fail to present a balanced picture, we must comment on other problem areas, especially those involving emotional disturbance and personality deficiencies.

It is obvious that many people in our society suffer from such pathological conditions and some are found among probationers. The probation officer would be remiss in his professional responsibility if he merely ignored such problems. He would also be remiss if he delved into areas beyond his abilities. As we have already said, he must be able to recognize such problems when he encounters them and, hopefully, make referral to proper persons in the community to deal with them.

This is often a process of longer duration than the probation officer can afford, even if he had the expertise. Also, resources for dealing with these problems may not be presently available in the community. In this circumstance the probation officer must, with the client, do some long-term planning to secure the therapy needed to enable the client to more effectively cope with his environment.

There is no conflict between such long-term planning, perhaps to continue after the probation officer is no longer involved in the matter, and practical efforts to resolve immediately pressing problems. Both can exist simultaneously and those involved can be working to resolve both conjointly.

The goal of future planning is to insure that the client can, without outside assistance, cope with his environment in a positive, legal and socially acceptable fashion. Both he and the probation officer must constantly work toward this end.

Chapter Four

PROBATION OFFICERS
AS PACESETTERS

THROUGHOUT THE HISTORY of penology those involved in working in the field have often been in the vanguard of change and development in penal philosophy and practice. They have frequently been the catalyst for innovation, and often the target of criticism for their "mollycoddling" of offenders as the result of new and improved methods. Correctional personnel have had to lead the way in most instances because the general community, due to lack of awareness or unconcern, has not been ready to move ahead with correctional reform.

Of course, those in the field have sometimes lagged behind general social development and change and have been forced to revamp out-dated procedures. In some instances, impetus for this has been legislative action in response to perceived needs for change due to personal philosophy of legislators or political pressures on them. In other cases correctional changes have been brought about through public demands or as the result of serious, and often very tragic, activity among correctional inmates which usually has triggered concern for change.

More often, however, the lag has been within the general public sector and has created serious hindrances to correctional change. This is part of the explanation for a slow, up-and-down development of correctional philosophy and practice.

Today, probation officers must continue this tradition of leading the way in developments in their field. There are sound reasons for taking the position that probation officers are pacesetters and there are several important ways in which they can fulfill this responsibility. These will be discussed within the framework of practical action which is the thrust of this book.

35

WHY PROBATION OFFICER SHOULD BE
PACESETTERS

Probation officers are not too much different from others in asking the *why* when told to do something. When we here say to him that he should be out front leading the way, it is natural that he would want to know why we take such a position. There are, perhaps, many reasons one could advance to support the position, but we will only discuss three of the major ones: the *helping profession* tradition of probation, the unique *position of knowledge* and the *power of expertise*.

The Tradition of Probation as a Helping Profession

Probation officers, probably following the lead of their social work colleagues, have long considered themselves as part of the *helping professions*. It is in this context that we have already made references to probation officer functions which are to *help, assist* and *work toward* resolution of problems.

Throughout its history, probation practice has included many activities under the *helping* umbrella, many of which involved the probation officer doing something for the client. It might be some kind of direct material or financial assistance to help get the client "on his feet"; or it might be some activity which helps him to work through some everyday problem. Perhaps it is some manipulation of the client's environment to relieve a source of pressure beyond his ability to handle; or it may be acting as a go-between for the client and some other agency in the community with which he must relate but with which he may be having difficulties of communication or service. It could be a matter of friendly advice on the technicalities of something the client is trying to accomplish for himself; or it might be a counseling effort in which there is a serious and progressive series of discussions designed to uncover, understand and correct some behavioral shortcoming of the probationer.

As we can readily see, there are all kinds of ways, degrees and levels of *helping*. But is this what *help* really means? Are these activities geared toward merely doing something for the client or are they planned toward the end of bringing him to the place where he is able to work through his own problems without the supportive or directive assistance of the probation officer? It should be obvious that merely doing something for the client, that is, just giving him something or solving some problem for him or easing some pressure point for him, will not be of most value to him in the long run because such action encourages him to continue a dependency on the probation officer's aid.

If, on the other hand, *helping* takes place within a framework of planned activity designed to enable the client to more adequately cope with his environment and function without resorting to illegal or antisocial behavior, then the probation officer's *helping* is of great value. In this situation he can do some things *for* the client, although most activity will be done *with* him, without fostering a dependency which in the long-run will be detrimental to the client and to the successful functioning of the probation officer in his duties and responsibilities.

The thing we are talking about here is the question of the *help* offered by the probation officer. One of the things he must keep in mind is that the assistance provided to the client must be important and meaningful to him. The things the probation officer does must be perceived by the client as meeting some felt need. The actions the probation officer takes must be understood by the client as relating to his welfare. If these things and actions of the probation officer are not meaningful to the client, they will be just things and just actions having no significant impact on changing client behavior. Thus they are merely a waste of time, energy and resources; something which the client, the probation officer and the community cannot afford.

A Unique Position

The probation officer occupies a unique position between the community and the client partially as the result of his assigned responsibility to protect the welfare of the community from the offender who has been placed under his supervision, and partially because he is the community representative to provide services to the offender. In this context the probation officer fulfills the function of a go-between and, in a sense, has a "foot in each camp." This accounts for his two-way responsibility to both community and client which we have already discussed. It also establishes the point of reference for exploring why the probation officer's position is one reason why he should be a pacesetter.

Vis-a-Vis the Client

By definition, all of the probation officer's clients have had at least minimal conflict with the legal authorities. In a large proportion of the cases they also have some history of antisocial conflicts to a greater or lesser degree. This means that the probation officer is exposed to a very wide range of problem people, places and situations as he moves about the community trying to fulfill his responsibilities. Because of the very nature of his job, he sees the needs and knows the demands of both the law-abiding society and the offender population.

His exposure, however, goes far beyond the relatively small number of offenders with whom he works. The offenders have families and relatives with whom he also comes in contact, and many of these are beset with problems similar to those of the probationer. In addition, there are neighbors and acquaintances of the client who are quite likely to share many of his problems. Thus, as the probation officer's contacts, exposure and area of work are extended beyond direct responsibility for the client, he takes on the enlarged group as *secondary clients*. The very fact of contact with the larger group entails some responsibility for them.

From this vantage point, the probation officer sees the scope and variety of the needs of a larger number of the citizens of the community. He is aware of the resources available in the community to respond to those needs, and he knows the gaps in those resources. He sees the results of needs existing but unmet, and knows the all too often tragic consequences of the failure of the community to provide needed resources.

Vis-a-Vis the Community

In relation to the community, the probation officer also occupies a unique position. His legal identify and his function were created by the community as part of the criminal justice apparatus for service to the community regarding those who offend against its laws. Thus, he works in and for the community and he and the community share responsibilities to one another.

The responsibility of the probation officer to the community, in addition to that of protecting its general welfare, is to perform his assigned tasks effectively and efficiently; to do his job and to be good at it. He knows what the community can require of his offender-clients in terms of their behavior and it is his function to enforce these legitimate requirements. Of course, he must be able to distinguish between requirements that are legitimate and realistic and those that are impractical and impossible to enforce. He may sometimes find himself in the position of an interpreter of offender problems and behavior to the community. This is the essence of his *go-between* functions.

Implicit in the relationship between the probation officer and the community is the responsibility of the community to provide the support, both financial and moral, he needs to carry out his assigned functions. The level of this support varies from place to place and from time to time in the same place, but the very act of creating the probation officer's position implies that he will be given the tools with which to do the job. Also implicit in this relationship is the responsibility of the community to listen to the "expert testimony" of the probation officer with regard to conditions and needs of those with whom he works on behalf of the community. Obviously, this is not always the case in real-life situations, but the community which does not heed the feedback provided by its own representatives is headed for even more serious and widespread problems.

If the community has not made necessary overt commitments of support and response implicit in its relationship to the probation officer, it is his responsibility to ask—even demand—that this be done. The probation officer has a right to ask for and expect to receive such support and, if it is not forthcoming, the responsibility to demand it. To do less is to be derelict in one's duty.

This reciprocal relationship, and the responsibilities of both parties implied in it, gives the probation officer a "foot-in-thedoor" position of strength in dealing with the community. This leads us to the next point of discussion, namely, the probation officer's *power of expertise.*

The Power of Expertise

Here we address the probation officer's responsibility to be a pacesetter because of who he is, the position he occupies and what he knows; in short, because of his professional expertise he must be a leader. Ideally, the individual probation officer has the knowledge and experience which make him professionally expert; certainly, the position he occupies implies such expertise. In any case, it is proper to expect the probation officer to exercise his responsibility to be *out front* as an expert in his field.

More than most others, the probation officer should be aware of existing problems in the community generally and for various individual citizens; he should be aware of needs not met and why they are so; he should know what resources are available, what are lacking and what specific resources are needed for response to specific needs. He is the professional with a special kind of knowledge of community needs and of ways to deal with those needs.

This provides the probation officer with the power of professional expertise. When this is coupled with the implicit responsibility of the community to listen to him, the probation officer should be ready to speak out; to use the strength of his position to aggressively lead his community in positive response to existing but unmet needs of the citizens of that community.

With this orientation to why the probation officer should be a pacesetter, that is, because of the tradition of probation as a helping profession, his unique position and his power of expertise, the next logical question is addressed to the *how to do it.*

IN WHAT WAYS MAY THE PROBATION OFFICER BE A PACESETTER?

There are probably many ways in which the probation officer can daily fulfill his responsibility to be a leader, even as he goes about many routine duties. Here we want to consider three of the more important ways which will undoubtedly include many of the more routine ones. They are concerned with agency development, advocacy and action for social reform.

Agency Development

We have already noted that one of the limitations with which the probation officer may have to contend is the lack of agency resources and leadership. We now take the position that part of the probation officer's professional responsibility is to individually work toward the overall improvement and development of his agency as much as it is his responsibility to extend and develop his own expertise. Of course, it will be more difficult to accomplish the former because he does not have the same degree of control over agency development as he does over self-development. We will be returning frequently to discuss self-development, so our present discussion will be limited to agency development.

Even the very best probation departments blessed with dynamic and wise leadership and with other resources, can be improved. As the world turns, situations and people change. So must the probation officer and the probation agency. Client needs may change, the nature of offenses may change and the nature of the clients themselves may change. This means that probation professionals must be flexible and have the ability to adjust and modify philosophies and practice in order to adequately meet changing conditions.

One of the unfortunate aspects of being an administrator in most organizations, whether business, public service, educational or others, is getting away from direct contact with organizational clientele. This often results in losing sight of client nature and needs, not because of lack of interest, but because of lack of contact and of attention being forced elsewhere. One of the things that the probation administrator desperately needs from line-level probation officers is information regarding what the conditions are and what is really happening out in the community. The unique position of the probation officer in relating to his clients and the community is one of bases for his responsibility to help keep his administration informed.

Another facet of this responsibility is to keep probation administrators stirred up; not to cause a hassle, but to demand action, leadership and adjustment where needed. This is not to imply that all administrators need to be goaded to movement. Rather, it is to emphasize that the probation officer has the right and duty to make reasonable demands that his agency administrators know of his needs in relation to his job functions and that they aggressively work with him to fill those needs. The probation officer who *knows the score* in his community and who passively sits by without demanding his agency stir itself to respond effectively to community needs is failing in his basic responsibility as a knowledgeable professional.

The probation officer can help his agency's development by making wise use of what facilities and resources are available in the agency without wasting them. In many organizations there are resources to do the job but, because they are not used to best advantage, they always seem to be in short supply. This is by no means to say all agencies have sufficient resources if only they were used properly; this is simply not the case. It is, however, to emphasize that the judicious use of available resources can greatly extend their scope and effectiveness.

An example might help to make this thought clearer. Some probation departments have psychological staff available to provide projective and diagnostic services for working with clients. If the probation officer makes referral to those resources in order to get professionally obtained data to help determine a client's potential for violent behavior or to set up a proper treatment plan for a client, he is making wise use of such resources. However, if he should make such a referral merely because he does not know what to recommend to the court for a client and he hopes the psychologist can tell him what to do, he is shirking his own decision-making responsibility and wasting scarce resources which could have better been used in other matters. Any waste of resources is deplorable and inexcusable for a professional.

The expansion and development of present resources and the cultivation of new ones is another way the probation officer can assist his agency's development. Many well-functioning and beneficial programs are the result of small beginnings when one person began to capitalize on a new resource. Volunteer programs in the probation setting have often begun this way. The probation officer may be aware, through his contacts in the community, of some such small resource which can be cultivated and developed to provide expanded services by the agency. If he does not remain alert to make use of such possibilities, the probation officer will miss some very valuable and viable resources and his own and his agency's work may be much less effective than it otherwise could be. There is really no way to say to the probation officer, "watch this, or that, or be on the lookout for the other." We can only admonish him to always be alert to opportunities to strengthen agency resources through development and cultivation of new possibilities where they may exist.

Advocacy

The probation officer can be a pacesetter by being an advocate, by speaking out, for general community needs and for specific client needs. This involves a twofold responsibility: to the community to help inform interested citizens of what are the needs of correctional clients, what things must be done to meet those needs and what will be the likely results if the problems are allowed to exist unresolved; and to the client to be a voice in his behalf.

Clients of the probation officer are among those persons most directly and dramatically affected by the lack of community resources and they are those least able to have any influence to remedy the situation. Most groups are at least beginning to organize to articulate their own needs, including unions of many kinds, professional associations, ethnic groupings, consumer groups, poverty groups, and even welfare recipients; but the probationer has no group to speak for him.

In his advocacy, the probation officer must speak out against the social conditions, injustices, rejections, isolation and stigma which spawn crime. He must take a strong and vocal stand in opposition to the existence of inadequate physical and mental health conditions; to substandard housing, poverty, discrimination, exploitation, unfair detention and unreasonable court delays; and to a host of other conditions which characterize the living situation of his clients and their contacts with the criminal justice system.

The probation officer should be in the vanguard of those who demand that adequate allocation of resources be made to deal with client needs. Throughout history, the government and the citizenry have been very reluctant to provide sufficient financial resources to properly carry out rehabilitative programs for criminal offenders. It is still so today in nearly every jurisdiction; funds are scarce and most government officials and private citizens are less concerned about correctional needs than they are about general tax rates. Consequently, correctional services have a low priority almost everywhere. The probation officer must raise his voice, both as a professional and as a taxpaying citizen of the community, to demand that correctional services be supported adequately enough to get the job done.

This kind of advocacy can be justified on several grounds: moral, in that any citizen who has basic needs should be helped to cope with his situation; professional, in that the meeting of these needs is the only hope we have to *correct* the offender; social, in that the correction of the offender provides the most effective means of protecting the welfare of the community; economic, in that it costs less over the long run to rehabilitate than to either pay the bill for crime detection or to incarcerate; and practical, in that if the probation officer does not speak out no one else likely will.

Action for Social Reform

Advocacy is commendable and necessary, but to speak out is not enough; there must also be positive action if lasting effect is to be gained. The emphasis here is not just on taking a specific position on issues relating to correctional needs and social conditions in the community and speaking out in support of that position; it is on active and sometimes aggressive participation to obtain the resources to meet those needs and alleviate those conditions. This emphasis is expressed in the old adage, "Actions speak louder than words" and in the vernacular "Put your money where your mouth is." The probation officer who speaks out in advocacy is only beginning to carry out this aspect of his responsibility. He must go to the next level, that of specific, positive, planned action.

As an individual, there is not a great deal the probation officer can expect to accomplish in securing the necessary resources to either meet broad correctional needs or change general social conditions. His best prospect for successful action is to join with various organizations who are working toward the same ends. Here he can be more than a lone voice or even merely one member of the organization; for it is here that he is most likely to be able to capitalize on his position of knowledge and power of expertise. In such an organization, he is dealing with individuals who are generally much better informed and who are far more interested in doing something about these conditions than is the case of the public generally. This concern can be the focal point of the probation officer's efforts to rally group support to use the organization's energies and influence to help rouse the larger community to action. Thus, he increases his own individual strength, energy and influence for social action many times over.

It may well be that in some communities there are no such organizations with which the probation officer can join forces. In this case, he may need to be the initial impetus to form a group which then can blend its strength and powers to influence others to action. Such a move will obviously need to begin slowly and small as the probation officer is able to convince one, then another and another citizen of concern and influence to join him. But such a small group can enlarge itself by convincing still other individuals to join in, thereby expanding its influence until it does have significant impact on the greater community.

Closely related to, yet a little different from, action to meet correctional needs and alleviate unhealthy social conditions is action directed at the prevention of criminal and delinquent behavior. This is a most important facet of the probation officer's responsibility to be a pacesetter in social action because it is the essence of much of his professional expertise. Prevention includes the general improvement of social conditions which may contribute to the development of environments, influences and opportunities for successful and rewarding experiences.

The probation officer must be directly involved in such prevention activities because it is his professional duty to help prevent individuals from becoming his clients and because, if prevention efforts are not effective and those individuals *do* become his clients, he knows much more about their situation and can probably more readily develop rapport with them than if he had never been involved. He also has some moral responsibilities toward such efforts simply because he is a citizen of the community and owes, as does every other citizen, the disadvantaged opportunities to share in his advantages.

Specifically what an individual probation officer may do to fulfill his responsibility to be a pacesetter and how he may decide to go about it will, of course, depend on local and personal circumstances. That is as it should be because each probation officer and his situation is different from every other and the need for flexible adjustments negates the establishing of hard and fast rules. But the underlying principle is the same for all; it is inconsistent with his position and professional responsibility for the probation officer to merely be a passive follower—he must be a leader.

Based on the various reasons we have considered in this chapter, the probation officer has an obligation to be a pacesetter, an obligation to his community, his clients, his profession, and to himself. His personal survival in his position and the welfare of his community may very well be at stake if he reneges on this obligation.

Part Two

PROFESSIONALISM

Chapter Five

THE PROBATION OFFICER'S PROFESSIONAL IDENTITY

I N RECENT YEARS there have been a number of articles in various correctional journals which have examined the question of whether probation officers are professionals. No matter what position the authors expound, they invariably stir up a lot of discussion among probation officers because many of them individually have not settled the question in their own minds. In the field generally, although to a lesser degree perhaps, organizations of probation officers also struggle to officially establish their position on the question. When reading the articles and listening to the discussions one begins to feel the intensity of the struggle and begins to sympathize with the search for a distinct professional identity.

There is a great deal at stake in the answer to the question in terms of its impact on probation officers as well as in terms of the meaning of the answer to society at large. So it is no wonder that responsible people in probation continue to write, discuss, struggle and search for a convincing answer. This chapter joins in that search and will take us into two broad areas of discussion: (1) an examination of the unity of specific factors which indicate that a particular field of endeavor may be properly referred to as a profession, and an analysis of probation practice in terms of how it does or does not fit the criteria; and (2) an attempt to specify just what is the professional identity of probation practice.

THE MEANING OF "PROFESSIONAL"

This term is used frequently and loosely in many different contexts to mean many different things, but generally those meanings revolve around three central, though broad and sometimes overlapping, ideas.

Professional may refer to someone who *really knows his business* and demonstrates a highly skilled competence, as a medical doctor, a lawyer, or a "really good auto mechanic." The term may be used to designate one who is paid for rendering specific services in contrast to voluntary donations of time or services, as a veterinarian, a professional athlete, or a "professional thief." Professional is also used to designate someone who demonstrates a high degree of dedication to his job despite adversity, as a minister, a soldier, or the performer who believes "the show must go on."

These three areas are, respectively, a matter of expertise, a matter of recognized position, and a matter of attitude. They are not entirely mutually exclusive; there is some overlapping. However, these three areas will provide direction for our examination of the meaning of *professional*.

A Matter of Expertise

One characteristic of a true professional is the mastery of his particular field of knowledge and practice; a mastery which is not attained overnight, but which takes long years of education, training and practical experience to develop the special competence which distinguishes him from others who only *dabble* in the field.

The beginning of gaining this competence is usually several years of formal education at the graduate school level, or its equivalent, where one is immersed in the study and discussion of the specific knowledge which makes up his area of specialization. Usually the student has already been exposed to most broader aspects of his own and related fields and this specialized in-depth study of more advanced theories, concepts and practices constitutes the basis of his mastery of the knowledge he will need in later performance. It is here that his philosophies, attitudes and basic directions of interests are crystalized. It is during this period of formal study that he lays the foundations of knowledge on which he will later erect his methods of practicing his chosen work in his own unique way.

Such formal study is only the beginning for the professional. This is usually followed by some sort of internship or practical training on the job, actually performing his specialty under expert guidance. This is a time of further learning, especially of the details of the functions which are to be the professional's life's work. It is a time of developing special skills on which he will routinely rely and on which he will call in emergency situations when there is no time for thinking or planning, only for acting.

Throughout his career the true professional will continue his learning, formally and informally, in order to keep abreast of the latest developments and improved techniques in his field of expertise. He does this because he knows that the world, its technology and its people are continually changing and that he, too, must continually update his knowledge and skills or he runs the risk of causing hurt or loss to those who depend on him, thereby betraying his trust.

Another dimension of this constant learning process is the accumulated wisdom and refined techniques of daily experience. As knowledge is applied to actual situations it is validated and made an integral part of the practitioner. Through such experience, built on a foundation of knowledge, the professional develops a special competence which enables him to fulfill the aims or purposes of the profession. It may even allow him to safely experiment with innovations which further develop his competence and the state of the art of his profession.

How do probation practice and the probation officer measure up thus far? There is, unfortunately, a serious lack of formal training as described above for most of the field. There are far too few graduate schools which specialize in the kind of study the probation officer needs as the basic foundation on which to build his practice. Educational requirements are not consistent around the country; indeed in some areas altogether nonexistent. Perhaps this is a major reason that educational institutions have been slow to develop a specialized curriculum for the training of probation officers. Most practitioners who do have graduate training have gone outside the field of corrections to obtain it or have put together a patchwork of courses as best they can.

Training on the job, actually performing his specialty under expert guidance, is available to few probation officers. Usually, the new officer is given a caseload to cover almost from his first day on the job. All too often he learns by trial and error without adequate supervision. The result is that his errors are often a trial to his clients, his agency and himself.

The individual probation officer can, as we have already discussed, continue the learning process on his own, keeping up-to-date on new developments in his own and related fields which may help him to more expertly carry out his functions. Certainly he can learn from experience; applying his knowledge to specific situations, being alert to make adjustments of methods and techniques based on the outcome of such application, thereby developing and continually refining his special competence.

While his formal educational background or his present opportunities for training may not be in the traditional mold of professional preparation, there is no reason why the probation officer cannot approach the continual updating of knowledge and development of special competence in a manner and with a dedication that is truly professional. To do any less does violence to the serious nature of his responsibilities.

A Matter of Recognized Position

Every true profession has a well-defined, clearly identifiable function which distinguishes it from all other areas of endeavor. This is not to say that the lines are always so sharply drawn that there is never any overlapping; it is to say that a profession must have an arena of activity sufficiently unlike others that its responsibilities and its practitioners can be distinguished from all others. This is the only way a particular area of activity can stand by itself without being swallowed up into something else. Anything other than such a distinctive entity will not long survive.

The basic reason for a clearly identifiable function is that it responds to a particular need, the meeting of which is important enough to designate a separate activity for this purpose. Life and health are valued enough to warrant special activities, the medical profession, to ensure their continuance. Social order is important enough to designate separate persons and institutions, the legal profession, to protect it. Whatever society values is generally protected and preserved through the designation of specialized functions and facilities.

One of the reasons these functions are so clearly distinguished is that their practice is based on a body of knowledge that is coherent, systematic and specialized. It is developed, expanded and refined especially to respond to the needs which are the reason for its existence. This body of knowledge is not usually understood by laymen as its assimilation may take many years of intensive study and application. It is also often couched in terminology of specialized meaning which makes it a mystery to all but the properly initiated. This is not by conscious design, but the end result is about the same as if it were; that is, the outsider is at a loss to understand, so he is forced to call in the professional for assistance.

Because the profession provides a socially valued function, the professional usually enjoys social recognition and sufficient recompense. Society is willing to pay for professional services it values through the granting of status, power and privileges to those persons performing those services. It also provides adequate monetary compensation in recognition of long and intensive preparation as well as valuable services.

Where do probation practice and the probation officer stand in relation to these criteria for a profession? In its present form probation is relatively new when compared to other fields of endeavor, although it has existed in concept for well over 125 years as part of the administration of justice. As such it has the clearly identifiable functions of serving as an arm of the court to provide rehabilitative care for those offenders placed under its supervision in lieu of incarceration. No other part of the criminal justice system performs this same function and probation is no more to be absorbed beyond identity within the broader field than is the profession of law, which is also a part of the broader field.

When it comes to a special body of knowledge, probation does not fare as well. The probation practitioner draws his knowledge from many disciplines, including law, biology, sociology, social work, psychology, psychiatry and medicine, among others. Within other disciplines and within the field of corrections there are continuing efforts to draw together and systematize those areas of knowledge which directly relate to the development, the treatment, the prevention and even the prediction of delinquent and criminal behavior. At the same time, efforts are being made, through research, to add to our knowledge in these areas.

Without doubt the probation officer's function is valued by society as fulfilling a necessary purpose; otherwise, the position would not likely have developed as it is today. Whether the motivation of society was out of generosity in providing worthwhile services to the offender or out of selfishness in providing for its own protection is not particularly important here. In either case, the function of the probation officer is of value to society, so he is recognized and delegated certain powers which identify him as a legitimate representative of society. However, the probation officer has a long way to go to gain full professional status in the community and acceptance as a professional among many who already enjoy that status. The general lack of adequate remuneration for his services, testifies to this lack of status for the probation officer.

A Matter of Attitudes

In addition to mastery of the knowledge and skills of his profession and recognition of his worth to society, the professional is also characterized by a responsible concern for effective service and the general advancement of his profession; by an attitude of dedication which says, "I believe in what I am doing, am committed to it and will do my very best at it regardless of the obstacles." This spirit of commitment is supported by the foundation of a sense of social responsibility which is responsive to the public interests, contributes to general social well-being and is accountable to the public for high standards of performance. The professional's attitude is one of service, of the best use of his knowledge and skills for the benefit of the society which accords him recognition and status.

This sense of commitment culminates in the development of a code of ethics and standards of conduct for himself and his fellow professionals. The professional subscribes to this ethic and these standards because he believes they are appropriate and necessary to the control and regulation of proper performance. They also serve to help develop a common sense of accountability to fellow professionals. In some professions these standards have been enacted into law in order to provide legal control over practice and strict sanctions for violation of the requirements.

A common sense of belonging and self-awareness as a professional draw many like-minded persons into a subculture where basic philosophy, values and attitudes are shared and much interaction occurs. This serves to reinforce personal commitments to the purposes and the ethics of the profession as each individual is constantly reminded of what it means to be professional. Out of this interaction grow formal local, regional and national organizations designed to help regulate the profession, provide continuing educational experiences, be the official spokesman for the positions of the profession and generally to work for the advancement and greater recognition of the profession and each of its practitioners.

In the matter of professional attitude, how do probation practice and the probation officer measure up? There should never be any question as to a sense of social responsibility or ethical standards of conduct. Generally, it is specified in the laws which create the probation officer's position that his work is in the interest of public well-being and he is accountable in a legal as well as a moral sense. It is hoped that the probation officer is keenly conscious of the responsibilities of his position because of the serious nature of his work rather than because of any legal requirements. It is hoped that he is committed to high standards of performance and personal integrity because of his concern for the worth and dignity of his clients rather than because of external restrictions.

The probation officer certainly shares a common culture, jargon, and purpose with his fellow practitioners as well as other workers in other branches of corrections. Most of these practitioners subscribe to the basic philosophy of social control and treatment of the offender for the welfare of all of society. They recognize their responsibility to both the client and the community to exercise sound judgment in the performance of their duties. They believe in the basic dignity and worth of each offender-client and diligently try to work with him to make whatever adjustments are needed to avoid future confrontation and conflict between himself and society. There are, of course, variations on these basic themes, but the similarities are generally stronger than the differences.

Like other groups, these commonalities have resulted in many formal organizations of workers in corrections; some very general and national in nature while others are quite restricted and local. There is some loose affiliation and cooperation among some of these groups, but no real interdependent relationship and unity of the sort necessary to develop a strong, aggressive and articulate organization. This is one of the unfortunate aspects of modern day corrections, one result of which is that the public is not made aware of the good being accomplished on the one hand nor of the serious lack of resources to do the job on the other. It is partially due to this lack of strong, formal organization that probation officers and other correctional personnel are not accorded the professional recognition and status that the importance of their tasks demands.

It is in this area of attitude that we may say the probation officer is in his own personal realm. There may be serious lack of educational institutions and curricula for the specialized preparation for work in the field; but this is something beyond the control of the individual probation officer. It may well be that he does not receive compensation which is commensurate with the importance and value of his services; and this, too, is something over which he personally has no control. However, he does control his own attitudes and need depend on no external force for their development. Here, he is "the captain of his fate, the master of his soul."

Because he does have control over his attitudes, there is no excuse for the probation officer to ever be anything short of professional in this area. In the matters of expertise and recognized position, he may be involved in a constant struggle to overcome handicaps resulting from the lack of opportunities that are forever gone and the impact of social forces outside himself which are not particularly susceptible to his desires. But, from the beginning, his sense of responsibility, integrity and ethical performance should be so high that neither he nor others should ever doubt that he is a true professional.

THE PROBATION OFFICER'S IDENTITY

The foregoing analysis of the requisite characteristics of a profession reveal some very serious shortcomings on the part of the field of probation so that in many respects we must admit that probation is not a generally recognized profession. However, this is more due to historical events and the relative youth of the endeavor than it is to the value of services performed or the manner in which the practitioner approaches his task. In this regard, it is more accurate to refer to probation practice as an *emerging profession.* Significant advances have been made in developing a specialized, graduate-level curriculum for correctional personnel which includes on-the-job practice under expert supervision. More and more, research into various aspects of illegal behavior and treatment of offenders is compiling and systematizing a distinctive body of applicable knowledge and experience and the field is now being credited with a special competence heretofore unrecognized. In many places the community is awakening to the value of services performed by correctional practitioners and is beginning to accord them the status and compensation they deserve.

As we have already noted, the probation officer more than meets the criteria in many other requirements for a profession, most notably in the matter of attitudes. This and the advancements being made as discussed above make it most appropriate to refer to the probation officer as a professional, which we have already done and shall continue to do. Yet, we still must consider what precisely is the probation officer's proper identity.

Law Enforcement Functions

The probation officer's job involves a number of police type functions, but he is not a police officer. He will, of necessity on occasion, use methods of surveillance and arrest as he deals with offender-clients who feel they can violate the law with impunity. But his primary aim is not to see how many lawbreakers he can find and he will not be sitting back waiting to pounce when one of his charges does something illegal. The probation officer in many jurisdictions is a peace officer and, as such, has some law enforcement powers and duties. A very specific part of his task is to enforce the terms and conditions of probation laid down by the court. Yet, his orientation must not be strictly toward police type activity, but toward treatment of the offender. He will have enough difficulty, because of his authoritative position as an officer of the court, in establishing effective rapport with the client without the added problem of having a *cop image* which usually arouses hostile feelings in most correctional clients. To be sure, the law must be enforced by the probation officer when necessary, but he must not be overeager to build a reputation for having the most arrests during the month.

Legal Functions

As we have already indicated, the laws delineate a number of legal responsibilities of the probation officer and he is an officer of the court; yet he is not an attorney, so he must be careful not to try to hand out legal counsel. Very often his clients will ask for legal advice from the probation officer, usually because he occupies the position he does and the client expects him to know the law. In order to function effectively the probation officer does need to know a great deal about the law; what his clients can and cannot do, what the law requires of him in the oversight of his clients, and other requirements encompassed in daily routine. Because of the very nature of his position, the probation officer should be as expert in probation law, both statutory and case law, and should be very familiar with criminal law in general. This is consistent with his position as a part of the administration of justice and should not interfere with, but rather enhance, his relationships with his clients. His expertise in law is not to enable him to dispense legal advice but to increase the effectiveness and ease with which he functions.

Casework Functions

Probation has long had a close relationship to the field of social work; indeed much of the impetus for the increased use of probation by the courts came from social workers. Perhaps, this is the major reason why much of probation supervision uses the social casework method of dealing with clients. No one could argue that probation practice owes nothing to casework practice, nor that casework is not a vital component of the probation officer's methods of dealing with clients; yet probation officers are not social workers, at least in the strictest sense.

There are many who would disagree with this position. Some would say that the use of casework principles makes one a social worker. Many psychiatrists, psychologists and ministers would disagree that they should be called social workers merely because they make use of casework principles and techniques.

None of this is to imply criticism or rejection of the social work field; it is simply a contention that probation officers (as well as other correctional workers), because of the particular legal and authoritative framework within which they practice, are somewhat different from social workers practicing with a voluntary clientele. The legal responsibilities of probation officers, including the law enforcement functions discussed above, places them in a different relationship to the client than does the social responsibilities of the social worker. This does not imply *better than;* it only implies *different from.*

Counseling Functions

Much of the probation officer's contact with clients is of a counseling nature, usually on a one-to-one basis, as is typical of the casework setting. In this role, the probation officer listens to the client talk about himself, his relationships and his problems; he serves as a sounding board and reflects back to the client the image the client projects to others, thereby helping him to get a clearer view of himself and his relations to other people. At times, the probation officer will help the client to examine all the alternatives available in a particular situation and will provide counsel regarding the consequences of each, thereby helping the client to make sound and wise choices. At other times the probation officer will need to be very directive in his counseling, giving the client specific rules to follow and setting out limitations on his behavior.

Although the probation officer makes use of therapeutic relationships in dealing with the client, he must draw the line between a more general counseling approach and psychotherapy. In his role of counselor, there are areas into which the probation officer should not intrude; serious emotional disturbances, medical problems, severe personality disorders, or extreme sexual maladjustment, for example. Typically, the probation officer is not trained nor does he have the experience to delve into such areas; in other words, he is not a clinician. He must know his own limitations and area of expertise and he must not go beyond the realm of his training, ability, or experience. He must also know what resources are available in the community to provide the level of service which he cannot provide. This leads to our next point of consideration.

Referral Functions

Although the probation officer may make referrals to other agencies in order to obtain needed assistance for his clients, he is not merely a social engineer manipulating people and things or merely allocating materials and resources.

Under no circumstances should the probation officer shirk his responsibility to forthrightly deal with the client and his problems so long as it is within the realm of his expertise. He has been charged with the overall supervision of the client; therefore, any problems exhibited by the client are of concern to the probation officer and it is his professional duty to try to do something about them. He does this himself when he can, but large caseloads may force him to refer some responsibilities to other agencies which can provide assistance to the client. This is realistic and acceptable because, if the need is beyond the scope of his time or ability, the probation officer still is responsible to obtain assistance where he can.

To do this he must be very familiar with the resources and facilities in the community on which he can call to help him meet his obligations. He must know what services they can provide so as not to unwisely use their time or dissipate their resources. He should also follow up every referral to be sure the agency and the client are working together, to provide coordination and feedback and to keep himself up-to-date on client progress. In other words, the probation officer's responsibility does not end with the referral; it continues as long as he has the client under his supervision.

Problem-Solving Functions

We have already spent considerable time discussing the practical problem-solving role of the probation officer, so there is no need to go into it again here. However, we do need to point out that the probation officer does devote a sizable portion of his time and energy helping his clients to deal with many very mundane, everyday affairs. For many socially adequate and well-integrated persons many of these cares are handled and problems are resolved quite routinely. There are, however, many probation clients who have never been taught to adequately deal with such matters, so for them the mundane and routine often becomes complicated, traumatic and insoluble. Perhaps it is in these areas that the probation officer can accomplish some of the most simple, immediately successful and most appreciated things that he can do for and with the client. The probation officer does help the client resolve many problems, but he is much more than just a problem-solver who operates an assembly line conveyer belt onto which clients may climb, slowly pass by his station, and have "something" done which sends them on their way with "everything all fixed up."

A Distinctive Identity

The probation officer is more than the sum total of the many aspects of these various functions which make up his job. The blending of these functions in the particular setting in which the work is performed makes probation a unique field of endeavor. He, along with other correctional people, has the responsibility for a specific category of persons; violators of the law. No other group of professionals has exactly this responsibility although they, too, work with lawbreakers: police, courts, attorneys, social workers, psychotherapists, social engineers and various problem solvers also all deal with law-abiding citizens. The probation officer has many functions which are related to those of several other professional fields; yet, he is not any one of them and is not to be absorbed into them. He has his own uniquely distinctive professional identity; he is a probation officer.

Chapter Six

THE PROBATION OFFICER'S PROFESSIONAL RELATIONSHIPS

N ow that we have established our position that the probation officer is appropriately considered to be a professional, we need to further examine his activity in this context. One of the most basic characteristics of a professional is the responsibleness with which he performs his duties; a solid sense of who he is, what his duties are and the proper way to go about performing those duties. In this chapter we will examine the many facets of this responsibleness within a framework of the professional relationships of the probation officer.

Anyone's relations with others are largely the result of the respective positions the individuals occupy and the roles they play. The tone of the relationship, the responsiveness of each person to the other and frequently even the physical setting are determined by how each sees himself and the other person regarding their relative positions and roles. As the positions and roles change, the relationship and its overtones also change because those involved modify their behavior and reactions accordingly. Failure, or inability, to do so in some situations would be indicative of serious emotional or personality problems. However, in most situations people are able to make adjustments as required or expected by a new set of circumstances.

The knowledge of what is expected in different situations and the ability to smoothly adjust one's responses as required are both part of the socialization process in our culture. Much of this is, of course, an unconscious learning as one matures; but some of it is conscious effort to learn new things, requirements and behavioral responses. This same situation is true of the professional. He unconsciously learns a great deal of a general and specific nature as he grows up and as he studies in his chosen field. But he also makes conscious effort to learn many specific patterns of behavior relating to his profession because they are the expected responses and, since they are new and different to him, it takes conscious effort to make them a part of himself so that they become *second nature* requiring little if any thinking before acting.

In his relationships to others who, because of their positions or roles, in some way interface with him in the performance of one or more of his functions, the probation officer must also make conscious effort to learn and internalize the expectations of the varying situations. Only in this way will he be able to relate to others professionally in such a way as to enhance the effectiveness with which he discharges his responsibilities.

The focus in this chapter will be on these responsibilities within the framework of the probation officer's professional relationships. We will thus move from the abstract to the concrete and practical. We will begin with the widest area and move through successively smaller circles, working inward to the probation officer himself.

THE COMMUNITY

We have already discussed the reciprocal relationship between the probation officer and the community, explicit in which is his obligation to work for the protection of the welfare of the community and implicit in which is the community's obligation to provide him the resources and support he needs to do his job. The very definition of this relationship involves a professional stance by the probation officer or he will not be able to adequately carry out his functions.

This reciprocal relationship is the basis for all the probation officer does. The community is the ultimate source of his position, appointment, authority, support and resources for discharging his responsibility. In turn, he is answerable ultimately to the community for the quality and effectiveness of his performance. As a representative of the community to the client, the probation officer represents community values and standards of conduct, not his own. Even though he may not personally agree with these community values and standards, if they have been enacted into law, his professional obligation is to support and enforce them. If they have not been made law but are only social expectations, the probation officer might still have to support them in order to help the client to at least avoid the sort of social conflict which could lead to stigma, exclusion from valuable contacts, or even illegal behavior. The probation officer has an obligation to assist his client to learn to live among his fellows without unnecessary conflict; this might sometimes mean helping him to see that he cannot possibly win in a continuing battle with the community, so it is often to his advantage to abide by most of the social expectations.

This relationship also involves a professional responsibility on the part of the probation officer to make the most judicious use of whatever resources the community is able to provide. These may be scarce, not because no one wants to provide more, but because that is the best the community can afford. The fewer the resources, the more important it is to use them wisely and efficiently. This sort of attitude and approach demonstrates the professional discharge of his functions by the probation officer.

An important corollary of the wise use of available resources is cooperation with other agencies and groups working to alleviate social problems in the community. Although probation personnel have a unique job to perform, much of what they do is quite similar to the things being done by individuals, organizations and official agencies in the community. Not only are there common goals with other groups; also many of the same clients are served by more than one group or agency. Cooperation and coordination become very important if the common clientele are to be optimally served and the common aims are to be achieved. There is no place for professional jealousy or competition because, if this is the case, everyone loses; the agencies themselves, the professionals, the general public, and especially the needy clientele. A hallmark of a true professional is his dedicated willingness to cooperate toward the goal of alleviation of these social problems even when others may not cooperate or may want to do things differently or may want to dominate the allocation of resources. It is not easy to function under such circumstances, but the professional keeps trying, because the end is so important for everyone involved. The probation officer must conduct himself in a truly professional way in cooperating with other groups in the community because he is a professional and because it will pay off in reciprocal cooperation from others in his efforts to obtain the necessary resources to allow him to do his job. As a professional, and a minority in the field, he cannot afford not to cooperate.

THE COURT

The court represents the legal thinking, standards and expectations of the community, functioning to interpret laws, decide disputes and impose legal sanctions for breaches of law. In his appointed role, the probation officer functions as an arm of the court providing information and services and carrying out certain wishes of the court. This relationship is not too difficult in small, homogeneous communities when the court and the probation officer have close contact and think much the same. However, most probation work is carried on in urban centers where there are likely to be varied views among many judges making up the court system; views that are strongly held and often forcefully articulated. A probation agency must work with all these points of view, attempting to satisfy the varied requirements of each while maintaining a consistent philosophy and orderly procedures. This is not a simple thing to do, so there will be failures. When this happens the agency should readily admit its shortcomings and try to be honest and candid in all their dealings with the judges and the judges should be equally honest and candid in turn.

The professional stand of the probation officer makes it encumbent on him to accord the court the respect due its dignity. After all, the court is a venerated social institution, it is the embodiment of society's laws and it is the administrator of criminal justice. As an officer of the court, it is unprofessional and unethical for the probation officer to criticize the court in public or to clients in such a way as to undermine confidence in the law and its administration. Of course, as with any citizen and especially as with a professional, he must work to correct the failings of the system. This may very well mean that he will speak out to demand necessary changes, but this will be in a constructive vein aimed at strengthening the courts rather than destroying their effectiveness. There are many changes which need to be made to make our courts more viable and responsive to human need rather than traditional precedent. The probation officer has a professional obligation to support the sort of change which will strengthen public respect and confidence for the courts. He can do this by doing a good job in his own functions and, as an officer of the court, fighting from within the system to bring about needed change.

Closely related to respect of the court is acceptance of its established legal function as the decision-maker in the administration of justice. Although other persons and agencies make decisions which frequently control input to the court, it is the court which has the final authority over determination of guilt or innocence and over sentencing; two actions which have tremendous impact on probation clients. The probation officer must never interfere with nor undercut this function of the court.

In order to make the best decisions the court must have factual, relevant and sufficient information. While some of this information comes from law enforcement officers, prosecutors, witnesses and defenders, it is the legal and professional function of the probation officer to supply much of the information upon which courts base decisions, especially in pronouncing sentences. It is his responsibility to provide pertinent and concise data as well as objective and appropriate recommendations.

The probation officer also has the responsibility to the court, as well as to the client, to provide the probationer with counsel and guidance in problem-solving, technical assistance in meeting his needs, specific direction as to acceptable behavior and control of conduct under threat of incarceration for illegal activity. These things the court has the right to expect the probation officer, as an officer of the court, to provide for those the court entrusts to his care. A further part of this expectation is that the probation officer will carry out the specific orders of the court, enforce the terms and conditions of probation and communicate to the court the progress or failure of the probationer. It is the court, not the probation officer, who has the final responsibility for and power over the probationer. The probation officer acts for the court in his oversight of the client; therefore, part of his professional relationship and responsibility is to provide feedback to the court as to the outcome of its decisions.

This relationship, however, is a two-way affair; the court also has some responsibilities to the probation officer if he is to fulfill his tasks and function at optimum level. The court must respect the honesty and integrity of the probation officer. The very act of requesting a presentence investigation and report implies such respect; and when the probation officer has endeavored to provide an honest and unbiased report, to disregard or to attack it not only makes the effort superfluous but also undermines the very reason for presentence reports. Of course, the probation officer must earn the respect of the court by performing his tasks in a professional manner. If he does not do so, the court's failure to respect the probation officer's integrity can very quickly destroy his effectiveness with clients and with other community agencies.

The court should also be aware of the practical tactical and procedural problems which exist with a heavy workload and a lack of sufficient staff, both of which are the case with most probation departments. While it is appropriate for the individual judge to communicate to the agency his particular wishes, philosophies, likes and dislikes, he should not try to be the administrator of the agency nor try to set policies for it. When a judge makes unreasonable or impractical demands on an agency or an officer, he creates pressures which can only result in a lesser quality of service for his and all other courts. It takes more than an order by a judge to get many things done. There are practical obstacles of time, space, manpower and knowledge which must be considered. Probation officers generally respond quickly and professionally to requests or orders from judges; but they are not all wise nor all powerful, being human and subject to human weaknesses. Whenever a judge fails to take these weaknesses into consideration, his orders will only worsen the situation by impairing the ability of the probation officer to respond and by lowering his morale. Even though he is a professional and tries to always so respond, he cannot perform at his best when under attack; especially undeserved and unfair attack. The court owes the probation officer the same kind of consideration and support it expects to receive. Like most relationships, that between probation officer and court flourishes best when built on mutual trust and respect.

OTHER AGENCIES

There are a number of community agencies with which the probation officer continuously interacts by the very nature of his job. Some of these are elements of the criminal justice system and others are not so identified. In both instances, however, his relationships must be characterized by professional understanding of the roles and functions of the other agencies, an acceptance of the basic integrity of the workers in those agencies and a willingness to work with them toward common goals. As we have already commented about other relationships, these too are reciprocal with the other agencies owing the probation officer the same understanding, acceptance and cooperation.

Although the basic philosophy of probation officers and police agencies differ, they find themselves with much the same clientele and often moving toward the same goals. The job of the policeman is the prevention and detection of crime, the apprehension of the offender when he is known and generally enforcing the law. The job of the probation officer is basically corrections, after the policeman has done his job. Obviously, each is greatly affected by the other; but each must respect the ability of the other to perform his assigned task. This means recognizing the basic and legitimate roles of one another as different in nature, so the philosophy and techniques should also be different. When the other person's job is different from mine, it is a mark of unprofessional stupidity to expect him to do it like I do mine.

Both the policeman and the probation officer must recognize that their common clients distinguish between their functions and often respond to them differently on that basis. The best way for these two professionals to work together is to get to know one another as individuals because, based on this kind of contact and knowledge, it is not so difficult to understand and accept differences of philosophy, function and method.

In addition to both being officers of the court and professionals, attorneys and probation officers also have in common the sharing of information about mutual clients. Whether prosecution or defense, the attorney has an important interest in conveying information about the offender to the probation officer and receiving information in turn. Although the roles of the prosecutor, the defender and the probation officer are distinct and do not usually overlap, there is a great deal of interfacing between them. Here again, there must be a mutual acceptance of the function of the other and respect for his ability and integrity. The adversary nature of criminal proceedings often seems to put the participants *on edge* with one another, but as professionals they cannot allow this friction to hinder them in each getting his job done.

There are other agencies in the community who frequently share the probation officer's clientele; such as welfare, schools, recreational programs and other social services and helping people. Because they share clientele there is often the need to also share information about the clients. Most agencies have policies and practices of confidentiality of information for their own and their client's protection. The true professional will respect the confidentiality of the information shared with him and will never use it for purposes other than those for which it was provided.

We have already noted, but it is important enough to bear repeating, that one vital trait of a professional is his dedicated willingness to work with others interested in the same ends and to keep on working in the face of adversity and frustrations. The problems that the various community agencies encounter can only be resolved through the teamwork of professionals who know what they are doing and who keep working at it together.

THE AGENCY

The law and the general community designate the position, the authority and the work of the individual probation officer through his agency. Without the agency, the probation officer is a private citizen, without official standing or professional status. In this regard, he is in a different position than are many professionals, especially those who are in private practice. The probation officer is a "public professional" because he works for a public agency. In most jurisdictions, there is no provision for a "private" probation officer; the position is reserved for those who are employed by public agencies. In this context, the agency is more basic to probation officers than it is to other professionals.

Because he is so dependent on the agency for his standing, the officer's relationship to it is of vital concern; he rises or falls with his agency. He must accept his role as a team member, not an autonomous agent; he must be careful to protect the name and standing of the agency; he must be sure that outside activities do not drain his physical and emotional energies, preventing him from giving his best to the agency.

As we have already discussed in another context, the probation officer has an obligation to help develop the expertise of his agency. While he is aware of the limitations of the agency's resources and programs and does not make unreasonable demands nor expect more than the agency can realistically give, he is also alert to opportunities to help expand and strengthen the agency's performance. In doing so, he is expanding and strengthening his own effectiveness and enhancing his own professional status.

The probation officer who is aware of his dependence on his agency is not critical of it, especially to outsiders. Of course, he has the right, and the duty, to speak out on internal issues because he is part of the team; but this is motivated by the desire to improve, not to tear down. The agency may very well be disorganized, mismanaged, or neglecting its responsibilities. In this case it is the probation officer's obligation to try to correct the situation by working within the organizational and administrative framework and its policies and procedures. If any or all of these things need to be changed, the professional approach is to endeavor to work out those changes by negotiation and gentle persuasion, not by destructive attack or subtle sabotage. Over the long run, he stands to lose far more than the agency from such negative action.

COLLEAGUES

The probation officer's professional relationships with his colleagues move in three directions; upward regarding his superiors, laterally regarding his peers and downward regarding his subordinates. All three directions are equally important for him and the accomplishment of his assigned tasks; he cannot afford to neglect any of them.

Unless he works alone as the sole person responsible for probation work in his jurisdiction, the probation officer will be part of a public agency with some form of organization of responsibility and authority. As a professional, he is aware of the importance of good organizational structure to get the job done and he respects this command structure and formal channels of communication. Even though he may become frustrated at times with a bureaucratic system and its red tape, he knows that this is a fact of public life; so, instead of letting it "get him down," he learns to adjust to its demands in order to carry out his functions. Rather than succumb to the deadening inertia often produced by the bureaucracy, he becomes thoroughly familiar with the system so that he knows how to minimize the pressures it creates. While he follows the formal channels of command and communication, he is also aware of and uses the informal channels in order to speed things up and smooth the way for formal movement. This is not to say that he disregards policy or that he undermines the organization; as a professional, he would not act in that way. It is to say that he is alert to take every legitimate advantage of his knowledge of how the system functions and ways to speed up the process in order to discharge his professional responsibility.

Another thing the probation officer owes his superiors, because they are responsible for his activities, is the willingness to admit he lacks the requisite knowledge or ability to get the job done when this is the case. He cannot pretend expertise if it does not exist. To do so will only hurt the client, hinder the work of the agency and make the probation officer appear inept. If he does not know, he should admit it to his immediate superior and ask for assistance to learn. That is one of the main reasons for superior-subordinate organizational structure. It is the only proper way to overcome such a problem. He must take the same stance when personal problems interfere with his job performance. It may not be necessary, nor even appropriate, to discuss these in detail with his superior, but he must be willing to recognize this situation and not let others assume that his lowered quality of performance is due to incompetence. Here again, an honest admission of a problem may be the first step in its solution and the best way to obtain organizational assistance to that end.

Laterally, the probation officer is likely to be involved overtime with a number of fellow professionals, his peers. These are people with whom he works in the same agency or has contact with from other agencies. A client may, for any number of reasons, be reassigned from one to the other: he may move out of one jurisdiction into another; he may have been under the supervision of one probation officer in the past and upon committing a new offense may now be assigned to a different one; the structure of the agency may require one officer to work with the client at one stage of the proceedings and a different officer at other stages. In any case, the officer who works even a brief period of time in the field will likely share many clients with his peers. As professionals, they must respect the work of one another. The officer who now has responsibility for a client may not agree with the way the previous officer handled the case, but he must remember that he does not have the same information and set of circumstances as the previous officer; if he did, it is possible he would have made similar decisions and dealt with the client in the same way. He must be very careful under these conditions not to criticize the former officer to the client; such action does not help the situation but only causes the client to wonder about *all* probation officers. One professional never attempts to enhance his standing with a client at the expense of a fellow-professional.

When it is necessary to transfer a client from one probation officer to another, they should communicate fully with one another to share knowledge of the client. In this way they help one another and certainly maximize their joint ability to help the client. Medical men share records, impressions and knowledge with one another about mutual patients; probation officers have a similar professional responsibility to themselves and the client.

In larger agencies, a probation officer might find that one of his clients shares a residence with the client of another probation officer. There are good casework reasons why one client cannot always be transferred to the other officer so he can work with both; for example, the rapport and working relationships already established may be destroyed to the detriment of the client. In this sort of circumstance, the two officers must coordinate their dealings with their clients so that differences in treatment, especially enforcement of similar terms and conditions of probation, are not discouraging or frustrating or harmful to either client. When they compare notes about their respective probation officers, things must be reasonably alike or they are likely to begin to "play both ends against the middle." It is so easy for one officer to inadvertently interfere with the other officer's work, negating its impact and falling into a trap that will eventually be to the disadvantage of everyone concerned because everyone will be set up for failure. As professionals, the probation officers cannot allow such things to occur.

Like most professionals, the probation officer is likely to have subordinates or support personnel working with him to help get the job done. These people are often involved in some sort of clerical work; typists, receptionists, telephone operators, secretaries and perhaps others. If the professional, whatever his profession, did not have such support it is unlikely he would function adequately, at least, not as well as he can with support. In some cases, he simply could not function at all. Because these people are so important to his being able to accomplish his ends, he owes them respect and consideration, courtesy and kindness. These are not "lowly people," but important components in his accomplishments; so he should not "lord it over" them. The professional human services worker will have at least the same feelings of warmth, acceptance and respect for his support personnel that he has for his clients. If he lacks these professional feelings toward them, he is not a true professional. Even from the selfish position of enhancing his own work and standing, treating support personnel with dignity and respect will pay off for him.

THE CLIENT

Perhaps this relationship is the very core of the probation officer's professional responsibility. We have already had much to say that touches on this relationship and there will be a great deal more in the pages to come. However, we do need to make some general observations at this point, leaving the details for later development.

It is the professional responsibility of the probation officer to provide the highest level of service and assistance of which he is capable to the client. He must never forget that the decisions he makes about the client deal with his freedom, his future and the way his life will go. He must use wise, informed and unbiased judgment; he cannot allow emotional feelings or beliefs to color his responses to the client. This relationship must be characterized by impartial but not disinterested treatment; an objective appraisal but not a coldly or clinically professional response; a genuinely warm acceptance but not a blind defense of his actions. There must be a balance between firmness and friendliness, choice and direction, advice and authority, freedom and enforcement.

The probation officer must avoid the trap of satisfying his own needs for acceptance, being the *good guy*, having others dependent on him, exercising authoritative powers, or any other personal needs in dealings with the client. As with any other person, many of the probation officer's personal needs are met through his chosen work; otherwise he would not likely be in the field. But selfish motivation or the satisfaction of personal needs at the expense of others, especially in a relationship where he has practically all of the power and advantages, is conduct unbecoming his position and totally unacceptable for a professional. For example, the probation officer's task is not to destroy or supplant existing relationships between the client and significant others in his life, thereby making him more dependent on or responsive to the desires of the officer. Rather, he should analyze those relationships, seek to enhance them and to build on those that are positive. He will never gain the respect of the client nor build a beneficial relationship with him by tearing down the links and lines of communication with those whom the client considers important to him.

A relationship with the client must be established which will allow the probation officer to take the client where he is and help him move to where he needs to be. Here the officer will assist the client to see the necessity of accepting the limits of behavior imposed on him generally by law and specifically by the terms of his probation. He will try to help the client to learn to function within these limits so that he can avoid the unpleasant and often painful consequences of illegal behavior. The goal is to enable the client to cope with his life situation in a way that provides both immediate and long-term satisfaction to him, all the while avoiding the sort of social conflict that resulted in his current restricted state.

One thing the probation officer must avoid at all costs is over-identification with the client. It is one thing to try to get through to the client and establish meaningful communication with him; it is another thing to become like him in appearance, speech, or mannerisms in an attempt to reach out to him. The probation officer can develop effective professional relationships with the client without getting involved in purely social situations with him. Unlike the doctor who can mingle socially with his patients and still maintain his professional medical standing with those patients, the probation officer cannot partake of the social life of his clients without losing some of the authority that must clothe his position if he is to function effectively. The patient may use the social setting to try to get free medical advice from his doctor, but the offender-client is more likely to use the social setting to break free of the restrictions imposed by his legal relationship to his probation officer.

Part of the professional responsibility of the probation officer is to set an example for the client in terms of behavior, attitude, language and appearance; an example which will help the client to understand some of the things he might have to do in order to gain the kind of social acceptance or recognition that he needs to allow him to function in his community without bringing undesirable consequences upon himself. Whether in the office or on the streets, in public or in private, the probation officer should always be aware of the image he is projecting to the client and his family or others who are important to him. This is not because the probation officer is so much concerned about his image *per se,* but because how the client sees him is part of his influence on the client for positive behavior.

There are countless little ways in which the probation officer makes an impression on the client for good or bad and which are often overlooked by the officer. For example, the probation officer stresses to the client the need to be on time for appointments because he is "very busy with lots of other clients," but he goes out for a twenty minute coffee break just five minutes before he has an appointment scheduled with the client. Which message gets across? Or the officer lectures the client about responsible behavior, but does not return the client's telephone call until he has called in several times. What is this "responsible behavior" thing, anyhow? Or the probation officer urges the client to be a man of his word and keep his promises, but does not follow through on promises to the client. How does one learn to be truthful under such circumstances? It may be very trite but it is still true that "actions speak louder than words"; the true professional knows the importance of this and behaves accordingly.

Finally, if the probation officer is to effectively work with his client he must be professional in his commitments to the client. This means that commitments are made with good judgment after careful consideration, not precipitously nor frivolously; and once the commitment is made, it is kept. The probation officer, perhaps more than most professionals, must be a man of his word because the very basis of all he can hope to achieve with the client is mutual respect and trust. If this is not present between the two, the relationship will be meaningless, unproductive and maybe even detrimental to the client. After all, if you can't trust a professional, who can you trust?

ONESELF

The beginning wide circle has now narrowed to as small as it can get; the individual probation officer's professional responsibility to himself. This is the place where professional ethics are really tested and are very important; here where no one else can see, where no reputation is at stake, where one's image is not on display. Yet, it is here, from within one's self, that there arises most of the basic professional behavior which is seen by others. If one finds it difficult to live with himself, he will not get very far in trying to help his clients learn to live in peace with others. If one cannot be true to himself, he will find it difficult to be true to others.

This idea is much more than moralizing; it has some very practical implications. For example, one thing the probation officer owes himself is to protect his personal and professional reputations for the good of the work he does. If he does not care what others think of him and conducts himself in an unethical manner, he will accomplish very little that is worthwhile and may even be denied the opportunity to try.

The probation officer also owes to himself to do the very best he possibly can in his work. He is not to vie for status higher than his peers; he is not to compete with other professionals for standing in the community; he is simply to be in competition with his own best self. He cannot afford to measure his effectiveness against that of others; if he doesn't measure up he will probably become discouraged and if he does he will probably be tempted to egotism. It is far more appropriate to simply strive to do the best job he can do, seeking constantly to improve but not fretting over someone who outshines him.

If the probation officer has a sense of responsibility of professional ethics, improper attitudes and conduct will mar his self-image; and a poor self-image severely hinders one doing his work in a *people-helping profession.* The very nature of his assigned responsibilities requires that he be at peace with himself and have a positive feeling of being worthwhile as a person before he will be able to effectively deal with the frustrating problems of his clients.

These, then, are some of the professional responsibilities and relationships of the probation officer. There are undoubtedly many aspects of his professional stance which have not been discussed in this chapter and may not be touched on elsewhere in this book. We have, however, gone into enough detail on a wide variety of relationships to show what we mean when we say that the probation officer practicing his work is a professional.

Chapter Seven

DESIRABLE CHARACTERISTICS OF PROBATION OFFICERS

W HAT MAKES A GOOD probation officer? What are the general characteristics and personal traits an individual must possess in order for him to function effectively as a professional within the constellation of relationships described above? Does it require the same kinds of abilities to relate to the court that it does to relate to the client? Can one perform well one aspect of these reponsibilities while failing in another, or are they so interrelated that weakness in one area will seriously affect performance in another area? These questions illustrate some of the implications the work and the professional responsibilities of the probation officer position have for the kind of person needed to adequately fill the position.

The thrust of this chapter will be to examine what characteristics are needed for one to perform probation work at the professional level we have been discussing. As we look at these various traits we will notice that some of them overlap with others and perhaps at times even seem to merge completely. We have distinguished between the various characteristics, however, for purposes of focusing more precisely on certain important aspects that might get lost were they to be considered in some other fashion.

There is one observation which must be made before we begin to discuss specific characteristics: underlying all of the desirable traits is the need for the probation officer to clearly understand the importance of his job. He deals with the freedom and the future of human beings; the things he does and the decisions he makes can have serious consequences for the lives of the clients and their families; he can have tremendous impact on the development of attitudes and behavior patterns in the clients; his influence can be felt in many ways unknown to him among his cli-

79

ents, their families and friends, and in the community generally. This understanding of the importance of his job is the foundation which supports the superstructure created by the unifica-
tion and interaction of specific characteristics. It also has important implications for formal education, on-the-job training and
personal growth as ways and means whereby those specific characteristics may emerge and be developed. No matter what are the
amounts of knowledge, the levels of skills, or the degree of energy spent, if the probation officer loses sight of the importance
of his functions he will be superficial and ineffective at best and
detrimental at worse. The very first and most basic lesson to be
learned by potential probation officers is the realization of what
he can do in that position and role to the lives of others. If he
is not awed by the depth of this responsibility he should get into
some other career and perhaps avoid doing serious damage to
some fellow human being.

Even the individual who is deeply impressed with the seriousness of the role of the probation officer must possess other
knowledge, abilities, skills and personal traits in order to do the
kind of job demanded by the serious nature of his task. It is not
true that one must *have a knack* for the job in order to perform
it well. The characteristics needed to make one a good probation
officer are not innate; they are learned in the course of growing
up and preparing for a career. Given the appropriate opportunities, anyone can learn the things and develop in the areas necessary to good probation practice. Some of the characteristics we
will discuss may be acquired through general maturation and
socialization, some through formal educational preparation,
some through specialized skills training and some through personal growth and development. Some may be learned almost unconsciously while others may be the result of specific effort; but
the important point is that they can all be learned, even later in
life, if one really wants to learn.

We turn now to our discussion of desirable characteristics of
probation officers, beginning with considerations of broad scope
and moving to more specific traits. The order in which we examine certain characteristics has no particular significance; every

trait is of vital importance, each being an element which combines with the others to make up the total person of the probation officer.

GENERAL SOCIAL MATURITY

This personal trait is developed, modified and expanded over the years as one grows from childhood into adulthood and beyond. Practically every experience and exposure which one has, in its own way and to varying degrees, contributes to the ever-changing and complex pattern of one's life that we refer to as social maturity. Much of it is the result of opportunity, to be sure; but part of the whole idea of social maturity is the ability to recognize areas in which one is lacking and to take action to fill in the gaps of experience that have been identified. This capacity for personal expansion and refinement is very important for the basic reason that no one person is likely to *accidently* experience all the many things that can make positive contributions to his personal development. The great men of history have usually worked to overcome weaknesses because they recognized that such gaps in their experience hinder the expression of greatness.

Understanding of oneself is basic to social maturity. If one is unable to handle his own personality in everyday life he will not be able to assist others in handling theirs; and the ability to handle oneself grows out of an understanding of oneself. This understanding includes a knowledge of the personal biases, the likes and dislikes, which are found in everyone. As a part of growing up and experiencing life we all develop preferences and prejudices. Many of these deal with quite insignificant matters, so do no harm to anyone. However, some can have serious influence on one's actions in very important issues, especially as they touch other people. The important thing is not so much what the biases are, but that one is aware that they exist and do have serious implications for behavior. Armed with this knowledge, one can take steps to minimize the negative influences of personal biases so they do not interfere with or destroy his relationships with others. Closely related to personal biases are individual motivations and ambitions of which the probation officer must also be aware if he is to understand himself. Knowing what gives one the drive to do what he does and the desire to gain a particular goal is important to total self-awareness as well as to the allocation of personal resources toward the attainment of optimum personal development. If one does not understand what motivates him, he is not too likely to be able to effectively marshall his resources nor correct a course of action even when he may be made aware that he has somehow gotten off course. It is highly doubtful that one who does not understand himself will ever be very effective in understanding his clients or helping them to know themselves in a way that contributes to long-lasting progress.

This understanding of one's inner self can project itself outwardly so that others see what is often called an *adequate personality.* The external manifestation is the only way the client has of judging how well the probation officer has "put it all together"; and if the client cannot see that this has been done, he will have no confidence that the probation officer can help him with his own similar problems. The client who can see the personal "hang-ups" of the helping person may exhibit considerably more insight than is shown by the helper because the inability to demonstrate a well-integrated self is indicative of lack of understanding of the self. It almost becomes a question of who is the helper and who is the client. In such a circumstance, the probation officer will not be effective in working with the client; and that is a loss that either can ill afford.

The socially mature person is one who thinks for himself. He is not likely to believe something just because he is told or sees it in print. He questions the validity of that which he does not know from experience; at least to the extent that it must be logical and, from other data available, appears to be sound. This is the individual who does not belong to a group or follows a career merely because his father did so; rather, he thinks through the issue and makes his own decision based on his own analysis of the matter. This is the man about whom others say "he stands on his own feet" or "he is his own man."

This is not to imply that he is self-centered or unmindful of the ways and views of others. To the contrary, he knows their views and understands why those views are held; but his own beliefs and methods are dependent on his own evaluations and decisions, not on the views of others. He listens to the arguments on all sides of an issue and responds with good judgment, not to emotional appeal. He considers the various facets of a question and, if he cannot agree with the urgings of those trying to persuade him, he tactfully establishes his own position and logically explains why he is doing so. In short, he trusts his own judgment and is not leary of taking a stand on an issue.

The knowledge that one does have a reasonably good understanding of himself and that he does project a genuine image of a well-integrated personality gives him social poise which stands him in good stead when circumstances are out of the ordinary and the routine has been upset. He is able to deal with the unusual situation from a position of strength which creates respect and confidence in those who observe or relate to him. Such an individual becomes a solid and stable force on which others feel they can rely in the face of change and disruption. There is a serenity which emanates from such a man and gives strength to those around him. He is in tune with himself and his environment and usually finds it rather easy to get others to follow him, trust him and respond to him.

Social poise helps one to be comfortable in his appreciation and respect for other cultures. He is not egocentric in feeling superior to them and he is not threatened by those who are different nor by those who are strong. Rather he is able to relate with understanding and communicate with compassion. He is at ease in all situations because he accepts and respects every other man for what he is and what he can do. He is a man in whom others can believe; consequently, he is a man they will follow.

WELL-ROUNDED EDUCATION

Education is the process of systematic development through study. It could be an informal self-study, but few people have the self-discipline necessary to see such a program to a successful completion; therefore, education here will be used to refer to formal study in a college or university. This is not to minimize the importance of individual study which is a process that should continually engage the attention and effort of every professional who wants to keep up with new developments and continue his personal growth. Rather, it is a defense of the necessity to follow and complete a prescribed and systematic course of study in order to begin to qualify as a professional probation officer.

No one seems to question the need for lawyers and judges, psychologists and social workers, or school teachers and CPA's to have formal education and certified competence in order to perform their assigned tasks in the community. We even have laws in some states to insure that the barber or beautician, TV repairman or auto mechanic and electrician or plumber are properly and specifically trained and equipped to do their jobs. But there have been many attacks on the probation officer and other correctional practitioners in terms of requisite education to practice this profession. The attitude has been, indeed, it has sometimes been stated, that all one needs to be a probation officer, a parole agent, or a correctional counselor is good common sense, a genuine liking for people and a desire to be helpful. There are also those who claim that one can only help the "street people" if he comes from the same background, preferably having been a "street person" himself.

This is simply not so. Today, we live in a highly complex society characterized by impersonal relations, stress on status, materialism, social discrimination and widespread corruption and disregard for the law. Citizens are increasingly having problems coping with such a society as evidenced by the rising tides of mental illness, emotional distress, antisocial conduct and criminal and delinquent behavior. The individual engaged in the professional *helping services* is more and more dealing with complicated behavioral mechanisms, neuroses and other personal disturbances. The probation officer's work with such persons is further compounded by the serious legal implications for both the client and the community as well as the serious social implications for the life and the future of the client. To meet the challenge of providing effective service in a setting of important and far-reaching ramifications requires the best education and training that can be provided. Anything less has the potential for socially dangerous consequences.

There is no way to accurately measure the benefits of a college education as preparation for a particular career, especially one dealing with attempts to change human attitudes and behavior. This is because there are many uncontrollable variables, such as the variety of specific course content which varies with major program, institutional offerings, individual electives and teaching approaches of professors involved; the unpredictable impact upon the student of various academic and nonacademic college experiences, exposure to individuals of prestige and influences of the general campus atmosphere; and the differential responses of the student to the many stimuli he encounters due to his own personality make-up and unique definitions of the stimuli. The formalized educational process thus has different learning results for different individuals; and this is as it should be. The process of education has never been intended as an assembly line turning out large quantities of identical products which vary only according to their "optional equipment" determined by their major courses of study. Rather, it is designed to be a systematic way for an individual to develop his knowledge, social skills, environmental awareness, analytical abilities, objectivity and ability to communicate. In short, the purpose of a college education is to develop a well-rounded and socially mature citizen.

Even though it is difficult to measure the impact of the college experience in terms of some specific training goals, there are several more general considerations which demonstrate some solid advantages in the probation officer having that college experience as represented by a baccalaureate degree. It is these advantages which form the basis for the possession of a four-year college degree as an entrance requirement for probation officers.

That four-year experience can provide some additional exposure to life and its workings for the young person before entering upon a career and, in so doing, give him more time to mature. Many people who enter the field of corrections do so at the beginning of their work life, often just out of college. The additional years of growing, learning and coming in contact with the world contribute to the general social maturity discussed already. Were it not for this additional time, some of these young people would have entered their work life much more unsure of themselves, more uncertain of the world around them and more unprepared in terms of maturity to engage in the important work which they have chosen to do.

One of the most outstanding characteristics of the correctional client is his history of failure in so much of what he has tried to do. This frequently results in expectations of further failure and a sense of hopelessness which hinders even minimal effort on his own behalf. He desperately needs some success experiences to help him gain the sort of confidence in himself which will unlock his energies and will contribute to further efforts for self-improvement. A failure will not likely be able to help a failure to become successful, but one who has experienced some success himself might be able to help another to be successful. Getting through college by meeting numerous short- and long-term requirements; learning to keep to schedules; being able to start at the beginning and gradually build according to a blueprint in order to fulfill specific requirements within a time span; and struggling with frustrating assignments until they are brought to satisfactory fruition, all indicate the number and variety of successful experiences which lend maturity and self-confidence to the college graduate. They provide him a sense of accomplishment, often in the face of adversity, which enables him to confidently relate to others in helping them to be successful.

The college experience also provides the probation officer with a broad knowledge of theory relating to social problems, cultural contributions, interpersonal relations, human behavior mechanisms, deviant behavior, individual development, family dynamics, group interaction, counseling techniques, personality development and many other social and psychological processes. All of these are necessary to the sort of understanding of the individual and his family which enables the probation officer to establish a positive working relationship with the client and to assist him in his efforts to cope with his circumstances. Many probation clients are quite sophisticated in criminal activity and, because of their backgrounds, are often very complex individuals. Relating to and communicating with these persons requires extensive knowledge of the principles of human behavior, both normal and abnormal. Without this kind of broad background of knowledge of human behavior, the probation officer would be able to contribute practically nothing to the life of the client. If he does not go to college to be exposed to and gain this knowledge, where will he learn it? Here we are talking about course content which allows one to explore and to learn about the hows and whys of human behavior, to learn "what makes people tick." The technical skills and specific procedures for getting the routine things done can be easily enough learned on the job.

In the course of his work the probation officer deals with a wide variety of clients on their own level, but with the goal of increasing their ability to cope with life. Thus, he needs to have some knowledge about a lot of things and be conversant with many facets of life. A broad educational background helps him to understand the purposes of many things and enables him to fit the pieces of life together so that he has a sense of direction while being flexible enough to cope with a variety of events and adapt to rapidly changing circumstances. A liberal college education can help to build this foundation for him.

More and more, the probation officer is dealing with a complexity of issues which require an intensive specialization of knowledge in order to properly perform his assigned functions. For example, he is caught up in the necessity of considerable knowledge of legal procedures regarding arrests, searches, probation revocations and other technical matters. Some states even require certain courses of study in these areas for probation officers. This specialization is more meaningful, and can be more adequately learned, if the probation officer has a broad, general educational background to serve as the basis and the framework for learning.

The probation officer typically has a great deal of direct and indirect contact with a variety of professional people in the community, such as judges, attorneys, doctors, psychiatrists, psychologists, school administrators and teachers. These are the professionals in the community who are responsible for the operation of the vitally important social institutions of education, administration of justice, physical and mental health and various social services to the citizenry. This contact may take the form of direct face-to-face communication, telephone conversation, exchange of written information, or reading of reports written at some time in the past. The effectiveness of such professional contact is dependent on mutual trust, respect for one another's integrity and confidence in the professional competence of each other. It is only through this kind of professional interaction that many functions important to the welfare of the community can be carried out.

The work of the probation officer is no exception; he is often dependent on the good will, trust and respect and cooperation of these other professionals to get his job done. Sometimes, it would be impossible to do the job, let alone perform on an optimum level, if he did not have the help and confidence of these other important people. It is highly unlikely that he will command the needed respect and confidence in his professional competence if he does not have the level of educational preparation that they consider roughly equal to their own. These people consider themselves to be professionals and will likely be reluctant to try to communicate on that level with someone they do not see as a fellow-professional. If the probation officer is known by them not to have had even a basic college education, which is merely the beginning of training for most of them, it will be difficult for them to accept him as a professional. If they do not accept and relate to him as a professional, it is likely that in both blunt and subtle ways this will be reflected in their trust of him and their respect for his competence. If they do not respect his professional competence, he will likely be hindered or even deterred from doing his best job. If he does not do his job on the highest level of competence, both the client and the community will be the losers and the potential loss is often of grave consequences.

To emphasize again: the probation officer must have a basic college education if he is to be accepted and permitted to perform as a professional in the discharge of his assigned responsibilities. The credibility and legitimation of the probation officer's person and position with other professionals is dependent on their acceptance of his credentials as a properly trained professional.

BALANCE BETWEEN IDEALISM AND REALISM

This very important characteristic of the probation officer is usually the result of a combination of general social maturity, a well-rounded education and considerable on-the-job experience. Developing these traits takes a lot of time and comes about in gradual increments. However, it helps to be aware of the important roles played by both a sense of idealism and hard-headed realism in the development of a balanced personality and method of approach to the task. This seems to be particularly the case for probation officers who are often responsible for a full professional function long before they have acquired much experience. A discussion of this needed balance between idealism and realism should, then, be of practical value at this point.

One criticism sometimes leveled against the probation officer is that he is idealistic in his philosophy, thinks all people are basically good and believes that his concern for and permissive treatment of the offender will save him from an evil society which is being unfair to him. It is true, of course, that many new workers in any of the *helping professions* tend to be idealistic and believe that, although others have failed to salvage the client, the worker will demonstrate that his brand of love and concern will succeed. Consequently, new probation officers are sometimes "conned" by the offender, do make mistakes of judgment and do get "burned" as a result. We really should not be too harsh with such eager new workers because one of the basic ways of learning anything is to try it out, perhaps make some mistakes, but learn from those errors. Fortunately, in all walks of life the consequences are not often a matter of life and death.

Actually, idealism is a positive, not always a negative thing. In most endeavors one needs the enthusiasm and drive which are the results of idealism. The probation officer, like many others dealing with human behavior, is often enough faced with very difficult, frustrating and thankless tasks. There is the temptation to become discouraged with lack of observable results, especially in attaining the more intangible goals of treatment. If one did not have some inner enthusiasm to keep pumping life into his actions, he would probably leave the field or, worse yet, *retire* on the job.

The probation officer should never lose his idealism nor his belief in the ability of people to change. He should never become cynical and suspicious in dealing with his clients even though constant exposure to so much of the seamy side of life may tend to warp his view of the world. To do so will cause him to lose sight of the importance of people and of the fact that positive good can exist in the midst of general decay. Basic to the ability of the probation officer to effectively relate to the client is a genuine acceptance of him as a worthwhile being and confidence in his potential for social readjustment. When these beliefs become tarnished through cynicism, the client will "get the message" and the probation officer's lack of confidence will be reflected in the client's responses.

Although it is vital that the probation officer maintain his idealism, his belief in the ability of people to change and his willingness to take risks for the client, this idealistic attitude must be balanced with equal parts of realism. He must be able to assess the world as it actually is, not as he might wish it were. He must have his feet on the ground, even though he may look to the sky. The general social maturity previously discussed will help him to know what life is all about and help to give him a sense of balance in appraising the total circumstances of a given situation. It is the realistic view which protects the probation officer from making serious mistakes when his idealistic concerns tempt him to take extreme action. This sense of realism is more or less synonymous with objectivity, a term often used to describe a necessary characteristic of those who want to be part of the helping professions. It is the realization that, no matter how hard he tries, he cannot save the whole world.

Another facet of this balance between idealism and realism has to do with the probation officer's past experiences. There are those who hold that a professional helping person cannot really understand his client because they generally come from different strata of society. These people claim that the helper best equipped to help is one who has already had the same experiences that the client is now having; therefore, in the correctional context, the best helpers are the ex-offenders, ex-addicts, ex-prisoners, etc. While it is probably true that the "street-wise" person is less likely to be "conned" by the client who is interested in his own advantage, it does not "take one to know one." There may be advantages to being intimately acquainted with the ins and outs of routine daily life as lived by most offenders, but it is possible to acquire such knowledge without actually living the same kind of life.

This may be done through various kinds of exposure to the routine of life. The alert probation officer can gain considerable insight into these matters by extensive reading in the area, often by those who have lived the routine. He can learn by careful observation of his clients' behavior, analyzing their attitudes, and discussing with them the details of their existence. He can gain the flavor of this life through participation in community activities involving the persons caught up in this atmosphere. He can share experiences of his clients through genuine feelings of empathy with them and a true caring for what happens to them.

As a matter of fact, the client often helps to educate the probation officer to his way of life when he believes in the reality of the officer's concern. When the probation officer is willing to admit his lack of knowledge of his client's life style, shows a genuine respect for the dignity of his client, displays a warm acceptance of the client as an equal and tries to understand what is needed to be of help to the client, he is likely to find himself the recipient of client efforts to assist him in learning enough of the details to increase his effectiveness.

Underlying this kind of exposure and feelings for his client is the probation officer's more general knowledge of the nature and principles of human behavior and interaction. If he can start with this base, be exposed to these learning experiences and cement them together with his genuine regard for the client, he can be even more effective than he necssarily would if his prime advantage was having lived the same sort of life. Just living the same sort of experience as someone else had does not mean that one clearly comprehends its meaning nor more completely understands the other person. There is more to life than mere living; there is also knowledge, effort, caring, understanding and a real desire to share and be of effective assistance to others. Hopefully, the true professional is more concerned with the latter.

ABILITY TO COMMUNICATE

It is probably correct to say that more problems arise in this world out of a failure to communicate than from any other, or even all other, sources. A corollary to this is that one of the most basic elements in human relations problem-solving is clear communication. It is totally impossible to understand another person, say, a client, and to assist him in the resolution of a problem without the ability to communicate.

Obviously, the term *communicate* in the context of helping the client, means more than mere talking or the use of some common language between two persons. It also means more than merely sending out a message, for there has been no communication until the message has been received and understood. Communication is the conveyance of one person's thoughts, concepts, feelings, beliefs, or ideas to another person in such a manner that the receiver comprehends them in the same way as they are understood and intended by the sender.

Communication is not automatic upon the message being sent; it requires an understanding reception also. Thus, it is not always a simple matter of saying something to someone; you may not really say what you mean or he may hear your words but give them his own meaning. Each one then acts in accordance with what he thought had been said, but each may be responding to a different message. This is how many serious misunderstandings occur between people in all walks of life and all kinds of circumstances. Clear communication takes some expertise which is developed through training, experience and effort. While this is true of both sender and receiver, it is probably more often true for the sender in that he must put forth some effort to be sure the message received is the same message he sent.

On the other hand, when the receiver is the professional helping person, it is an added responsibility on his part to be sure what he is receiving is that which is sent. It is not enough for the probation officer to simply listen to the words being spoken by the client; the probation officer must look beyond the mere words to be sure he gets the basic meaning of the message. By virtue of his training in interpersonal relations, his position as a representative of the community and the importance of his assigned functions, it is his professional responsibility to take the lead and insure that clear communication takes place between the client and himself in both directions.

The probation officer must be skilled in two-way verbal communications, both conveying clear messages to the client and clearly understanding the messages the client is sending. A large portion of the probation officer's time is devoted to conversation with clients, usually on a one-to-one basis. If he does not have the ability to clearly communicate verbally, both sending and receiving, he will waste a lot of time. He must be aware of the *static* which often occurs between sending and receiving; as when words are used which are not familiar to the other person so he does not grasp their meaning, or when emotionally charged terms are used which have special meanings to the receiver but not intended by the sender, or when the tone of voice conveys a message which is different from the words being used. Since both the client and the probation officer will act on the basis of what each thinks has been said, the officer must always make sure that the communication between them has been clearly understood by both.

Another large segment of the probation officer's time is spent in preparing written communication, most often in the form of reports to the court concerning his clients. Here too, it is vitally important that he have the ability to clearly communicate. There are *noises* which interfere with written communication, as they do with verbal, because the same problems exist regarding the use of unfamiliar words and emotionally charged terms. There is no problem with tone or noise interference, but the coldness of the written word can also be misunderstood simply because the reader does not have the advantage of hearing the tone used while speaking the words. This written communication takes on serious import when the court passes sentence based on the information in the probation officer's report. Not only must that information be accurate, it must also be conveyed in such a way as to have its accuracy and meaning clearly understood. Here again, this skill takes training, experience and effort; but implications for the client's future and the professional responsibilities of the probation officer require him to put forth whatever effort is needed to insure clear written communication.

There are ways to convey a message other than through either verbal or written form. Two which are very important should be mentioned here. One of these has to do with the entire impression the probation officer makes on the client as they relate to one another. The officer must relate to the client on a human level, not as a precise impersonal clinician. He must come through as a warmly real person; he must convey a genuine acceptance of the client as an important personage in his own right; he must communicate to the client that he sincerely cares. This is not done merely by so stating to the client; rather, it is made clear to him by the many little and often unconscious ways in which he is treated. If he is treated with dignity, respect, and politeness, he will "get the message" that the probation officer accepts him. If he is handled fairly, openly, and directly, he will realize that the officer really cares. All of this conveys a message to him, and that is what is meant by communication.

Another nonverbal way the probation officer can communicate

with the client is by setting a good example for him to follow. This is not to say that the client should be and do exactly as the probation officer; that would be artificial and impossible. It is to say, however, that the probation officer must not demand of the client what he negates through his own behavior. He cannot allow himself to imply to the client, "do as I say, not as I do." As quickly as anything, this attitude will hinder the effectiveness with which the probation officer relates to the client. After all, if it isn't thought important to him, why should it be thought important to the client? By his own behavior the probation officer conveys messages to the client, and if those messages are different from the things he has been saying, they can negate the real meaning of verbal exchange.

Because so much depends on the effectiveness of his verbal, written and nonverbal communication, it is an area of extreme importance to the professional practitioner. Some people, by the time they reach adulthood, have already developed a *knack* for such clear communication. Others may need to learn even after they have decided on a professional career. Good communication is not magical, innate, or automatic; it is learned. It is learned through the development of a simple but precise vocabulary, through being carefully aware of the emotional tone of a situation and through conscious effort to understand how one's message is being received. It takes study over a long period of time and experience gained through a process of output, feedback and adjustment. But good communication methods can be learned; they must be learned by the probation officer because the payoffs are of such great potential and the failures are of such serious consequences.

ORGANIZATIONAL ABILITY

One cannot overemphasize the practical importance of good organization on the part of the probation officer. Generally, his caseload is much larger than anyone can adequately handle, but there is much which has to be done on each of the cases. If the officer is not well organized to make the most judicious use of his limited time, much which is vital will not get done. Both the client and the community are the losers.

The probation officer must establish priorities according to the pressing needs of all his clients, hoping to be able to at least deal with the most serious and immediate. This means that careful analysis and planning for his entire caseload is a necessary procedure which must be regularly updated according to changing situations and demands. In addition, he must be alert enough and flexible enough to adjust to unexpected changes or demands. Without good organization, he will not be able to care for the unexpected and at the same time continue to carry out various planned activities.

On a very practical level good organization means clear definitions of procedures and the development of routines, when this can be done without his getting in a rut which can be deadening. It means establishing schedules and keeping to the deadlines; it means setting up necessary record keeping systems and faithfully doing the clerical chores that keep them current; it means assigning everything to a specific place and keeping it in place; it means periodically checking out the seldom done or seldom used things to be sure they are in good working order if needed; it means making time for the mechanical things necessary to keep daily routine in good order.

It is a temptation for a busy and perhaps overworked probation officer to let the more mundane chores go unattended in favor of the less tangible and usually more satisfying processes of dealing with the clients. But no one can keep straight all the demands of a large caseload unless he keeps records of who needs what when. No one can get reports ready for court on schedule unless he is aware of the deadlines. No one can remember all the things to be covered in those reports unless he has records on which to rely. No one can meet all the demands thrown at him from all angles and from a wide variety of circumstances unless he has a systematic way of maintaining control.

The alternative to good organization is a helter-skelter way of trying to do too many things, all absolutely necessary, at the same time. The interests of economy and efficiency demand good organization. The uneven flow and tremendous variety of client needs demand a systematic approach. The professional competence of the practitioner under many different pressures demands well-organized procedures. The serious consequences of missing something vital because of a hit-or-miss attitude demand good organization. The probation officer who is not well organized will discover that his frustrations are many times greater because of it and it is doubtful if he can long survive, at least as an effective practitioner of his profession.

SELF-DISCIPLINE

Discipline is defined as a state of order and control within which the probation officer operates; order and control which he has developed within himself, growing out of the rule and authority of ethical and professional responsibility. The key concept in self-discipline is control; for the probation officer, self-control in relation to himself and in relation to his clients.

The probation officer exercises self-discipline in many ways; some of which have already been mentioned in the discussion on organization and some of which will appear later in discussions relating to other topics. Here, we want to make a few observations in order to show just what is meant by self-discipline.

In relation to himself, the probation officer exercises self-discipline by continuing to learn and keep up-to-date on developments in his field. One legacy of his college experience is that he has learned the process of learning; a process which requires scheduling, meeting requirements and deadlines and which by its very operation teaches self-discipline and the necessity of good organization to efficient output. As a practitioner, this same learning process is continued because he has learned that it is the only way to avoid becoming antiquated.

The self-disciplined professional always maintains his basic honesty and integrity and is not willing to compromise principle. He does the ethical thing, even when no one is looking or when no one else cares. He maintains his self-respect even if he has to forego some pleasurable experience or be thought too rigid by others. Without this kind of self-discipline, he is not really a professional.

There is also the thought of self-control in relation to the client. This includes such things as an even-tempered approach to dealing with the client so that some necessary stability of relationship is added to his life. It means the recognition of personal biases, and objective and fair treatment of him even when emotional states may tempt one to behave otherwise. It means the maintenance of a helpful relationship built on openness and kindly "straight-from-the-shoulder" frankness. It is the kind of personal control of action, emotions and attitudes which professional ethics demand.

There are many personal characteristics which have not been included here, but which would also be desirable for the probation officer. Someone else might want to group the traits differently or possibly feel that certain ones should receive more emphases because they are a bit more important. However one may feel about these points he probably will agree that the characteristics we have discussed are all necessary.

This is not to say that the probation officer must possess all these traits to perfection; that is impossible. We do not intend to try to make him look like a paragon of virtue; we recognize that he is human with shortcomings and failings like any other. But the importance of his function and the impact he can have on so many people require that he work hard to learn and train himself so that the failings are kept to the minimum.

Chapter Eight

THE EXERCISE OF GOOD JUDGMENT

THE LEVEL OF THE PROBATION officer's competence is frequently assessed on the basis of how well he independently makes decisions and exercises sound judgment. Many people knowledgeable of just what the probation officer's task is are very much aware that he deals in important commodities: the freedom, the future, the daily life of the client. If he lacks the ability to exercise sound judgment, he will have serious negative impact on the client. If his judgments are sound, he will likely have a helpful influence on the client and a positive impact on the community.

The validation of the probation officer's professional status, especially among other professionals, also involves his ability in independent decision-making and the exercise of good judgment. If they determine through their contact with, observation of, or knowledge about the probation officer that he cannot make decisions or act independently, they will not accept him as a professional. In like terms, if they discover that his judgment is faulty and not to be trusted, he will not be accepted by them as a professional.

Much of the probation officer's activity with the client is confrontive in nature as he works to help the client accept responsibility for the consequences of his behavior. This effort is sometimes met with resistance or even hostility by the client. In such a highly charged atmosphere things can go wrong so easily, especially if the probation officer lacks good judgment, and the consequences can be disasterous for attainment of the goals of the probation program.

Thus the estimation of the level of probation officer competence, his professional standing among other professionals and the effectiveness of the probation program are dependent upon the exercise of good judgment by the probation officer. The use of good judgment is a blending of positive attitude and proper action which conveys to others that one knows what he is doing and is in calm command of the situation. This adds strength and stability to any setting and gives one "the edge" of control in an atmosphere where confrontation and suspicion might prevail.

Obviously, the probation officer should exercise good judgment at all times in every situation. However, there are several specific areas in which the exercise of good judgment is particularly pertinent to the position and functions of the probation officer. He should be careful to exercise good judgment in the recognition of his role, in the use of his authority, in the way he deals with the client and in his personal conduct.

RECOGNITION OF ROLE

The probation officer must know, understand and accept his own particular position and role in the process of administering criminal justice and treating the offender. His is a specific function related to that of the other criminal justice components, but not interfering with them. To understand his own role, he must be able to clearly delineate the roles of the other components and not infringe on them. The law enforcement officer has the task of detecting crime, gathering evidence and making arrests. The prosecutor's function is to decide what matters will be prosecuted and try to present evidence sufficient to warrant conviction. The defense attorney must be sure to protect the rights of his client and provide him the best possible defense. The judge has the responsibility to make legal rulings in the matter and decide what the sentence will be. None of these various functions belong to the probation officer and he should never try to assume them as his own. He will be busy enough if he properly carries out his own functions.

It is not enough to simply know what are the roles of the other principles; the probation officer must also accept them for what they are and learn to accommodate his role to them. This does not mean that any one role is subservient to another; it does mean that they should all dovetail with one another, each fulfilling its own function in the justice process without interfering with the orderly operation of the others. When one accepts and feels comfortable with his role because he feels it is important and because he clearly understands how it interfaces with others, accommodation is not difficult.

For example, in relation to the court, one of the functions of the probation officer is that of a recommender, not the final decision-maker. He functions as an adjunct to, not in lieu of, the court. His role here is very important because he gathers the information, prepares the evaluation and makes the recommendation which courts rely on and most often follow. But even if the court does not accept the probation officer's evaluation and recommendation, he should not fret about it. He has done his job and now the court is doing its job; and that is as it should be. The only way one can survive and maintain his sanity is to do the very best he can at his tasks and leave the rest to the other components of the system without worrying about how they will do their jobs.

This also implies another aspect of good judgment in the probation officer's recognition of his role, namely, that he will refrain from public criticism of the other components of the justice system of which he is a part. Because of his close relationships with law enforcement, attorneys and judges, the probation officer will quite likely see and know about actions and decisions they have made with which he does not personally agree. He does have a right to his own opinion, but he must remember two things: unless one clearly understands the role of another person, he has no right to be critical of his performance of that role; and there is nothing which can destroy one's own position so quickly as chipping away at the foundations of other positions on which his depends. Although as an insider the probation officer may feel he has valid comments to make, he should be very sure that they are not made in a setting or in such a manner as to undermine public confidence in other parts of the justice system. Without their cooperation and support the probation officer will find it very difficult and frustrating to try to do his job. So, while he should be willing to discuss mutual problems with them, he cannot afford to *put them down*. He needs them.

USE OF AUTHORITY

The unique thing that the probation officer shares with other correctional workers, but which is different from most casework and counseling positions, is his cloak of legal authority. This is an awesome authority which carries with it the power to restrict a client's actions, deprive him of his liberty and in many other ways exercise control over his life. This is obviously something not to be taken lightly by the probation officer because it has such far-reaching and serious consequences. It is also one of the most difficult things for many probation officers to learn to handle in a confident and judicious manner. There are a few observations to be made on this point which might help the probation officer to more effectively deal with the authority he has.

It will help a great deal if he remembers that his authority is not personal but has been delegated to him from society by law through the agency. In and of himself, the probation officer is a private citizen with no more authority than any other citizen. But in his position as a probation officer, duly appointed by his agency as one of society's representatives in the community, he takes on authority to act in behalf of society. This view of authority will allow the probation officer to be much more objective and discreet in the way he uses the authority of his position to work with and on behalf of the client. It prevents him from succumbing to the temptation to retaliate when the client does something of which he does not personally approve or which displeases him. If he falls into the trap of using his authority to personal ends he will seriously hinder, if not completely negate, rehabilitative work with the client and will bring reproach upon himself and his profession.

Authority must always be used constructively; to accomplish something with and for the client, not to tear him down or intimidate him. Although probation may involve a great deal of surveillance and control over the client, it is not a matter of being on the lookout to "get the goods" on him. The probation officer cannot afford to allow illegal or destructively negative behavior to go unchallenged. Part of his job is to confront the client with the realities, including painful consequences, of his behavior and this will sometimes involve action by the probation officer which may not be pleasant for the client. Yet the probation officer must always be aware that part of his task is to help the client understand what is happening to him and why. This cannot be done if action is taken in a lord-it-over-him manner. The probation officer must never get caught up in the I-can't-let-him-get-away-with-it syndrome in which he sets out to gather all the evidence he can in order to "have the goods" on the client to support a revocation of probation.

This sort of orientation or motivation is sure to lead him to an emotional and unwise use of authority which could in a moment undo the positive good which may have taken many months to build up. Besides, as we have already discussed, there is much more to the probation officer's responsibility in working with the client than just insuring observance of the law; there is also the challenge of assisting him to learn to cope with his problems and environment in a more effective and acceptable manner.

There are times, of course, when the probation officer must make use of his authority to enforce the law or the terms of probation, because the client is behaving in such a way as to be harmful to himself or others, or because his behavior is so serious that it cannot go unnoticed by authority persons. This is a legitimate and constructive use of authority. Sometimes the line between the proper and the personal use of authority is difficult to discern, but the probation officer should never make use of his authority just to demonstrate to a client that he can do it.

Another facet of the wise use of authority has to do with how the probation officer talks about his authority. The probation officer who says to a colleague, "You know that guy I busted last month here in the office? Well, I convicted him of ———," has a problem with authority. The officer who says, "I remember him, I sent him to prison three years ago for ———," has a problem with authority. This kind of talk is usually not an innocent expression of fact; rather, it indicates a person who might easily misuse or abuse his position of authority. It also indicates a probation officer who has not learned to properly delineate and accept his own role in the process of the administration of justice because it is not he who *convicts* or *sends to prison;* it is the court. This is more than just talk; it is authority which he exercises or that which is exercised over him. Until such a person more clearly understands his functions as a probation officer and comes to grips with his problem with authority, he will not be the kind of person who, with firmness and compassion, can help someone else make adjustment to his own difficulties in life.

Attitudes and actions like these seem to be appeals to the ego of the probation officer or be ways of meeting some of his own personal needs to be important, be respected, have power. In any case, they indicate personal problems which render him less than adequate to do the kind of job a probation officer must do. The most dangerous and offensive thing a public officer can do is to use the authority or power of his official position to meet his personal needs. Under no circumstances can such an action be legitimate or acceptable. The probation officer must be careful to analyze his motives and be alert to avoid even the hint of such activity. It is not an easy thing to do, but if he understands himself as a person, understands and accepts his role as a probation officer and exercises good judgment, he is not likely to have serious difficulty in this regard.

TREATMENT OF THE CLIENT

There are, of course, many situations and opportunities in his ongoing relationship with the client in which the probation officer can and must exercise sound judgment. In a real sense, these probably occur every time he makes contact with the client and perhaps even in collateral contacts about the client. All of these are important because in some way, even though it might appear insignificant, they affect the overall relationship between probation officer and client. However, our discussion here will be limited to only two aspects of the use of good judgment in the treatment of the client. They revolve around the concepts of self-determination and flexibility of adjustment to changing circumstances.

The concept of self-determination is not only basic to the development of our nation in the early days of its history, it is also basic to effective human development. It is a key principle in the philosophy and practice of social casework and is what correctional counseling is all about. This idea that the individual has the right to live his own life, to decide his own destiny, to make his own choices is a strong force in the makeup of free men. There is a heavy emphasis in American culture on rugged individualism and we admire the man who can "stand on his own feet, shift for himself, and become a self-made man." At the same time, we feel some compassion for the weak and needy so long as his problems are not of his own making. The problem is, however, that we sometimes have difficulty in distinguishing between those for whom we should have compassion and those who have no right to make demands on us.

The probation officer can easily fall prey to this problem because he is in almost constant contact with many weak, needy and dependent persons who look to him as a person of strength and a source of help. At the same time, he is expected to use his expertise and authority to force these same persons to become self-supporting so as not to be a drain on society. Sometimes it is difficult for him to know where to draw the line, but he is required to draw it, so he must use good judgment in doing so.

One of the major goals of correctional counseling, as it is of all casework, is to help the individual find his own solutions to his problems and to avoid excessive dependency on anyone else to do for him. This is the essence of the principle of self-determination as a part of the philosophy and practice of casework. The probation officer's focus is not to make decisions for the client, but to help him learn to make sound decisions on his own. He will help the client to clearly identify the problem, determine the possible and feasible alternative solutions to the problem and see the consequences of each possibility; but it must be the client who ultimately makes the decision. Then the probation officer may have to help him learn to live with the decision he has made. All in all, the probation officer is ever alert to avoid fostering client dependency on him or on others, so he is careful not to make decisions for the client although he will be making decisions for himself about the client as part of his function.

Flexibility of adjustment to changing circumstances is another area in the treatment of the client in which the probation officer must always exercise good judgment. Consistency of requirements for behavior, of relationship, of treatment is very important to help give the client some additional stability in his life. But consistency is not mechanical sameness; it encompasses the flexibility needed to maintain the treatment plan in the direction of its goals. There is no conflict between consistency of treatment and flexibility to adjust to varying circumstances, but the meshing of the two does require the exercise of sound judgment by the probation officer.

Action which is appropriate, even necessary, under one set of circumstances may not be the proper action in another situation. The probation officer tries to help the client to comprehend this in his decisions. He must also see this distinction in his own decision regarding the client. Part of the professional expertise of the probation officer, as well as part of the idea of good judgment, is knowing how to act and when to act under what set of circumstances. An intelligent assessment of a situation and sound judgment regarding it will go a long way toward successful treatment of the client, whatever may be the specific goals of treatment.

PERSONAL CONDUCT

The probation officer must be very careful to exercise good judgment in two broad areas of personal conduct; in on-the-job behavior and in off-the-job behavior. Both of these are of vital importance because both can have serious impact on job performance. One is usually judged more or less superficially by most people and the judgment is based more on the general impression they get than on specific actions. The image one projects can have serious implications for effectiveness in performance. For the probation officer, much of his effectiveness and success depends on how he is defined and perceived by the client. Like others, the client reacts to what he thinks he sees in the probation officer. Consequently, the way the officer "comes across" to the client, that is, the image he projects, has a lot to do with effectiveness of performance. With this orientation, it can be seen that using good judgment in personal conduct is of the utmost importance.

We have already discussed many aspects of both on- and off-the-job conduct and others will be dealt with in other contexts in later chapters. Here, we need simply mention a few additional thoughts that are not dealt with elsewhere.

Discretion is a cardinal virtue for a probation officer, and nowhere is it more needed than in his personal conduct. He needs, for example, to be discreet in what he says to clients and others, using good judgment as to vocabulary and content. But he also needs to be discreet about where and to whom he talks. There are many comments he might safely make to colleagues without fear of misunderstanding, but he must be careful about making the same comments in public where they could be overheard and misinterpreted by the uninitiated. Public coffee shops, hallways and waiting rooms are not proper places to discuss cases with anyone; colleagues, attorneys, clients, or anyone else. This applies to both on- and off-the-job conversation, whether it is a serious case discussion or casual conversation.

This is not to say that the probation officer can never discuss a case with others except in the privacy of his own office; it is to say that he must use good judgment about discussing cases no matter where he is. And—need it be said at all?—he must never discuss the case of one client with another client. After all, "if my probation officer will talk to me about another client, I can reasonably expect that he will blab to someone else about me." Imagine what that thought might do to the relationship of trust and mutual respect one is trying to establish with the client.

The worst aspect of the probation officer's failure to exercise good judgment in the recognition of his role, use of authority, treatment of the client and personal conduct is that it hurts everyone. Poor decision-making or errors of judgment will work to the detriment of the client, the agency, his colleagues and himself. And there is no substitute for good judgment; no matter what the level of education and training, length of job experience, or contriteness after the fact, errors of judgment carry their own consequences. The probation officer must be ever alert here to *do the right thing* as required by the situation and not depend on anything or anyone else to get him out of it. It is his responsibility to exercise good judgment.

Part Three

PERFORMANCE

Chapter Nine

THE PROBATION
INVESTIGATION

IN GENERAL, the probation officer has two major functions: conducting investigations and writing reports for the court; and supervising those persons placed in his care by the court. The later, which has to do with the individual already on probation, is probably the function most people would think of in terms of describing the probation officer's job. However, the former is of equal importance in the overall philosophy of probation and one needs to be careful that it receives its share of attention.

We cannot, in the scope of this book, cover all the details of such things as interviewing and good writing which might be appropriate; many books have been written on these subjects in other areas and are available for careful study. We can, however, profitably address ourselves to most of the major considerations in these areas as they specifically apply to the probation investigation and report. This examination will be brief but will deal with the most salient points and will establish a proper frame of reference for the practitioner who will want to later explore on his own some of the finer points of interviewing and writing.

The probation investigation is not unlike most any other examination of a situation which will be followed by a formal report and recommendation. Its primary uniqueness lies in the fact that it has to do with court processes and the provision of information to the court for its use in arriving at a disposition of a matter. Often the statutes of a state require, or at least make provision for, this investigation as well as the content of the report. These statutes vary from state to state, so we cannot focus too much on their requirements. We can, however, discuss the probation investigation in more general terms which will apply to any jurisdiction. The specific legal considerations will be left to the individual reader to explore according to his own jurisdictional setting.

PHILOSOPHY OF PROBATION INVESTIGATION

The authorization to conduct a probation investigation is usually specified or implied in the statutes of the state, and this is sufficient. However, this authorization is also an integral component of the very philosophy of probation as articulated by the spokesmen in the field and which often is the specified foundation for legal requirements. The underlying principle is to provide adequate and accurate information to the court to enable it to make an intelligently appropriate decision in the specific matter. This principle comports with the idea of an individualized approach to the administration of justice; an idea which is the very heart of the concept of probation. Thus, the probation investigation is a legally sanctioned action which is rooted in and expresses a basic social philosophy of criminal corrections.

In conducting the investigation the probation officer is exercising his role as the representative of the community in regard to the handling of offenders. This gets us back to our previous discussion of the probation officer's recognition and acceptance of his role in the criminal justice process. It is vitally important for him to remember that he represents his department and its legally constituted authority and, by extention, the courts generally as well as the community which provides for his function. He does not represent himself nor even his own values in the strictest sense; he is the servant of the community and, especially in his recommendation, is often the spokesman for the community in terms of protecting its own welfare. The probation officer must never forget this basic responsibility to the community.

The probation investigation, coupled with the report resulting from it, consists of four major components: gathering data, analyzing data, developing a plan of action and making a recommendation based on the data. The data gathered is basically social rather than legal. Of course, legal information of several kinds may well be a part of the data collected, but the thrust is not to establish legal culpability; rather, it is to develop a complete portrait of an individual who has violated the law. Hopefully, the data will be factually accurate, but many things will come to light in the investigation which are hearsay rather than legally admissible as evidence. However, if these things help to provide an accurate picture of the behavior of the offender, they are appropriate to the investigation and report. In his report, the probation officer should be careful to designate the different kinds and levels of substantiation of information he is using as a basis for his conclusions.

By analysis of data is meant answering the questions, "What does all the information mean?" "Exactly what does it tell us about the offender and his behavior?" This means that what the probation officer must do is more than merely describe the offender; he must interpret the underlying meanings of the information he has gathered. He must narratively paint a dynamic picture of the offender as a whole person with strengths and weaknesses, attitudes and feelings, past behavior and future potential all clearly shown for the decision-maker to see, study and decide how to handle.

The question of what to do with the offender is, ideally, based on what he is like and how he has acted. The plan of action to which the probation officer addresses himself grows out of answers to such questions as "What are the needs of the community and the offender in this particular situation?" "What are the goals to be attained?" "What are the specific courses of action needed to reach these goals?" When these questions are answered, the probation officer is ready to make his recommendation to the court; a recommendation which is the logical conclusion of the data gathered, the analysis of the information and the specification of a plan of action. It is the component of the process of investigation which "ties up the package," making it ready for delivery.

Another important element of a philosophy of probation investigation is the recognition of the importance of what is usually the initial contact between the probation officer and the offender. It would be difficult to overemphasize the importance of the first contact for both the agency and the client because it sets the stage for so much which will follow. We have already commented on the long-term impact of first impressions, and it is just as crucial here because it can set the pace for later relationships and actions. Of course, this nor any other contact can be so routinized as to become standard; the nature of the initial contact will vary according to a myriad of particular circumstances. However, some general observations would apply in every case.

It is important for the probation officer to realize that apprehension usually blocks meaningful communication and, without such communication, gathering and analyzing necessary data will be severely hindered. One of the first things the probation officer should do is to explain to the client the meaning and purpose of the investigation process and give him an overview of what it will cover. He would do well also to explain the nature of further court proceedings and outline the possible alternatives in disposition. Generally, the more fully the client understands what is happening, the more concerned and cooperative he will be. Besides, it is his freedom and future which are at stake so he has a right to be told what is taking place regarding himself.

The initial contact, as all others, should be characterized by courtesy and friendliness, by firmness and a matter-of-fact approach, by concern and recognition of the dignity of the individual. This is the first step in the treatment process which will hopefully be followed up in the same atmosphere; so these kinds of attitudes are very important for establishing the sort of therapeutic relationship which is so basic to working with people who have problems.

PROCESSES OF PROBATION INVESTIGATION

What the probation officer does from the time he is assigned a probation investigation until the report is ready for delivery to the court should flow orderly, smoothly and without delay. There are, of course, many intervening variables over which he has no control but which can seriously hamper the investigation. With careful attention and planning, however, the probation officer can avoid many of these interferences and minimize the effect of others.

This can be done by being familiar with exactly what information will be needed and how it is to be incorporated into a written report. Legal, judicial and administrative requirements to be met must be clearly in the mind of the probation officer as he gathers material because they give direction to his activity. It is also necessary to plan ahead from the moment of the assignment. He needs to immediately review the various tasks to be done and establish priorities, especially in a time frame of what is due first or what must be done in order to lay the ground work for later tasks. Another way to avoid problems arising is to be sure to get started as soon as possible; do not delay, time has a way of disappearing and future dates suddenly become today. Delay will almost always return to haunt you.

After these general observations, it is appropriate to look at the specific steps involved in the investigation. Agency policy may dictate certain kinds of things be done or forms be used and these may not be reflected in what will be discussed below, but the suggestions will generally be applicable as guidelines in most investigative processes. Following them will help the probation officer to approach his task in an orderly manner and will assist in the most efficient use of his time. To facilitate discussion the specific steps are organized into four phases—pre-interview, the interview, collateral contacts, and post-interview.

Pre-Interview

Since most agencies require some sort of monthly workload reports from the probation officer, his first act after being assigned a new case should be to record the assignment in whatever way is appropriate for the required reports. If this is done as new cases come to him, it will help to insure that none are inadvertently laid aside and thus forgotten or even lost. It is also the best way to provide an accurate count of the number of cases received.

The next step is to schedule an interview with the client. The question of time is vital here because the probation officer must be careful to do what has to be done to meet the deadline of the date his report is due in court. Making an appointment may be as simple as noting on one's calendar to see the client on a particular day, or it may be as complicated as having to check through many sources merely to determine where he can be reached. It may involve sending an appointment letter or making a phone call; in either case he probably will need to allow time for the client to arrange his affairs in order to make the appointment, especially if he is employed and will need to take any time off the job. Time is also a consideration in that the probation officer may need to do a number of things prior to interviewing the client, many of which may require a lot of time. Be sure to make a note on the calendar to remind you of the appointment time as well as the date due in court.

Prior to interviewing the client, the probation officer should review all information available to him regarding the client and the offense. This would include arresting agency reports of the offense and interviews with witnesses, any notes made during intake interviews, prior probation reports if any exist, and any reports made available by either the prosecution or defense. In the course of reading these reports the probation officer should make notes of questions to be asked the client, facts or other information to be verified, other contacts to be made and reports to be requested.

Information and reports from other agencies should be requested as soon as their existence is known. Replies often take some time and the time the probation officer has to get his investigation completed is usually limited; thus, delay in requesting information will frequently mean it will not arrive in time to incorporate into the report; and the data might make a significant difference in the recommendation.

Before the interview the probation officer should always check out any previous arrest and court records the client might have. Previous contacts with law enforcement agencies and the courts are important aspects of the client's life and behavior patterns. These need to be discussed with him to get an idea of his motivations, his feelings about the events and how they have affected his life style. This means that the probation officer must have information about these incidents before he interviews the client.

These pre-interview steps are vitally important for many reasons. The act of beginning with them will help to set in motion the entire investigative process and, if they have been done properly, will force the "ball to keep rolling." This helps to insure the probation officer will not forget some important step and that he will meet his court date deadlines. Just as importantly, these pre-interview actions will prepare him to discuss with the client in more appropriate and effective terms the various things that must be covered. It is unfortunate, but true, that frequently the probation officer will be able to interview the client only once; if he is not prepared to cover every important item during the one sitting, his report will have serious gaps of information and will thus be rendered far less valuable than it should be.

The best way to avoid this problem is to be well-organized in his preparation, get these pre-interview actions started and be alert to any hint these items might provide as to other sources of information or directions of investigation the probation officer should pursue.

The Interview

When all the above steps have been taken, the probation officer is probably as well prepared to interview the client as he could be. Being well prepared is vitally important to an efficient use of the limited amount of time available, but it also provides a psychological boost to the probation officer because he feels confident and in calm command of the situation. This element, in and of itself, will help him to be more relaxed, alert and clear-headed, thereby increasing the effectiveness with which he gathers and evaluates information from and about the client. There is no satisfactory substitute for being well prepared.

After this preparation, however, the probation officer should be careful to be prompt for his appointment with the client. This is a matter of good organization and professional attitude. Even though a veteran probation officer knows that many clients are lax about promptness for appointments, he must remember that it is *he* who is the professional. Just because a client may be late is no valid excuse for the probation officer to be late. This is not merely a matter of being nice to someone else; it is an example of using the little things to get messages across. One thing the probation officer probably needs to focus on with the client is his sense of responsibility. Promptness for interview appointments help to set an example of the kind of responsible attitudes he is trying to help the client develop. Part of this consideration is advance notice to the client, if at all possible, in the event the officer has an emergency requiring cancellation of the appointment. But merely routine matters should never be allowed to interfere with the work to the extent of causing cancellations. Not only does this have an adverse effect on the client's impression of the probation officer; it also tends to pile up the workload for later times, the end result of which will likely be less time to do the job which means a decline in quality of work.

Throughout the interview process, as well as during preparation for it, the probation officer must be thorough in his work. He must be careful to "cover all the bases" which the situation and the requirements of the report dictate. He must be alert, think and anticipate what might come up. He must look ahead, always aware of what the next step is to be. As a matter of fact, part of his mind should be moving ahead to anticipate the next step while the other part is still dealing with the matter at hand. Only this kind of alert thoroughness will enable the probation officer to maximize his time and resources to keep up with the workload while operating at the highest level of quality; and this is the approach which must be taken by the well-trained professional.

The most important "stock-in-trade" for the probation officer in dealing with the client is the one-to-one, face-to-face interview. As a counselor, this two-way relationship is the major casework technique that he can use to carry out his responsibility and reach his goal of assisting the client to cope with his situation at least to the extent of avoiding legal conflict due to his illegal conduct. The probation officer has this personal one-to-one contact with the client in two broad settings: in the interview necessary for the preparation of the probation report; and in the ongoing supervision phase of the probation process. In the first setting, the *inter-view*, or *looking within*, is for the purpose of gathering information to form a broad and clear picture of the client in order to assist the court in sentencing decisions. In the latter setting, the probation officer is still trying to *look within* but for different purposes. Rather than providing a general picture, the focus is usually directed at specific problem areas, behavior patterns, or immediate concerns which are to be dealt with during the probation period.

There is a great deal to the "art of interviewing" which cannot be covered in this section. Many books and feature length articles have been written on the many facets of the subject, including theory, practice, various approaches and techniques and problems arising from specific applications of several sorts. Probation officers are encouraged to study these sources, especially those written expressly for the field of corrections, in order that they may know and effectively practice good interviewing techniques, without which they will be lost in a profession which depends so heavily on the personal interview. Here, we will limit our discussion to some considerations which are most applicable to the kind of interview conducted as a part of the probation investigation. Most of the comments will also be appropriate to regular interviews in the ongoing supervision phase of probation and should be kept in mind for use in that context.

Even before the interview begins there are things to be done. The probation officer should try to plan specifically for each interview. We have already touched on some considerations along this line in terms of making notes of questions to pursue while he is reading reports. He should take time before the interview to integrate these notes with all the information he has at the time in the light of what he knows about the offense and the offender. All these things should be organized in such a way as to flow smoothly from one point to another and so that nothing important will be missed. We cannot stress too often the necessity of planning and organization for the most efficient and effective use of time and resources. The probation officer who is well-organized and plans ahead will be able to accomplish twice as much in the same amount of time, and of as high or higher quality, as the probation officer who lacks organization and planning skills.

The setting for the interview is another important factor to be considered. Physically, it should be as private and comfortable as possible. The fewer the interruptions and distractions the more effective will be the process. It is recognized that in many agencies this is a difficult arrangement to make and many probation officers have learned to adjust to surroundings which are much less than ideal. This same sort of ingenuity should be put to work to make the physical setting for the interview as conducive as possible to the gathering of data which is its purpose.

There is also a psychological aspect to the interview setting. This includes the impression the physical surroundings make on the client. The kind of office decorations, pictures and furnishings which tend to overwhelm or antagonize the client should be avoided. Office decor should reflect the personality of the occupant, but it should also reflect appropriate professional attitudes and be designed to put clients at ease, not to make them tense or apprehensive. Accoutrements of authority are not necessary as wall decorations to impress the client of the probation officer's position. The few times this is necessary, it is better accomplished through verbal communication than through ostentatious display. The interview atmosphere should be pleasant and characterized by relaxed friendliness and courtesy. It is usually not necessary to scare the client; he is not as likely to communicate freely when he is tense and afraid as he is when he is relaxed. And, after all, the purpose is to get him to communicate, not to withdraw.

Even when one has tried to make the physical and psychological setting as conducive as possible to good communication, there are many things that can interfere. For example, if the probation officer uses jargon or a vocabulary not understood by the client, he will not make himself clear; and if he cannot get the client to understand him it is unlikely that the client will communicate in such a way as to enable the probation officer to understand him. Plain language in common usage is the most effective way to communicate to most probation clients. Other kinds of "static" or "noise" which interfere with good communication in the interview may come through to the probation officer as obstinacy on the part of the client. If he is anxious and uncertain he will not likely respond to questions in the best way; hesitancy due to nervousness or mistakes due to tenseness may be interpreted as withholding information; or attempts at levity due to anxiety may be interpreted as insincerity. Not only should the probation officer try to put the client at ease by telling him what the interview is all about, he should also be very alert not to misinterpret what the client says or does, or does not say or do. The client may be trying but is so "uptight" that he is stumbling all over himself. Part of the probation officer's skill is to distinguish between this situation and deliberate hostility, "conning," or lack of sincerity; all of which will hinder good communication.

The attitude of the probation officer also has an effect on the willingness of the client to communicate. If he maintains a non-judgmental attitude he will not cause the client to be "turned off," thereby blocking communication. It is just as difficult for the criminal offender to talk to someone who is always critical of him as it is for the rest of us. The probation officer does not indicate to the client that his behavior is acceptable, but he also does not label the client as "bad." As the old cliché goes, "I accept you but not your behavior." All of us feel more comfortable and can communicate more freely with someone who shows an interest in us as people; the probation client is no exception. Most of the time, when he feels the probation officer accepts him as a person and treats him with courtesy and dignity, he will easily discuss his life, his actions and his feelings; in other words, he will share the kinds of personal data the probation officer needs in order to complete his picture and arrive at his recommendation.

The probation officer needs to be sure that he is in control of the interview. While it is exploratory and of necessity must take in a lot of territory, he cannot afford to be too nondirective; he simply does not have the time to allow the client to ramble wherever he may wish to go. The interview is usually more directive in the investigation phase than it is in the supervision phase. This is not to imply that there will necessarily be more time for interviews in the latter phase; it simply means that the purposes are different and there will be less need to complete a certain process by a given time due to court dates. So the probation officer must remember the purpose of the investigation interview, channeling the discussion where needed and following leads at other times. He must be flexible to change his role and his method as the situation changes so that he is always working at maximum efficiency and effectiveness for the purposes of the interview.

Throughout the interview process the probation officer must be sure to listen. He will not learn anything about the client if he is doing all the talking; except, perhaps, that the client knows how not to talk! He must listen, listen, listen! Listen with his ears to what is being said; with his eyes to physical postures and movements as it is being said; and with his mind to what is not said. He must be careful to listen, not just to hear but to understand; and from the understanding to be able to develop a general picture of the client. If the probation officer will listen alertly, he will not only gain information needed for his report to the court, he will also pick up clues for future treatment considerations.

This approach to interviewing is far from a routine mechanical operation; it is a process of human communication in two directions which can only be developed through training, experience, practice and genuine concern for others. If the probation officer tries to function in any other fashion he will be signally unsuccessful.

Collateral Contacts

The primary purpose of the probation investigation is to learn as much as possible about the client. There are many sources of information in addition to the client himself and the

The Professional Practitioner in Probation

probation officer should be alert to determine how to tap these sources. Additional information may be obtained from arresting officers, victims, witnesses, coparticipants, prosecution and defense attorneys, family members, employers, schools, other social agencies, other correctional agencies, doctors and psychologists, to name a few. This does not mean that the probation officer should try to contact all these possible sources; some are not appropriate to the particular situation, and he may be limited in time so will not be able to contact all those which are applicable. The basic principle is to contact everyone necessary to secure all the information he needs for his report.

This will usually mean establishing some sort of priority according to who would be the most productive source, who is available and how much time can be used for this purpose. The major reason for making collateral contacts is so the probation officer can gain information from people who have known the client in various circumstances over many years and thus supplement what he has learned and observed through his own limited contacts with the client. Because the time he has to spend with the client is limited, objective data gathered from thoughtful collateral sources becomes even more important to a full and clear portrayal of the client to the court.

Whatever the time limits, there are some collateral contacts that must be made. The probation officer should always contact the victims of the criminal offenses he is investigating. Even if he gains no information in addition to that already reported by the arresting agency, at least the victim is not forgotten, an all too frequent occurrence, and the probation officer will probably make a friend for his agency. He should also contact the arresting or referring agency if the reports hint of problems not explained in the reports. He should always contact any person or agency specifically requesting an opportunity to provide input to the investigation. He should always contact other probation or parole agencies if the client is already or has recently been under their jurisdiction. He must always coordinate and exchange information with other probation officers in his own agency who are conducting probation investigations on coparticipants.

When the probation officer uses information in his report which he has gleaned from collateral sources it should always be so identified. This means that, during the process of making the collateral contacts, the source of information provided should be told that he will be quoted in the report and permission to do so should be requested at that time. Some people will respond differently when they know they will be quoted and this could slant their data. However, the honesty and integrity and professional approach of the probation officer will not allow him to mislead or misinform a source of information as to how he intends to use the information. His only choice is to be frank and candid and do the best he can with what he is given.

Post-Interview

After the probation officer has gathered all the information he can, or has time and resources to gather, there are some things he should do before he is ready to write his report.

It has been assumed that he was making notes as he was conducting the investigation; now we make it explicit. If he does not make notes as he goes along he will be lost as he begins to complete his written report. He should not rely on his memory to reproduce conversations with the client or collateral sources; it is too easy to forget important material or confuse what one person said with what was said by another. He should make his notes on paper which is large enough not to get misplaced or even destroyed. Each sheet should be identified with the client's name so that things do not get mixed up if several files are in use at one time. The probation officer should also number, date, and initial each page of notes. This takes only seconds but may save hours later in getting things organized for the report or if he is called upon to verify when he talked to whom and what was said at the time.

The probation officer should also discuss the entire matter with his supervisor before he writes his report. This procedure is required in some agencies, but it is good practice to follow even if it is not policy. It keeps the supervisor informed in the event he must take some action on the matter in the absence of the probation officer. It helps to insure that planned action is legal, according to agency policy and realistic by providing a double check on it. It is also appropriate as a *trial run* of information for the report in that it will probably expose gaps or weaknesses in the data, will help the probation officer to organize and crystallize the data and will help him anticipate what questions may arise when the report is considered in court and how to best be prepared to answer them. This practice is also a good training exercise, showing the officer where he might not be "up to par" in his data gathering and allowing the supervisor to suggest ways of correcting or improving the officer's practice.

Throughout the entire investigative process the probation officer must remain alert to pick up and follow clues that will be useful to his purposes. He must also think ahead and be one step in front or he is likely to feel he is not in control of the situation. Not only is this a frustrating and disheartening experience, it is also destructive of high quality work and interferes with job satisfaction. The task the probation officer is performing in the probation investigation is too important to permit it to be hampered, especially by some factor which is entirely within his control. He will have enough problems from external and uncontrolled sources, so he must be careful that his own actions, attitudes and approaches are alertly and thoughtfully professional.

Chapter Ten

THE PROBATION REPORT

THE LOGICAL AND SPECIFIED end of the probation investigation is the production of a written report. The probation officer cannot write a complete and useful report unless he does a complete and objective investigation. A good investigation helps to ensure a reasonably good report because it serves as the foundation for and the building blocks of the report.

Few probation officers will ever become successful novelists or biographers because of the practice they get in writing reports, but most can learn to improve on the quality of their reports if they so desire and put forth a little effort. The effort will pay off in terms of personal satisfaction from knowing one has done his job professionally and from the awareness that it will be used to help accomplish worthwhile goals. It is toward this end, helping the probation officer improve his report writing, that this chapter is directed.

AN IMPORTANT DOCUMENT

The probation report is a very important document for many reasons, not the least of which is its purpose or use. The decisions which are made and the actions which are taken and which are based on the information contained in the report, make it a document of prominence, not to be taken lightly. The following section will discuss this aspect in more detail, underscoring the importance of the report.

The fact that the probation report becomes a legal document also indicates its importance. This is not to imply that it is always an evidentiary consideration, though in some cases it may be. It simply says that the probation report is formally and officially filed with the court of record, thereby becoming a part of the official court file. It provides the information which is the basis of many actions taken by the court and it is sometimes a factor in matters taken on appeal.

The probation report is also an important document because it is the most tangible and readily observable product of the probation officer and of his agency. It goes to many places in most jurisdictions; to the court, the prosecutor, the defense counsel, to correctional institutions and to many other correctional and noncorrectional agencies. It is the only thing that many persons and agencies know about the function and competence of the probation department. It is one of the major things on which the agency is judged by outsiders and, whether he likes it or not, the probation officer is always judged by the quality of his report. This is probably as it should be, because he is responsible for the professional quality of his work, whether it is tangible or intangible. It is just that the more tangible is what others can observe and they make judgments, sometimes sweeping and inaccurate judgments, on what they observe. The probation officer would do well to give careful attention to the production of his report.

The value of the probation report will be in direct ratio to the care, diligence, and skill used in the investigation and in the report. A poorly done and inadequate investigation and report will do more harm to the client, the court, the agency and the community than no report at all. This is because many people look to the report as a means of helping them to make vital decisions; if they are misled by an inadequate report, those decisions will likely be worse than if they had gone on more limited, but more valid, information.

PURPOSES OF THE REPORT

Although the overriding purpose of the report can be summed up in one simple statement, to convey a picture of a personality, it is necessary for greater clarity and understanding to expand somewhat on the statement. Said another way, the probation report contains information which becomes the basis on which some very important decisions are made, so one of its major purposes is to provide information regarding the offender.

This information is necessary for the individualization of justice; for the court to consider in making an appropriate disposition of the matter based on the particular situation and personality. Of course, this is the basic foundation of the philosophy of rehabilitation in which the concept and practice of probation are rooted. This is the justification, both philosophically and legally, of the probation investigation and report as well as the process of supervision which follows; it is the justification for the probation officer's job, and it underscores the real importance of the report.

The individualized approach is carried through as the report also provides information for treatment considerations after the court has made its decision. If the offender is committed to a correctional institution, the probation report usually is sent to the institution where it provides some basic data about the individual. Theoretically, and often in practice, this data becomes part of the classification process in which a program of rehabilitation is developed to fit the particular needs of the offender. It is important because it contains information gathered in and from the offender's immediate environment "back home" which is usually beyond the resources of the institution to provide.

On the other hand, if the offender is placed on probation, the information in the report can enable the probation officer, whether he is the report writer or someone else, to quickly begin to work with the client to get at the resolution of those things which contributed to his illegal behavior in the first place. If the report is thorough and has clearly depicted the client and his situation, it will be possible for the probation officer to be broadly aware of the scope of his activity with the client in the months ahead and will enable him to take quick action, if needed, without much loss of time due to having to become familiar with the client and his circumstances.

The way judges, correctional institutional personnel and other probation officers use the report in their decision-making and working with the client will be in direct proportion to the way they see the report writer's integrity, objectivity and professional expertise as evidenced in the written report. His usefulness to those who must depend on him for an accurate and dynamic picture of the offender is determined by the quality of the report which he prepares and presents to them for action and decisions. He must do his job in a thoroughly professional manner.

CHARACTERISTICS OF THE REPORT

An understanding of the purposes and importance of the probation report is basic to turning out useful reports. Beyond this basic understanding, however, there are some very practical considerations which will help to make the probation report more useful in fulfilling its purposes. We will explore some of these in this section and the one immediately following.

The probation report should be characterized by candor. It should be as professionally objective as it is possible to be, containing the most reliable information available and verified where necessary or feasible. No attempt should be made to second guess the judge or to slant the report according to his likes and dislikes. By no means should any part of a report be faked; if you do not have the information or it was impractical to try to get it, say so. There is no reason for the probation officer to be other than open and frank about what he wants to say in the report. Of course, what he says should be accurate, relevant and expressed in a tactful manner; but it is better to be candid and come straight to the point than to "beat around the bush" or try to impress the court with one's ability to double talk and hide simple thoughts in roundabout reasoning.

Another characteristic of the report should be conciseness. This means brevity, not skimpiness, through selection of the things to include in the report. The idea of selectivity will be more fully discussed in the next section. Here, the point is to be as complete as necessary according to the situation and specific purpose of the report, but not to be verbose. One aspect of conciseness which some probation officers overlook is that, if the report is long and tedious, no one is going to bother reading his "beautiful product."

Continuity is also an important characteristic of the probation report. It should begin at the beginning and end at the end, with as few detours as possible in between. Following a good outline will help the probation officer to organize his data in this way.

But another aspect of continuity, the logical flow of ideas and conclusions, is up to him and a formal report format will not help very much. His data, interpretations and conclusions should flow smoothly one from the other so that even a cursory reading will reveal the logical connection between them. Such a report will be very useful to decision-makers and will be appreciated by them as it saves much time because it is easy to follow.

One other vital characteristic of the report is clarity. A report that cannot be readily understood is of no value to anyone. It must be, as someone has said, an exercise in clear communication. The probation report is not intended to give its writer a vehicle to show off his verbal skills; it is intended to convey a clear and dynamic picture of a particular person. When it fails to do so, it is useless to those who need to depend on it. In the sentence construction and grammatical usages it should be clear; in the conveying of basic data it should be clear; in the expression of the writer's own ideas it should be clear; and in the logic of its conclusions it should be clear. Nothing less will be useful or acceptable.

CONTENTS OF THE REPORT

In most jurisdictions, by statute or judicial policy, the contents of the probation report are specified, although in fairly broad terms. This gives the probation officer some overall direction but makes allowance for considerable discretion about what specifics to include. Here we are getting to the question of selectivity which we mentioned earlier. This is an important question because it addresses itself to what material will be included in or excluded from the report; and this, in turn, has implications for the quality and usefulness of the report.

Selectivity

The probation officer who has done a thorough investigation will always have far more material than he can use in the report. He learns many details of events and situations which are not relevant to the purposes of the report, but he also discovers many minor items which may be used; thus he must decide what is appropriate to be included in his final report to the court. This is not an easy decision to make because much of it is a matter of judgment as to relevance and someone else, including his supervisor or the judge, might see it differently. Probably, selection of what to put into the report from the mass of information he has is about the most difficult and delicate part of writing the report.

The report is expected to include enough but not too much data, so the writer must weigh his detailed information to determine what is most appropriate and useful. The report must, in its entirety, be relevant and pertinent to the situation and to the purposes for which it is to be used; it is not to be padded with trivia or information which may be interesting but of little practical value. Although this is not an easy process, the probation officer can improve his selection ability by being thoroughly familiar with and following a well-organized report format, by following the concept of *need to know vs. nice to know* and by learning from his experiences as his supervisor, the judge or others point out to him ideas about the quality of his selectivity. Hopefully, the following discussion about contents of the report will also help along this line.

Circumstances of the Offense

Information about the offense of which the client has been convicted is an important part of the report, not only because of what it might convey about his general personality and behavior, but also because the judge needs the information to help him make decisions regarding matters which are not known to him as in the vast majority of cases the accused admits the offense without a hearing. This information should be factual in terms of what arresting agency reports say about the offense and statements of witnesses. It is not the probation officer's job to establish guilt in this regard, that has already been done by the court. All he need do is simply state the facts, avoiding unnecessary minutae and legal jargon not commonly understood by laymen, and he must be very accurate with dates, places, names and amounts. For example, it would be appropriate to include the date, place and name of the person arrested while driving a stolen auto; but the inclusion of a description of the auto and its license number would be superfluous information unless the auto had been identified as being used in the commission of other offenses.

The probation officer should not quote lengthy arrest reports unless his jurisdiction requires it. Rather, he should briefly and factually summarize them, giving a clear and simple picture of what happened. Of course, very complicated situations will require more space and information than will the simple minor offenses, but most can be concisely and clearly conveyed within the scope of a few brief paragraphs.

Social History

Personal and social history information is needed to depict the individual offender. In many jurisdictions, most of the statistical kind of data is contained on a face sheet of some sort which is usually the first page of the probation report. Where this is done, the probation officer should be careful to fill out the face sheet completely and accurately. He should give attention to details which, while perhaps not too important for his immediate needs, may be of great significance in future actions. For example, it may not mean much to the investigation to have an accurate address of a sibling or other relative of the offender, but if he should later move and cannot be found, the address of someone who may know where he is becomes very important. The face sheet should also be neat and legible so the typist can read and transcribe it accurately; it saves everyone time later on.

Personal information should be gathered and presented in such a way as to convey a living, dynamic picture of a real person. It must be meaningful in terms of depicting the client and in relation to the needs of the reader of the report. This will frequently mean an expansion, in the body of the report, of the statistical information contained on the face sheet. But it does not mean all that data will merely be repeated in narrative form. Rather, the significant items will be explained in terms of their contribution to developing a clear picture of the individual and as they support interpretations and conclusions of the probation officer about the client.

Collateral Information

Collateral information can be a very significant factor in providing additional data about the offense and the offender. We have already discussed this in the section on probation investigations, so we will not discuss here the gathering or the importance of such data; rather, we will focus on making use of it. Collateral information can "cover the waterfront" and may be new data or supplementary to that already gathered. Some of it will be in written form and some conveyed to the probation officer verbally. Some will come from friends and supporters of the client, some from sources which are against him and some will be from neutral sources. Some will be factual and can be documented, but most will likely be hearsay.

All of these things are factors to be considered in trying to determine the value of the collateral information. The probation officer must weigh the sources of the information and not be swayed by the nature of the relationship of the source to the offender. He must look beyond emotional presentations and try to ascertain the validity of the data as objectively as possible. In this regard, it is important to repeat something we said before, namely, the probation officer should always identify the source of his information so that the reader can also weigh the objectivity of the source. There is nothing improper about using hearsay information in the report; much of the data collected will be hearsay. But as clear a distinction as possible should be made between hearsay and documented data, and hearsay should not be treated as legal evidence.

It will sometimes be appropriate or necessary to attach to the report copies of lengthy documents, letters, or reports from other sources (as psychiatric evaluations). When this is done the data should be incorporated into the probation report by reference to the document and it should not then be repeated in the report itself. This is a duplication, and waste of time to read, which is unnecessary. This particular comment should not, however, deter the probation officer from using quotations from written documents in his report if needed; and certainly he should not merely attach a supplementary document to his report simply because it exists. If it is of limited value in its entirety, extract only the pertinent parts for inclusion in the probation report and do not attach the document.

The Evaluation

The evaluative section of the report is probably the area where there is the widest variation of interpretation as to what it should contain. The position taken here is that this is the place to evaluate data already presented in the report; it is not to be a repetition of that data or rehash of it in different terms; it should not introduce new information not previously contained in the report; it should be an analysis of all the data gathered in the investigation and included in the report; it should be directed toward answering the questions, "What does it all mean?" and "When we take all the disjointed facts and descriptions and put them all together, what kind of person appears?"

The idea is to paint a word picture of an individual in such a way as to help the court decide what is to be done with that individual. This can be accomplished by analyzing key concepts which will help to describe the client, such as his attitudes and motivations; patterns of behavior, including type and length of the patterns; the risk to the community posed by the offender; strengths he possesses which can be utilized in a correctional program; weaknesses which need to be overcome; and potential he has for future lawful behavior.

The evaluative section is a place where the probation officer can most effectively demonstrate his expertise in his function. It is expected that this will be his evaluation of the client and his conclusions about what should be done next. He should not hedge on his evaluation or conclusions and should not be afraid to take a firm and positive position, provided, of course, that he knows what he is doing. If he knows that there is validity to what he wants to say, he should say it in clear and firm tones with no "beating around the bush." When the probation officer backpedals and does not take a firm position, it weakens the authority and value of the entire report. If he really is the expert, as he should be through training and experience, he is failing in his professional responsibility when he refuses to take a firm position because he is afraid of criticism. If he is on solid ground and can substantiate his conclusions, he should not hesitate to say so; if he cannot do this, he should either do a more thorough investigation to enable him to do so or move on to some other line of work.

This section should be done in clear, simple language and construction; it should not be flowery in style nor aimed at trying to impress the reader through the use of technical or professional jargon. The idea is to communicate, not complicate. This can best be done by using a vocabulary which will be clearly understood by the reader. The mark of a true professional is to be understood in his communications, not to confuse the situation by using uncommon terms or double talk without meaning. If the court cannot follow the probation officer's reasoning and conclusions, of what value is the report?

The Treatment Plan

A plan of action should follow the evaluative section. The proposed plan should be based on a combination of the needs of the offender and the needs of the community, both of which must be clearly delineated in this section. The probation officer should never propose a plan of action to the court without explaining why he believes it to be the most appropriate one to follow. This will sometimes require an explanation as to why other alternatives have been rejected. At other times it may require the probation officer to outline the advantages and limitations of several alternatives so that the court can decide between them if it does not accept the officer's conclusions. In every case, the plan should contain the probation officer's prognosis of the effectiveness of his proposal which includes information of how the client feels about it and how he is likely to respond to the proposed plan. Special concerns of the community should also be noted because they do have an impact on the potential success of the proposed plan as well as on the decision-making process of the court.

This section is, of course, the logical conclusion of the evaluative section; therefore, they should be in harmony with one another without discordance. The arrangement of the section should follow a sequence logically leading up to the recommendation to follow. This will usually mean that various alternatives will be explored and explained and reasons given for those which are rejected. Then follows a description of the plan of action which the probation officer believes to be most appropriate with the reasons for the conclusion. The potential for success, including both client and community concerns, is next developed. Now the probation officer is ready to formally state his recommendation.

The Recommendation

Requirements of the recommendation section will vary, from one jurisdiction to another, all the way from no recommendation at all to a detailed recommendation which includes number of days in custody and/or specific terms and conditions of probation. We will proceed here as though a recommendation is at least permitted, if not required either by statute or judicial policy.

The recommendation should, then, logically flow from and be justified by everything that has preceded it in the report. This includes the nature of the specific offense, the character and motivation of the offender and the concerns of the community, because all are part of the decision as to what sentence is to be pronounced. How the probation officer arrives at this decision is explored fully in the next chapter, so here we will mention only a few things which are needed to complete the train of thought.

The probation officer must be sure that his recommendation is legally permissable according to the laws of the jurisdiction. He should also be alert to ensure that it is within the policy framework set either by the courts of the jurisdiction or by his agency. While there are those who would object that this is an infringement on the professional function of the probation officer, it is also a practical fact of life that he has his position and authority by virtue of agency existence. Therefore, it is foolish and useless for him to try to function within such a setting with which he is not in agreement. It is better, for both him and the system, for him to move on to a setting in which he can be comfortable and useful.

As has already been implied, the recommendation must be appropriate to the total situation to which it is to be the resolution. A very practical part of this consideration is that it must be realistic in terms of feasibility of implementation. This means that proper facilities and resources are available, that the conditions of probation can be enforced and/or carried out and that there is some legitimate expectation that the plan will at least help to resolve the problems or circumstances which led the client to this point. This consideration, too, will be more fully explored in the next chapter.

DICTATION OF THE REPORT

Here we turn to some of the mechanical aspects of preparing the probation report, but these are quite important to its final production. Failure to consider and devise efficient mechanical processes will result in poor work which will be dissatisfying to both the writer and the reader.

Obviously, the first step is to organize the notes and other materials to determine what will be included in the report. These should be arranged in the same sequence as the report outline which the probation officer will follow. He should also read over the notes to refresh his memory of them and to correct or clarify items that may not be clear to him as he goes along. Taking a few minutes to get organized will save considerable time and frustration after he begins his dictation.

We are discussing dictation here for two major reasons: most probation agencies use some form of mechanical dictating equipment; and this is much faster for nearly everyone than is writing things out in longhand. Thus the probation officer should learn to dictate well in order to conserve his own time as well as that of the typists who do his reports. He must be sure that he knows how to mechanically operate whatever dictating equipment is provided him because improper operation can be frustrating and very costly of both time and repair of equipment which breaks down through misuse.

Do not be afraid of the machine. Speak into it as though you were simply telling someone about the case in an organized way. Do not allow the presence of the machine to subtly cause you to become stilted in expression or at a loss for words. Do not get *mike fright*. Learn to make the machine work for you to save time and effort and to contribute to a more acceptable end product.

When dictating, keep in mind the problems you can create, or prevent, for those who will later type the report. Know the basic procedures for helping the typist do a faster and neater job of her part of the preparation of the report and do not be hesitant to develop new techniques for this purpose. You will win friends and be prouder of the end product. Thus, in dictating, always speak clearly and not too rapidly; spell out uncommon proper names and unusual words, especially if they are technical in nature, and be sure you are correct in the spelling. Do not allow the machine to run while you are thinking of what to say next, but also avoid constantly clicking it off and on. Gaps of silence and lots of "clicks" are annoying to the transcriber. If possible, make your own corrections on the tape; if you cannot erase, be sure to mark the correction and give proper instructions. Do not get to the end of the dictation and then decide something should have been put into it someplace earlier. If this happens, give the transcriber a note so she can listen ahead and get it correct the first time. Remember that the more you try to make the transcriber's job easier, the better will be the final results of your report writing efforts.

POST-DICTATION ACTIVITY

After the report is typed, the probation officer should read it very carefully for errors; either typographical or in his own expression. As you read, think! Think if this is really what you wanted to say. Is it clear so that the reader will not misunderstand what was intended? Review the reasoning to be sure it makes as much sense "in the light of day" as when you first spoke into the microphone and that it is supported by basic data in the report. To take a few minutes for such a review will be a good check on one's work and may save him embarrassment later if someone else notices faulty reasoning or some other serious error.

Corrections should be made judiciously in terms of the degree of seriousness and closeness of deadlines. The report should always be signed by the probation officer, indicating he is willing to take responsibility for and defend its contents and conclusions. All this should be done as promptly as possible after it is returned to him from the typist. This is particularly important if corrections must be made or due dates are close.

Many times it will be necessary or appropriate to discuss the report with clients or attorneys before the court hearing. This should be done with courtesy, frankness, tact and discretion. The probation officer must be careful that he does not act outside his authority, especially in those jurisdictions where the probation report is not routinely made available to all parties.

POST-COURT ACTIVITY

Whenever it is feasible, especially if the client is placed on probation, he should be seen by the probation officer. Many things could have changed since he was interviewed in the investigative phase, so the probation officer should verify the client's residence, job and plans for the immediate future. This will help to maintain contact with him and continuity of case handling.

The probation officer should also be alert to feedback from the court or attorneys who read his report. Often their comments will be helpful to the probation officer in improving the quality of his report writing. Take such comments or suggestions for what they are worth and try to incorporate them into the next effort. After all, these people are likely to be much more objective in their appraisal of the report than is its writer.

Chapter Eleven

WHAT SHALL I RECOMMEND?

THE PROBATION OFFICER conducting probation investigations is often faced with making decisions of great importance. He must decide what to recommend to the court; the court most often follows his recommendation; therefore, the decision the probation officer makes has far-reaching ramifications. It is vital that he know how to make valid and sound decisions. While this is not an easy process to follow, it is not a magical power that can only be inherited from the mysterious past; it can be learned! The thrust of this chapter is to delineate the factors involved in decision-making and thereby, hopefully, aid probation officers in their mastery of the process.

GENERAL CONSIDERATIONS

There is no substitute for general knowledge, experience, maturity and sensible judgment in the decision-making process. It is difficult in decision-making processes, as it is in many other areas of endeavor, to draw a hard and fast line between *do* and *don't*. In any situation dealing with human behavior there are many variables which can alter the climate for decision-making. To be aware of all the variables and to keep track of their changes is more than most people can do unless they are well-trained and fully organized. However, there are some general "rules of thumb" which can be used to assist one in his decision-making tasks.

The more one is firmly grounded in the knowledge of the philosophy and general processes of decision-making, the more valid will be his choices. The probation officer must also be aware of the specific circumstances under which he operates in his decision-making because, as we shall later discuss, there are professional, economic and political pressures impinging on his decisions. This calls for a mature ability to judge just where the do/don't line is, even under fluid conditions.

139

Admittedly, there are calculated risks in making such a judgment. Some mistakes will undoubtedly be made, but they should not be compounded by too much second-guessing. One must learn from his mistakes; but to continue to rehash them will only tend to make one "gun-shy" and overly cautious. This condition will stifle initiative and hinder the steady flow of necessary decisions in even routine situations.

Sound decision-making also requires a systematic approach to the consideration of the data on which a specific decision is to be made. This is not the same thing as a mechanical approach, which implies that everything fits neatly into pigeon holes, can be precisely regulated and output is the result of mechanically fitting pieces together according to a standard diagram. Rather, to be systematic means to consider all the basic data, analyze all the realistic alternatives and to arrive at a decision as the result of carefully thought-out procedures.

A simple three-step procedure will illustrate this kind of systematic approach:

Step One: What are we trying to do? Determine the objective. In probation, this is tied into general rehabilitative philosophy and into community protection, but we are basically trying to decide what to do with a specific defendant in a specific case.

Step Two: Why do we want to do this? Because it has value? is worthwhile? is realistic? is feasible? is a social good? Also involved here is the question, what are the consequences of not reaching the objective? Costs? Benefits?

Step Three: How do we accomplish this? What is the best way to reach the objective? What are the alternatives, and which is the most effective and efficient?

The mere act of following a systematic procedure designed to cover all facets of a matter helps one to improve the quality of his decision-making.

One other general comment is appropriate. A unique factor in the probation officer's decision-making is rooted in the basic philosophy of probation in terms of both community protection and individual rehabilitation. There must be a sound balance between the *search for alternatives* based on individual need and the *need* to incarcerate based on the welfare of others.

Finding this balance is not easy, but it is the probation officer's responsibility to make the decision. A systematic consideration of all the variables is the only way he will ever be able to consistently do this job. He certainly will sometimes need to rely on the input which can be provided by others; as psychological reports, information about prior behavior on probation or parole, school reports or other collateral contacts. He will use this information, but *he* must make the decision; no one else can do it for him. If he depends on someone else to make the decision, he is "copping out" and not discharging his professional responsibility.

Let's turn now to examine several specific considerations which form the basis for the probation officer's decision-making.

IMPACT ON THE COMMUNITY

As has already been noted in this book, the probation officer has a dual responsibility: the protection of the community and the rehabilitation of the offender. There can be no question that the protection of the welfare of the community takes first priority.

The community is very often unaware of specific defendants in its midst who may endanger its welfare, though it may be broadly aware of and in some fear of the general "crime problem." In this framework, and because of his knowledge of specific defendants and their violence potential, the probation officer often stands between the defendant and the community's welfare. Any action on his part which fails to take into account this very serious concern is an irresponsible action which attacks the very heart of professional integrity.

There is a real sense in which almost any defendant released into the community represents some degree of risk. When the probation officer has recommended release and the defendant does do some harm to the community, the probation officer must assume a portion of the responsibility. (On the other hand, if the defendant never acts destructively, no one ever congratulates the probation officer for his good judgment in recommending release. It's all part of the job!) This degree of risk must be carefully weighed by the probation officer and balanced against his responsibility to help protect the welfare of the community.

One other very important consideration with regard to impact on the community is simply that some offenses are so reprehensive and repugnant to the community that probation should not be considered a viable alternative. The American Bar Association takes the position that probation should not be granted if *it would unduly depreciate the seriousness of the offense.*

The probation department is a public agency, as the probation officer is a public official. This means that all authority of the position ultimately derives from the community which, through its elected representatives and approved laws, has established the position and the agency. It also means that they both are responsible to the community for every action taken on its behalf and in its interest. It is a serious responsibility to be charged with protecting the welfare of thousands of others, and the probation officer who approaches this part of his task in a lax or unthinking manner is not keeping faith with the source of his existence.

IMPACT ON THE OFFENDER

This is the other part of the probation officer's dual responsibility and it too is a serious concern with far-reaching ramifications. The major underlying principle of probation is the concept of an individualized approach to rehabilitative treatment in the administration of criminal justice. Concern for impact on the offender gets to the core of this basic principle.

The probation officer's decision will obviously have considerable impact on the offender; it is his freedom which is jeopardized. But the main concern here has to do with the impact on the offender in terms of individual treatment needs. After all, he is the one person on whom the criminal justice system has now focused as the result of his offense. It is his actions, past and future, and his personality with which the system must now deal. It is he who must now be incarcerated or placed on probation.

It is he who now requires, in correctional jargon, "rehabilitative treatment."

This chapter is not to discuss treatment modalities *per se*. Suffice if here to briefly comment on the offender's capacity and potential for positive response to whatever treatment modality is deemed appropriate, because such potential is at the heart of the choice of treatment processes. The defendant's capacity to respond positively to the greater freedom from restraint in the probation setting is a very crucial consideration in the decision not to incarcerate. If he cannot function in and benefit from the opportunity to readjust his life patterns in the free community, why place him there? Why not confine him, work with him until he has gained more control of himself, then release him to the freer setting of the community?

There are individuals who can only be treated in a closed, controlled setting because they have not developed the inner restraints necessary to coping with life's problems without resorting to violations of the law and/or antisocial behavior. Again, the American Bar Association believes that one major reason for incarceration is when *the offender is in need of correctional treatment which can most effectively be provided if he is confined*. This position recognizes the common human problem of needing external restraints to enforce disciplined conduct. It also implies that some needed treatment facilities and resources will be available in the institution which are not available "on the streets." We will come to this thought shortly. The point to remember here is that the offender's capacity to respond to treatment process and the potential level of that response, are crucial factors in the probation officer's decision-making task.

Another factor which is often overlooked in this area of impact on the client is the principle that all actions have some kind of consequences. The consequence of violation of rules (or laws) is some action to force the individual to assume full responsibility for his behavior. The offender violates the law which forbids a particular course of conduct. A representative of the society imposes some sort of penalty on him because of his behavior. This penalty is the legal consequence of his conduct, emphasizing that he must accept personal responsibility for his actions.

The response of the probation officer, as the representative of the community, to the conduct of the offender should flow naturally from this position. When he acts in a manner designed to hold the offender accountable for his conduct, he is not acting capriciously or unreasonably; he is administering therapeutic discipline. Any failure to carry out this kind of action is a neglect of the basic responsibility of the probation officer and the position he occupies.

AVAILABILITY OF RESOURCES

A crucial factor in the probation officer's decision-making is the availability of the resources necessary to implement the treatment program suited to the individual's needs. After the needs have been established, there must be a match of need and resource. This cannot be a cursory consideration; there is too much at stake for that. Only a "hard-headed businessman" approach will provide the realistic appraisal required to make an adequate judgment about the appropriateness of the resources.

The resources under discussion here would include treatment programs specifically geared to deal with the problems and needs of the offender; the physical facilities and equipment necessary to work with the simplest or the most difficult manifestations to make a meaningful impact on treatment goals for the offender; the financial support to ensure the viable beginning and ongoing operation of the appropriate treatment processes; and the public support to make the use of all the other resources an effective approach to the resolution of the problems besetting the offender and which are within the scope of the correctional concern.

A basic question for the probation officer to ask in his decision-making is: what are the resources needed to meet the needs of this offender and where may they be found? The philosophy of individualized treatment and rehabilitation dictate that the offender should be sent to where the resources are available, even if this is the correctional institution, if this is the only place where the resources are. On the other hand, unless the offender poses a definite threat to the community, if the resources are only available "on the street" in the local setting, that is the place for the offender, even though there may be some public feeling that he should be behind bars. There is always some risk involved in such matters, but taking a risk with wise discretion is sometimes the proper way to act. After all, what advantage is it to employ elaborate techniques to establish individual need if no effort is to be made to connect that need with the resources designed to meet it? That sort of "blind justice" makes a farce of the entire criminal justice process.

PATTERNS OF BEHAVIOR AND ATTITUDE

Here the probation officer considers the basics of who the offender is and what he has done. The focus is not merely on prior illegal behavior but is more general in its concern, including both positive and negative, legal and illegal, social and antisocial conduct. Neither the good nor the bad, alone, will give an adequate picture of the offender; so the probation officer must ask, from a framework of general considerations: What kind of a person is he? How has he behaved in the past? What are the strengths and the weaknesses possessed by the offender? The whole man, past and present, is a necessary consideration for judging what he may be and do in the future. No attitude or pattern of behavior should be dismissed out of hand because any information which helps to give a more complete picture of an individual is significant to the probation officer's decision task.

The complexity and intensity of attitudes and behavior are important, also. Are they situational and passing or are they chronic? Is it a matter of minor, surface involvement or a deepseated problem? If the behavior under consideration involved criminal offenses, were they aggressive, assaultive, violent or were they property offenses or "victimless crimes"? Is the behavior a nuisance or an annoyance or is it threatening and risky for others?

Another important consideration has to do with the length of behavior habits and the frequency and continuity of that behavior. How deeply imbedded is the behavior and how long has it persisted? In a positive vein, this has to do with stability; of job, residence, family relationships, financial reputation and other factors. In a negative vein, it has to do with instability as manifested in these same or other factors. Is the stability or instability of long-standing duration?

Attitudinal patterns of the offender are also of vital importance in developing a complete picture. Are they generally mature, responsible and realistic? How does the offender view himself in terms of criminal orientation? Does he exhibit embitterment at society for the things that have happened to him? Is he possessed of some substantial degree of self-control and does he have the ability to effectively deal with frustrations without falling apart? What are his attitudes toward his normal obligations; familial, financial, occupational, social? How does he view authority and is he amenable to necessary restrictions? Attitudes often determine overt action, so they constitute a crucial consideration in the probation officer's decision-making.

Part of past patterns relates to the effectiveness of previous treatment programs, if any. How successful were they? What was the offender's adjustment to the changes such programs were trying to bring about? Did he demonstrate any personal motivation to change or improve his way of functioning or coping or readjusting? Was there retreat into old patterns rather than sincere attempts to manage his life?

Whenever the probation officer makes a recommendation, he is predicting future behavior: if his recommendation is to deny probation, he is predicting that the offender would likely behave in such a way as to represent too great a risk or the potential for change is not worth the effort which would be invested; if it is to grant probation, he is predicting that the offender's behavior is likely to pose no threat to the community. Although such predictions cannot be with scientific precision (the vagaries of human nature and personality preclude this), accuracy can be improved through the careful consideration of available information. We can only predict future behavior based on what we know of past conduct, present attitudes and motivation and potential for change. The more we know, the better we can judge the future; and there are numerous clues to assist us if we will look for them. For example, the offender's behavior during the investigation process may be a good indication of his behavior if he is placed on probation. A sincere and prudent man would be careful to cooperate, keep appointments and present himself in a good light in order to convince the probation officer he is worthy of "another chance." If he is uncooperative, hostile, or unconcerned in this situation, it is highly unlikely that he will behave more positively once he is placed on probation.

SUPPORTIVE FACTORS

Along with attitudes, patterns of behavior, and ability to respond to treatment efforts, another important aspect of the offender's situation is in the area of supportive factors and relationships. It should be obvious that the offender who possesses strengths of the sort that we have already discussed, employable skills, or other positive attributes, offers something with which the probation officer can work to make a treatment program effective. However, the main thrust of this particular section deals with supportive relationships.

Social scientists emphasize that man is a social animal needing other human beings in order to survive and function. They speak of *significant others* who have great influence on the socialization and behavior of the individual. *Others* are just as important to the criminal offender as they are to law-abiding people. So the nature and quality of supportive relationships becomes an important factor in the probation officer's decision-making processes.

Very often the offender coming to the attention of the probation officer has a history, sometimes a very long history, of poor relationships with others; especially with others in authoritative positions or in positions which would allow them to make positive contributions toward the offender. This history of failure has often culminated in the offense which brings offender and probation officer into contact and it usually sets the stage for whatever relationship develops out of this contact. If the probation officer is able to even begin to demonstrate a positive supportive relationship with the offender, he has taken a vital first step toward helping the offender cope with the problems in his life and to see that good relationships can be developed with authority figures who are in a position to assist him.

It is not always possible for the probation officer to get off to such a good beginning during the time he is conducting the initial investigation and making a decision as to what to recommend to the court. There are, however, other supportive relationships which are significant for his decision and which must be examined.

These include family members who are loyal and care what happens to the offender; who have not "washed their hands" of him and are willing to offer whatever assistance they can, even if it is limited to moral support; who can provide comfortable acceptance of him as an individual; who will not plague him with recriminations for embarrassing the family by his actions; who themselves conform to lawful demands and are concerned that the offender also so respond; who want him, believe in him and can make him feel he is worthwhile. One of the strongest supportive influences impinging on the offender is such a family.

An employer can also provide considerable support if he is loyal to and believes in the offender. Even if this support is purely on economic considerations because the offender is a good worker, it can still be very helpful in providing continuity and stability of employment. If the offender loses his job and is forced to face the rejections of prospective employers who do not want to take a risk with a *criminal*, it can be a devastating experience for him and make subsequent attempts at readjustment extremely difficult and highly frustrating. A supportive employer is a very important stabilizing influence in the offender's life.

There may also be significant extra-familial groups who can provide supportive relationships for the offender. Social or fraternal groups to which he belongs; a church group; a specifically organized group, such as alcoholics anonymous or a drug abuse treatment program group; or simply a group of good friends and associates; all can provide strength, acceptance, moral support, specific kinds of assistance and warm friendship which may make the difference between success and failure on the part of the offender.

Another supportive relationship not to be overlooked is the community-at-large. This ties in with, but is the "other side of the coin" of our previous discussion of impact on the community. A great deal of the potential for success or failure of the offender is conditioned on whether the community is willing to "give him another chance." If the offense is so reprehensible or the offender's reputation is so poor that the community does not want the offender in its midst, the pressures on him will likely be so great as to virtually preclude any sort of positive adjustment on his part. He will feel the pressures of jobs denied, evidences of unacceptability, or even active agitation as the community looks askance at him. On the other hand, if people are willing to give him the opportunity to prove himself, their support could be the boost of encouragement or provide the feeling of belongingness which could help propel the offender into an energetic and effective resolution of his problems.

These, then, are the major factors for the probation officer to consider and which will assist him in making decisions. When one looks at the totally integrated concept of individualized treatment of offenders, he sees that all these elements apply to everyone in some degree and all are pertinent to the consideration of what shall be done with the offender.

To pull it all together is not a simple procedure. It is easier said than done! This is one of the major reasons why a systematic approach is needed, not to become merely mechanical in adding up the pluses and minuses, but to be sure all the factors are considered thoroughly. Inclusion of all these considerations will not guarantee success, or even decisions without error; but it will greatly reduce the probability of error.

Chapter Twelve

CONSISTENCY IN PERFORMANCE

A CENTRAL CONCERN of legal scholars and reformers for many centuries past has been the inherent inequity of the human system of criminal justice. There have been attempts of various types to right the wrong and make the process of administering justice more fair and impartial. Efforts to codify the common law rulings, to "make the punishment fit the crime," and to develop *rehabilitative* programs and facilities all represent attempts to make the application of *justice* more objective and less susceptible to human whim and error. One philosophy is to define every offense and set a penalty for its commission, automatically and without exception applying the same consequence to every violation of that law. This uniformity of *justice* is seen as the only way to "treat everyone exactly alike." Another philosophy is to define offenses and set the necessary penalties, but to focus on the offender rather than just the offense, allowing for variation of penalty according to the circumstances. This differential application of *justice* is seen as being more in keeping with the principle of equity and of rendering what is merited.

And so it goes, back and forth. Scholars still debate the question, "Is equal treatment of unequals true justice?" To be sure, the discussions and the attempts to make the administering of justice more equitable have resulted in tempering the harshness of justice in some regards. But great disparities still exist on a very wide scale and both the administrators and the recipients of justice are still concerned with the inequity, sometimes voicing that concern in loud and vigorous terms. Yet the problem remains unresolved.

Various studies cited in the report of the President's Commission on Law Enforcement and Administration of Justice demonstrate the wide disparity of sentences between Federal judicial districts as well as within the same districts and among judges of the same urban court. There is also a considerable variation in sentences handed down by the same judge for the same type offense at different times. All this is noted, not to be critical of judges, but to make the point that serious inconsistencies exist in sentencing practices, whether it is viewed from a geographic, organizational, or individual perspective.

REASONS FOR DIFFERENCES

Among the factors contributing to these differences is the personal orientation of the decision-maker, the judge. For many reasons, which some may feel are irrelevant, the judge may have very strong attitudes about how certain offenses or kinds of behavior should be handled. He may take a strict position regarding violent offenses or those which have moral overtones or those which violate a public trust. Another judge may take a more liberal stance regarding some of these, but be strongly repelled by deceitful kinds of conduct. Still others might be characterized as being strict on all offenders while some might be considered "easy" on all offenses. Obviously, background of experiences, formal and informal training, philosophies of life, interpretations of the law, and many other personal factors will influence the basic orientation of the judge. Being human, he is just as subject to these variables as anyone else and it is impossible to totally discount these forces. Nor should we want to do so; because these kinds of differences are what sparks discussion, discovery, development.

These disparities also reflect differences between laws and philosophies of different jurisdictions. The existence of different statutes in the various states is part of the American tradition of local political rule. The more strict or more liberal interpretation of laws may well reflect the differing methods developed to deal with differing problems in different geographical areas. While there are many who decry this situation and strive for a uniform national criminal code, believing that the differences are unjust, there are important reasons to consider local needs. The wide discrepancies that exist between geographical regions may not be ideal, but they are real; and they must be recognized and approached from that perspective.

The individualized approach to the administration of justice is also a reason for differences in sentences. The rehabilitative philosophy of tailoring the sentence to the needs and circumstances of the offender in order to best accomplish the correction of illegal behavior will always mean a difference of sentence and treatment. This is as it should be, at least regarding individual differences, but it still does not resolve the difficult problems of personal differences between judges or differences between geographical jurisdictions. The attempt to apply an individualized sentence and treatment approach is obviously subject to human errors of judgment as to needs, prejudices against certain *types* of offenders, and biases regarding particular kinds of offenses. While it is impossible to completely control these human variables, it is possible to reduce their impact, as we will be discussing later.

THE NEED FOR CONSISTENCY

These differences, called "unjustified disparity" by the crime commission report, create serious adverse effects on the general public, the criminal justice system, and on the offender. Several national surveys conducted in recent years by opinion poll organizations indicate that the public generally believes the courts deal much too leniently with criminal offenders and that *justice* is not being properly meted out. Over the long run, this attitude will severely undermine the confidence of the general public in the criminal justice system, thereby contributing to its ineffectiveness and perhaps even its eventual collapse.

The offender probably never sees disparity of sentences as being justified, especially if he is the recipient of the harsher sentence. Typically, criminal offenders view any sentence, however mild, as undeserved punishment and any restriction of freedom as unjustified interference. When a truly inconsistent sentence is added to this already negative attitude, it makes a rehabilitation plan almost impossible. Under this condition the offender will not likely accept what is happening to him as a viable treatment alternative, a basic prerequisite for any sort of corrective success.

There are many problems created by the severity vs. leniency of sentence polarity which has been the result of differing philosophies of correctional treatment. To some degree, there is a polarizing of philosophy within the entire field of criminal justice, though there are also many who stand somewhere in between. The general public is pretty well grouped at one end or the other of the severity-leniency continuum. The results are conflicting approaches which sometimes negate one another, competing requests for limited funds, a lack of solidarity and cooperation which is necessary to success, some duplication of facilities and services and a vast waste of time and effort. This confusion of positions, which keeps individuals and groups apart and which defeats its own end goals, is probably the greatest bane to the criminal justice system. So long as the various components of the system are not more compatible in basic philosophy of what to do about criminal behavior, there is little likelihood of success in dealing with this serious social problem.

We need to realize that it is not a question of severity or leniency of penalty which will be effective; it is a matter of consistent application of the penalty. The certainty that legal behavioral standards will be enforced, that the enforcement will be swift and that it will be equitable; this is the knowledge and attitude which must prevail if we are to make our criminal laws and justice system effective.

Not only must we avoid unjustified disparity of sentence, we must also avoid uniformity. To treat all offenders convicted of the same crime exactly alike is uniformity, but it is not justice and is not in keeping with a rehabilitative philosophy. Uniformity is sameness, regardless of immediate circumstances. Consistency, on the other hand, involves harmoniousness, compatibility, logical connection; there is room for difference, but there are reasonable bases for the differences. The legal principle of *what a reasonable and prudent man would do* is based on consistency, for there is a logical connection between reason and action. The sociological concept of community tolerance limits regarding deviant behavior is based on consistency because it implies rather general agreement at the extremes but some acceptable variation within the *normal* range; and this is compatible with the welfare of the community.

In the criminal justice system, consistency in handling the offender is an equitable balance between sameness, in recognition of the stated penalty, and difference, in recognition of the need to consider the individual situation. Consistency is a prerequisite for fulfilling the needs of the offender while providing for the protection of the community. This is, in fact, the concept of individualized justice which is the foundation of the philosophy of rehabilitation. The effectiveness of correctional practice is just as dependent on consistency of treatment as the effectiveness of childhood development is dependent on consistency of discipline. Any other approach will be a frustrating waste of time, effort and manpower.

Consistency is needed on all levels of correctional practice; national, state, local, and personal. It is highly unlikely that we will ever attain national consistency; there are too many cultural, jurisdictional, political and economic barriers to that goal. Since all areas of a given state are subject to the same laws, consistency on this level should be easier, but still there are political, jurisdictional and perhaps other practical reasons why this, too, is only an ideal goal.

Locally, most of these barriers should disappear, but they frequently are still very formidable. Political pressures, personal orientations of decision-makers, manpower and procedural problems in the criminal justice system, levels of competency and workload and many other factors operate to hinder reaching the goal of consistency. But, as we have stated previously, the probation officer has an obligation to assist his agency to develop, to meet the demands placed on it and to fulfill its stated mission. Consistency is one of the evidences of growth and professionalism which must characterize the agency. Consistency is a central component in a sound organizational approach to the practice of probation; the agency must have a common and unifying philosophy to give direction to its efforts to reach its goals and objectives. Any sort of effective professional training for probation agency personnel is necessarily based on consistency. Program and budgetary planning for the future are partially based on projected total workload growth, which is based on consistency of handling cases at the recommendation level. Consistency can also serve as a defense against public pressure in a specific case because the agency can show that it was handled in a way which is compatible with other cases which did not elicit such pressure.

Consistency is needed on the personal level also. The ability to analyze a situation and take action which is consistent with basic principles but at the same time allows for unique circumstances is a mark of personal intellectual and emotional integration. This is a crucial individual characteristic of the probation officer who desires to maximize his potential to be successful in his job. Consistency is also representative of the professional stance which should characterize the probation officer's attitude and approach to his work. A vacillating *on again-off again* method of performance cannot be accepted as measuring up to professional standards.

It is also important to maintain consistency on a personal level, because the probation officer's recommendation is often where the problem of unjustified disparity of sentences begins in that what judges decide is most often the same as what the probation officer has recommended. This may be interpreted to mean that probation officers generally agree with the judge's position as to the proper disposition of a case, and so recommend. On the other hand, it may be interpreted to mean that the recommendation of the probation officer carries a lot of weight with the judge. The latter is undoubtedly the case. A very high percentage of defendants before the courts plead guilty and the judge must often sentence many defendants each day, knowing little about them other than the initial impression each makes in his brief appearance before the court or the information presented by the probation officer. The judge does not have the time for careful consideration of all the ramifications of the sentence he imposes; so he depends on the probation officer to inves-

tigate, determine the impact of the alternatives on the defendant and the community and to communicate this information
to the court with a recommendation for disposition. It can be
seen then, that consistency by the probation officer is a crucial
consideration.

HOW TO MAINTAIN CONSISTENCY

A very important question comes to mind here: How does the
probation officer arrive at and maintain consistency of performance? Our attempts to answer this question will be focused on
the personal level because that is the only area where the individual has great control over what takes place. There is not very
much he can do about consistency on a national or state level or
within various components of the criminal justice system on a
local level. He has little control over, although he may have some
influence on, consistency within his own agency. He does, however, have a great deal to do with whether or not his own performance is consistent; he can determine to what extent his actions will be compatible with individual considerations without
uniformity or getting into a rut (defined by some wit as a grave
with both ends open). In other words, the probation officer can
avoid a deadening sameness; but how?

Knowledge

The beginning point is knowledge. The probation officer must
be knowledgeable regarding the individual offender; of his background and social history, of his patterns of violations of law,
of the specific circumstances of the offense, of the offender's
motivation and attitudes, of all the many factors which make
him much like any other human being yet unique unto himself.
It is not easy to make decisions which seriously affect another
person even when one knows him well; it is a tragedy to make
such decisions when one does not know him at all. The probation officer must be very conscious of this principle and not be
nonchalant about such conclusions and decisions. If you do not
know these things about the offender, be reluctant to make a recommendation about him until you can gather more data. Of
course, there are times when the processes of the system will not

allow this extra time, in which cases the probation officer must be extremely cautious about his conclusions regarding the offender and his recommendations for judicial action.

Knowledge of the alternatives available for dealing with the offender is also essential to consistency. The probation officer must know what are the legal alternatives in the particular situation, why these alternatives exist, what each can provide in terms of meeting the combined needs of the offender and the community and what has been the experience of success with each in relation to individuals similar to the one now being considered. Without this kind of knowledge, the probation officer's recommendation will always be a *hit or miss* guessing process. Lack of knowledge of the alternatives and what they can provide is just as serious a hindrance to consistency and justice as is a lack of knowledge of the individual offender.

The development of this knowledgeable expertise will require a lot of study and effort on the part of the probation officer; study and effort directed at learning how to gather data about people, programs and resources, and how to analyze that data for its real meanings and implications. This process may require the agency to provide training programs and practical experiences to assist the probation officer in learning. If these do not already exist, the probation officer should demand that the agency set them up to provide him the opportunity to learn.

Objectivity

Objectivity is also a key element in consistency. If the probation officer is biased in any regard, he will not be able to attain consistency, other than to be consistently biased. If he does not have the ability to look at a situation and an offender with openness and comprehension of all facets of both, he will not be able to bring consistency to his task. Of course, it is very difficult for anyone to be totally objective because everyone grows up with likes and dislikes and with biases in favor of or against many things. Recognition of the existence of these biases is the first step toward being able to make decisions or take actions without the biases causing one to be one-sided in what he does.

The probation officer is almost always dealing with people in situations which are permeated with the potential for emotional conflicts. He deals with people who are "in trouble" with the legal authorities, with victims who are upset and angry over what has happened to them, with well-meaning citizens who know "what should be done with all criminals" and with pressures which are brought on by conflicting laws and policies concerning what is in the best interests of both the offender and the community. Caught in the middle of these potentially explosive cross-currents, the probation officer cannot afford to lose his head; he must remain as objective as humanly possible.

This means that he cannot allow himself to be unduly influenced by emotional considerations; his own or someone else's, either in favor of or against a particular action. He must be careful to deal with outside pressures diplomatically while resisting the force of those pressures to push him in a particular direction which does not consider and account for all sides of the issue. He must also be careful of internal forces generated by personal prejudices or biases, whether they are ethnic in origin, based on spurious principles, or merely personal inclinations. He must not permit himself to deal with either people or situations in a stereotyped manner. Each must be approached as though it never before existed, which, in fact, it never has, and treated accordingly to its own unique requirements. This is what is meant by professional objectivity, which in turn is a key consideration in the development of the kind of consistency necessary to deal with criminal offenders justly.

Realism

Another important consideration for consistency is realism. The probation officer must always deal with people and situations as they are, not as he wished they were. He should never *con* himself, and should help his clients to see themselves and their world as they are. If the probation officer is not capable of looking at a situation and see it as it is, he should return to the "study area" for additional work until he is able to look at life squarely and not through rose-colored glasses. If he *cons* himself it will be very easy for his clients to *con* him also; and he, the client and the community will all be losers for it. Without this sort of realistic approach to life and to his work, the probation officer cannot hope to perform consistently.

Realism as discussed here should touch all aspects of the probation officer's job. He must not only see the circumstances of the client's situation as they are, he must also be realistic in his appraisal of the needs of the client and of the resources available to meet those needs. It is not enough to think, or write reports, in idealistic terms; because idealism, no matter how inspiring, will not come to grips with the cold facts of problem situations. There must be the practical realization that solutions to problems must be just as concrete as are the problems. This is the kind of realism that matches solution to problem in a way that takes cognizance of all the circumstances of both so that the end result is substantive, not illusory. And it is this kind of realism that brings consistency to the actions of the probation officer while allowing for flexibility to satisfy the unique situation.

Evaluation of Work

In order to establish and maintain consistency, the probation officer should periodically analyze and evaluate his work. It is not a waste of time to regularly pause and reflect on the different clients in their unique settings with which one has recently dealt. This analysis should include some comparisons of clients with similar circumstances to see how they were treated the same and how they were treated differently. If everyone was handled in exactly the same way, the probation officer is getting into a rut because his clients are different enough to require different handling to realistically meet their needs. If the differences in treatment cannot be solidly substantiated, then the probation officer is allowing biases or just plain carelessness to affect his actions. When he makes such a comparison and sees unjustified disparities, he must determine why they exist and take action to correct them.

This is not an easy matter; it is very difficult to be scrupulously honest and objective about one's own work. The tendency is to rationalize and go easy on oneself. This is where another person can be of great assistance and is why the probation officer should seek out his supervisor for help. Someone else who knows the various facets of the job and who can make an independent analysis of the comparison of actions can more objectively recognize discrepancies and determine probable causes. This is one of the functions of a supervisor of professional practitioners; so the probation officer should seek his assistance in this regard in order to maintain consistency in the performance of his duties.

Disparity and inconsistency can never be completely eliminated; there are too many human factors which result in error. But this should not be a stumbling block to continued effort to reduce disparity. The conscientious probation officer would take the position that inconsistency in his work, especially where the consequences can be serious, is a perversion of justice. A professional or even a simple concern-for-people attitude would not tolerate such perversion, but would work diligently for its elimination.

As some writer of bygone days has said, consistency is indeed a jewel. This is especially so in the field of criminal justice because consistency is the only way for fallible human beings to even begin to approach the concept of justice. Justice is equity, fairness, impartiality, rendering what is merited. This is the way the offender is to be treated; but the treatment of all offenders must be compatible and harmonious with logical connection when there are differences. There can be no real justice apart from consistency.

The kind of consistency discussed here is not intended to suggest a panacea of any sort. Rather, it is seen as a way to help fulfill the probation officer's responsibility to actualize the concept of individualized justice.

Chapter Thirteen

CASELOAD MANAGEMENT

W E HAVE ALREADY spent some time in discussion of caseload management during the time of the probation investigation and report, where we covered such topics as general organization of one's work, establishing priorities in accordance with time schedules, planning ahead and adequate preparation to move from one step to another. This chapter will deal with caseload management during the time of supervision of the client who has already been placed on probation. There are, of course, many areas of overlap where the same thoughts would be applicable to either phase of the probation officer's work. But the longer-term considerations of follow-up supervision involve some facets of caseload management which do not apply to the investigative processes. These differences constitute the major reason for separate consideration of caseload management in the two phases of probation work.

Caseload management is a crucial consideration whatever the size of the caseload. If it is large, as is likely the case in most places, the probation officer must be careful not to be *spinning his wheels* for lack of knowing where to begin. It is easy, if one feels overwhelmed by the magnitude of a situation, to spend a lot of time doing nothing but fretting over what to do first. There is the likelihood that, because there is so much to be done, most things will be done very superficially and without meaning merely because that is the only way one can even begin to keep up with the flow of paperwork. This obviously will have serious consequences for the general attitude and approach of the probation officer: he may become very frustrated by not being able to keep up with the work; he may become disillusioned because he is not doing what he thought probation work was all about, working in depth with people in trouble; he may simply give up the struggle and resign himself to a superficial noninvolvement

161

which keeps the paper moving but does nothing to resolve client problems; or he may quit and go into some other line of work. All these possibilities indicate the importance of good caseload management practices to the large caseload.

These practices are equally important to the small caseload, but for different reasons. Here the problems include becoming bored with the feeling that there is so little to do, especially if the caseload is relatively stable and not very active. This is as much a question of the kinds of cases assigned to small caseloads as it is one of how the probation officer approaches his casework activity, but it should be of concern to him. Another problem is *busy-work,* where the probation officer tries to find things to do to maintain the appearance of being busy or to protect his cushiony assignment to a "lazy man's workload." Small caseloads which allow for considerable involvement of the probation officer with the client are good, so long as the officer is capable of using that involvement wisely to assist the client, an attribute that some probation officers do not possess. There is also the problem of *overkill* where actions are unnecessarily repeated and accomplish nothing except a waste of time and probably bore and frustrate both the probation officer and the client. Another danger of small caseloads is the possibility of creating client dependence on the probation officer simply because he is so much involved and so readily accessible when anything goes wrong or needs to be done. This is precisely the opposite effect the work of the probation officer should have. These things all point to the vital importance of good caseload management to the small caseload.

Caseload management means different things to different people, depending on their orientation to casework and paperwork. As used here, it includes general organization of workload, a system for classification of cases, case recording and completion of required reports on case activity.

GENERAL ORGANIZATION OF WORK

Judicious management of a caseload requires an orderly concept of what is to be done and an organized way of going about it. The probation officer should be ever on the alert for ways to save time without diminishing effectiveness. One way to do this is to be sure no time is wasted because of his failure to be prepared. There should always be something at hand to do if plans do not materialize. For example, he has a long schedule of office appointments and a client misses his appointment. Does he simply sit and wait for the next client to show up? No! He has paperwork handy so he can work on it or he makes a phone call that he has not yet had time to make.

If he is well organized, each day's work will be planned in advance the day before or the first thing in the morning. He should be aware of appointment times, cases to be dictated that date, contacts to be made and other things to be done. These should be arranged in an orderly fashion to meet deadlines, take advantage of travel time and fill in the odd moments with things which need to be done. The typical probation officer has many demands on his time; some vitally important, some fairly pressing and some which can be worked in at any available moment. He establishes daily priorities and fills in slack time with the items which are flexible in their demands.

If he organizes his work well, he will be surprised at how much more easily it flows and how much can be done in a short while. He will also cut down on the inevitable number of hours worked over the usual eight-hour work day. He will be more relaxed as he works, less drained at the end of the day and much more likely to feel satisfied with the day's accomplishments. Not only will this affect his job performance, it will also have a pleasing impact on his home life because things will go more smoothly and serenely if he is not so tired and drained; and consequently less irritable and on edge. This may sound like a lot to attribute to good organization, but the physical and psychological result of one's feelings of accomplishment are, at the same time, like a soothing tonic and an inspiring urge. And the real secret of more-than-usual accomplishments is a well-organized way of tackling the job at hand.

One aspect of being well organized is some system for keeping track of work due dates. There is no established system which one could recommend; every one should develop a procedure which is comfortable, yet effective, for his own needs. Systems that are in use range from the very simple to the sophisticated; but, as a general rule, the simpler, the better. If a process is so cumbersome or time consuming that it hinders getting the work done, it defeats its own purpose. Many agencies have ample clerical help so that the probation officer does not actually operate the procedure himself. Where such assistance is available, it should be used to maximum capacity. In many cases, however, the probation officer becomes a "do-it-yourselfer." Here, a simple listing of work due on a daily calendar would be sufficient, especially if he made it a daily practice to look ahead a few days to be familiar with what is coming due in the near future.

A planned approach to field contacts is another element of well-organized practice. The probation officer should never head out to make field contacts without a plan that is akin to a "circuit" schedule. Barring emergencies, calls in the same geographical area should be grouped together to reduce time lost in traveling from one point to another. Addresses should be kept up-to-date and, if he is moving in unfamiliar surroundings, studying a street map beforehand will considerably reduce unproductive "looking for" time. Sufficient stops should be planned so that he can quickly move on if he is unable to contact a client. Few things are more wasteful of time than an unplanned itinerary which does not provide for contingency secondary stops when the primary ones fail to materialize as scheduled.

Some method for periodic case review is also essential to a well-organized approach to caseload management. No matter how good a case classification scheme is devised, regular review is the only way in which the probation officer can gather up the loose ends of a case and pull them together in such a way that he can grasp the dynamics of the situation and make intelligent plans as to how next to proceed. This review should be at least quarterly and should involve a written summary of all case contacts during the period. There should be a description of the goals of the efforts, problems encountered, how they were attacked, to what extent they were resolved, what remains to be done and how it will be accomplished. It should be possible for someone not familiar with the case to read the quarterly summaries and get a clear picture of the movement of the case, including the impact of the probation officer's efforts. The summaries should be read by the supervisor so that he can keep up with what the probation officer is doing with the case and can make suggestions as to alternative approaches, point out any errors of judgment made in working with the client and spot weaknesses which require further training.

CLASSIFICATION OF CASES

The underlying principle of probation is the individualized consideration of what to do with the criminal offender. As we have already noted, both the legal and philosophical bases for everything the probation officer does is the careful selection of which persons will likely benefit from a program of control and treatment in the community, and the application of time and resources on an individual basis. It is very easy to lose sight of this principle, especially with a very large caseload, as is typical of so many jurisdictions. There must be a way whereby the probation officer can allocate his time and efforts in an organized and realistic way designed to provide as much assistance to every client as he needs. In some jurisdictions this may be the impossible ideal, but even here a method of classifying cases in the framework of need and time considerations will go a long way toward a proper allocation of resources.

Any probation officer who is even halfway organized or who is not in a rut has already divided his caseload into categories based on how often he needs to see each client. This division may not be official or formal; it may be merely a mental note that one client does not need as much assistance from him as do others. This is a rudimentary form of case classification usually made necessary by the size of the caseload and made possible because the probation officer knows enough about the clients to separate them according to what they need from him. Such a process is usually reflected in the frequency with which the officer has the client report in or with which he goes out to see the client. The less assistance the probation officer estimates the client needs, the more infrequently he will be seen.

Some such classification scheme is necessary to avoid the inefficient and ineffective use of the probation officer's time and energy. A routine, stereotyped way of supervising each client in the same manner is the exact opposite of the concept of an individualized approach to correctional treatment. Every client is not alike, does not have the same needs and does not require the same degree or type of assistance from the probation officer. To treat them all alike is therefore a waste of valuable resources. On the one hand, the client with greater needs will be deprived of the assistance which may help to lead or restore him to more adequate legal and social functioning. On the other hand, the client who has strength to make it on his own and who needs to be given the opportunity to show what he can do may be smothered into frustration and rebellion through oversupervision. Either way, clients' needs are not being met and valuable time and resources are being expended where they do no good. Many of these problems can be reduced through a sound system of case classification.

There is probably little disagreement among professional practitioners in probation that some case classification scheme is necessary in order to make most effective use of available resources. The differences appear as one considers just what form the classification plan will take. Schemes which have been developed range from the very simple and basic in design all the way to sophisticated and detailed plans requiring minute numerical ratings and total scores which are supposed to indicate precisely what is needed for a particular client. For the average probation officer it probably makes little difference which is thrust upon him, because it will be mostly paperwork anyway. He may well comply with the required processes and complete the necessary forms and computations, but throughout the course of supervising the client he will make many adjustments of plan and time according to the need at that particular moment. These adjustments will not likely be reflected in the paperwork in the case file but will probably be more effective in meeting client needs than the elaborate point system in the case file. This is not something about which anyone should be alarmed; it is the reality of dealing with people in dynamic situations and in a world of constantly changing pressures and directions.

It is also indicative of a basic principle of life: use the simplest means which will effectively accomplish the desired end. The simpler the classification system, the less frustration it will cause in its implementation. However, the analysis of client need and the allocation of probation officer time and resources should not be left to chance; this is the haphazard approach which has so often failed in the past and, in the process of failure, has cast the concept of probation in a bad light. There must be some simple but organized system of case classification which will help the probation officer to avoid the pitfalls of both under- and over-supervision. The question is, then, what sort of classification system will be effective?

We have already discussed the need for a simple and easy-to-follow system; simplicity is the first prerequisite for effectiveness. The second requirement is a positive orientation. Many current classification schemes focus on the weaknesses and shortcomings of clients which will require a great deal of the probation officer's time to help the client overcome. Such a negative focus tends to establish an atmosphere of espectation of failure with the question being, "What can we do to keep the client from failing?" In such an atmosphere both the probation officer and the client are caught up in defensive tactics which leave little time or energy for growth or development. This negative attitude is so pervasive that most conditions of probation established by the courts for probationers are expressed as a series of *shall nots*. While we cannot overlook the necessity of setting limits on behavior for the client, a more positive focus will bring more satisfactory results. The approach should be to identify the strengths of the client which can be expanded to decrease or overcome the weaknesses and increase his potential for success. If the *shall nots* were cast in positive terms it would help to establish an atmosphere of expectation of success; the emphasis then being, "What can we do to help the client succeed?" The psychological impact of the positive approach can go a long way toward helping to establish self-confidence and to getting the probation supervision process off to a good start.

What factors should be evaluated to help determine what are the positive aspects on which to develop a supervision program? Basically, the same factors one considers in deciding if the offender is a suitable candidate for probation in the first place. Some of these, which we have already discussed, include evidences of stability in employment and family life, attitudes conducive to readjustment of behavior, evidences of prior successes and support from family or other community groups.

Other factors which should be considered are those that experience has shown are related to the risk of reoffending. These include (1) age: generally, the younger the client the more likely he will reoffend; (2) prior criminal behavior: the younger the client was upon first arrest the more likely he will reoffend, offenses against property are more likely to be repeated than offenses against person and persons with a history of institutional commitment are more likely to become recidivists than those without such experiences; (3) drug or alcohol use: the more deeply the client has been involved in substance abuse the greater likelihood of failure on probation; (4) marital status: married clients are generally better risks than single clients without such ties; (5) community involvement: the individual with roots in the community and a stake in its functioning will likely be more successful on probation than one without these roots; (6) and financial status: the client without great financial pressures will be less likely to succumb to temptations for easy dollars than the one who is always without resources.

These various factors help to focus on specific needs of the client which must be met in order to assist him to cope with his environment in a more legal and socially acceptable way. The essence of a good case classification scheme is to realistically match available time and resources to client need. This will frequently be impossible in any ideal sense; there just isn't enough time and there aren't enough resources to meet all client needs. But, within that which is available, the probation officer must make realistic allocations to meet as many needs as possible. As we have already indicated in other areas, this will require establishing priorities and being alert to changing demands. If the probation officer will allocate his time and resources to the areas where they will do the most good and will be alert for ways to expand and increase his effectiveness, he will find that many other situations will take care of themselves.

An effective classification scheme will also provide for progress on the part of the client which will be accompanied by a modification of the supervision time and resources allocated. As problems are resolved, needs are sufficiently met and the client demonstrates increased ability to successfully cope with his situation, the probation officer reduces the amount of time and resources allocated to that client and reallocates them to someone else. This helps to emphasize the client's personal responsibility for his own behavior and well-being and moves him toward the eventual removal of all restrictions and supervision processes. This is, after all, one of the major goals of the probation program and the case classification plan must provide for such development and change of circumstances.

CASE RECORDS

Probation officers generally feel they are "people-oriented" and seldom like the paperwork processes necessary to keep up with caseloads. One does not need to like the paperwork, but a clear understanding of its necessity and importance will help to make the chore more acceptable and will help him to be more professional in his approach to his *people* work. It will also make him more effective in dealing with clients because less will be left to chance or overlooked due to lack of reminders.

Probation officers spend a sizable portion of their time gathering data and recording it in some form, either in probation reports to the court or in case records maintained in the agency files. While he may not be enamoured with this process it is a very important part of his job; so much so that without case records a great part of what he does would be ineffective or useless. Time studies have shown that from over one fifth to over one third of the probation officer's time may be devoted to various forms of record keeping. Even without considering its impact on effectiveness, the time spent in case recording would justify a considered and organized approach to the task.

Other people are also deeply involved in various aspects of case recording. Stenographers, transcriber-typists, file clerks and other clerical support personnel probably spend more time than does the probation officer on keeping records up-to-date and in good order. The time that supervisors, or others, spend in reviewing and approving case records must also be considered in evaluating their usefulness against their costs. The agency has a tremendous responsibility to train all members of its staff in good case recording processes. No one should ever assume that the probation officer who is an effective casework counselor will necessarily also be good at case recording. It takes some time and effort to develop the ability to record contacts, interviews and impressions in a way that is meaningful to all who review the records and to the casework process itself. The probation officer owes it to himself, his profession and his client to develop this ability either through training and opportunities provided by his agency or through other efforts on his own if the agency does not help. The importance of good case recording is too great to be ignored or left to chance or, like Topsy, to "just grow."

Purpose of Case Records

There are many purposes for case records. We have already discussed the probation report, the purpose of which is to convey to the court a dynamic picture of the offender. In many jurisdictions some records are required by statute, so case records help to ensure that legal and administrative responsibilities are properly met. In the context of our present discussion of the processes of probation supervision, the case record becomes the repository of the facts and the dynamics of the case. It contains the pertinent dates, places, people, events and movement needed to sketch a picture of what is happening with the client. The overall purpose of such records is to facilitate the total treatment program which has been established in mutual discussion by the client and the probation officer.

Case records are needed for proper case planning. To accurately and concisely record what the facts are and what is happening helps to organize one's thought processes about the total situation and to chart the appropriate course of action. The records help to clearly determine the goals of the probation process and indicate progress toward those goals. It is impossible for any probation officer to keep all the facts about many different persons and situations in his head and to keep them separate and distinct from all others. They must be in written form so he can go back over them to refresh his thinking about a particular client without getting him confused with someone else. If he does not have these written reminders he will overlook significant influences and facts which will hinder his effectiveness with the client. He might even confuse clients with one another, thus projecting the impression of unconcern or causing the client to wonder if the probation officer is capable of assistance or worthy of trust. In any event, if the facts and dynamics of the case are not kept straight, the probation officer will fail in his responsibilities to both client and community.

Accurate and comprehensive case records are also essential as the basis for decision-making on many crucial aspects of supervision. After working with a client for a while, the probation officer may discover that the initial treatment plans are inadequate and are not accomplishing the original goals; the plans may need to be discarded and new ones developed. Without good case records on which to rely, he will not be able to determine the shortcomings of previous plans or to delineate how new ones differ and so offer more potential for success. Decisions often have to be made regarding legal action by the probation officer in behalf of or against a client. Such efforts must be substantiated by the records in the case or courts will not take the action requested by the probation officer. To grant requests for early termination and dismissal of a probationer, courts require the probation officer's records to show compliance with the conditions of probation and demonstrable ability to lead a law-abiding life. The only way to substantiate a request for revocation of probation is for the case records to show in clear detail the failure of the client to comply with the orders of the court.

With current trends toward tighter legal controls on the probation officer and his supervision of the client, accurate and comprehensive records kept up-to-date will be more and more crucial in the discharge of his responsibilities to both the community and the client.

Facilitating the smooth transition of the case from one probation officer to another is an additional important purpose of good case records. Although good casework practice would favor continuous treatment by one probation officer, there are times when some other person must take over the case. This is the situation when the officer is out of the office and an emergency arises that must be handled by his supervisor or a peer; or it may be that the regular officer is ill or on vacation when some sort of help is needed. There are also many instances when the case must be transferred from one officer to another, as retirement or resignation of the regular officer. In all these instances good case records are necessary for the substitute to be able to assist the client. A perusal of the case record will provide information about the client and what he has been doing; it will tell what the treatment plan is, what steps have been taken to implement it and what progress has been made toward the established goals; and it will give the substitute some idea of how to approach the client's present need. Without good case records every change of probation officer would be like starting all over again for the client. The time thus wasted and the frustrations created could negate much of the good already accomplished. For the smooth transition of a client from one worker to another, whatever the reason for the change, there is no substitute for accurate and comprehensive case records.

A corollary use of case records is to provide the probation officer and his supervisor a basic record upon which to evaluate his casework practice. In discussing consistency of performance, we suggested that the probation officer periodically analyze and evaluate his work. Good case records provide him with sufficient data on each of his cases to make such an evaluation. They are important, too, for his supervisor to evaluate his skills and performance in working with the clients, to determine his level of knowledge of casework functions and to judge the degree to which his work is well organized. All these insights assist the supervisor in his function of helping the probation officer to grow and develop in his job. They reveal where he is in learning the job, what are his strengths and special skills and what weaknesses are apparent which must be overcome. Good case records can contribute importantly to the overall learning and development of the probation practitioner who desires to be at his professional best.

Content of Case Records

Most of the time there will be an abundance of information of various kinds which could be included in the case record. It will frequently be the case that all the information cannot be included simply because there is too much of it. Selectivity of material then becomes very important. What we have already noted on this topic elsewhere can also be applied here. In addition, it is necessary to make several points specifically applicable to case records as part of the ongoing supervision processes.

The question of what to record has implications for effectively implementing and following through on the treatment program. Thus the record should contain data about the client's activity; what he is doing and what is happening to him. It should show the impact of various events and actions on the client and include the probation officer's impressions and conclusions about the meaning of these things to the client and their implications for the treatment program. The record should also note situations, events, or actions which demonstrate progress toward the established goals of the treatment program.

The record must also include notations of failures on the part of the client and actions which are contrary to the orders of the court because such items have serious implications in possible legal actions in revocation proceedings. Notes as to specific behavior, such as missed appointments, unsuccessful efforts by the probation officer to contact the client at home, at work, or by phone, unfulfilled commitments to act on a particular matter; these facts of client activity, lack of action, or failure become the record on which legal action may be based. More and more, the probation officer is being drawn away from the usual casework practices in dealing with this sort of failure, and is being drawn to a legalistic, adversary-type proceeding to respond to negative behavior by the client. When this is necessary, the case records will be useless as substantiation unless they contain factual data as to dates, times, places, people, events, actions, circumstances and so on. As noted above, even data regarding unsuccessful efforts to contact the client may become important in proceedings dealing with a client's failure to report. While it is in fact the client's responsibility to report, the court may take no action unless the probation officer can demonstrate that he has made extra effort to get the client to comply with court orders. Most judges are extremely reluctant to jeopardize a probationer's liberty unless there are ample and solid grounds for doing so.

Techniques of Case Recording

The why and the what of case recording are not complete without the how, because it is the how that makes for clear communication of the data recorded. As we have already noted, the material should be accurate and comprehensive to its purposes. The records must be maintained with professional objectivity and honesty, clearly delineating facts of client behavior from interpretations of the probation officer. The material should be organized in such a way as to enable one to read easily and chronologically the activity in the case and to quickly grasp a clear picture of what has transpired. The terms and language used should be easily understood and should simply convey the story of the case.

Whether the probation officer records his notes during an interview or afterwards is probably of little consequence so long as he is sure to be accurate. In all probability, there will be recording both during and after interviews. The surest way of getting data accurate is to make notes on the spot, during the interview discussions. These need not be elaborate; they can be in crude form in order not to lose the information. After the interview, the probation officer should transcribe his notes into an organized and more detailed recounting of the discussion and should record his own impressions and analyses of what has taken place and what it all means.

Probably the most useful way to keep case records is to record, in chronological sequence, a narrative account of each contact or attempted contact. Some of the more routine contacts and failures to reach the client will be very brief, containing just the factual data of time, place and event. Others will be much more expansive and will recount important topics discussed, information or directives issued and plans for further action. These will also often include the probation officer's interpretations at the time, not left for analysis at a future date when he is far removed from the occurrence.

There should also be periodic summaries. Here the individual contacts are brought together and examined from the perspective of a greater time span. In this way the reader of the case records can more clearly see patterns developing, growth occurring and progress being made toward treatment goals. The periodic summaries also provide a more concise and easier-to-read account of case activity than provided by the details of each contact. This sort of overview can tell a great deal about case movement and the probation officer's ability to work with the client. If a client is to be transferred from one probation officer to another, the case record should contain a summary that takes the client and his situation from where the first officer found him, through their mutual efforts to realize the goals of the treatment plan, to the point where he is to be turned over to the second officer.

COMPILATION OF NECESSARY REPORTS

A discussion of caseload management would not be complete without some mention of the statistical reports found in every governmental agency. The laws of some states require monthly and annual reports of matters handled by the probation department; reports which usually have their beginning in the activity of individual probation officer caseloads. To meet these requirements many agencies require monthly statistical reports from probation officers on such things as numbers of probation reports completed, cases added to the caseload, cases removed from supervision and a breakdown of reasons for the removals. It would be nearly impossible for the agency to meet its requirements if the probation officer did not keep careful track of his work load.

These same figures also have important bearing on budgetary considerations for the agency because staffing requests and patterns are generally based on workload data. Thus it is vital that the probation officer maintain accurate statistical records of workload ebb and flow.

Obviously, these considerations are administrative and are not the direct responsibility of the individual probation officer. However, they would be difficult without his input of data, and his concern for and professional commitment to his agency dictate careful record keeping and conscientious reporting to the agency to help it meet its needs. After all, if the agency suffers, the probation officer suffers; so cooperation is to his own advantage.

Chapter Fourteen

COMMITMENT TO EXCELLENCE

E XCELLENCE IS A TERM describing a condition which is above the ordinary; an excelling or surpassing the expected standard; the state of something unusually good for its kind, or of exceptional merit. It is the idea of superiority. This is the term which should describe the performance of the probation officer in every aspect of his work. Although it describes the extraordinary, the probation officer should strive to reach the level of performance where *excellence* is the description of his ordinary work. In other words, his personal goal of performance should be on a level a notch above others. This is not meant to refer to an egotistical attitude about his work; rather, it is meant as a goal toward which he always aspires.

Setting this goal and the attitude of dedication to get there are vital to actual performance on an excellent level. In the same sense as the probation officer helping his client to set goals and to strive for their attainment, he must determine where it is he wants to go and how he must get there. Working toward a specific and attainable end is just as important to the kind of organization and dedication required to put forth his best effort for the probation officer as it is for his client in his own situation. In other words, the same principles of motivating client action to reach goals apply also to the probation officer's motivation regarding the quality of his work.

The importance of the work which is the probation officer's responsibility demands excellence; anything less is not good enough because the stakes are too high. The work is important to the community in terms of its general well-being and safety because the probation officer has, with others, the responsibility to help ensure behavior which is not disruptive or destructive to the peace, a condition without which the community could not long survive. The work is important to the courts and other

177

agencies of the criminal justice system in terms of their orderly functioning because the probation officer plays a part, is a cog in the wheel, which is related to the others in such a way that failure to properly do his job will result in increased activity or even slow down of the other components. The same principle holds for other agencies in the community, especially those in the "people helping" services, because there is often a great overlapping of clients and interdependence between those agencies and the probation agency. A let down in quality of services provided by any agency will probably result in further burdens on the others.

The work of the probation officer is also very important to the client in terms of resources for problem-solving and his personal freedom because the courts have placed him in the position of reliance on the probation officer for the fulfilling of needs and control of liberty. The probation officer can have such an awesome impact on the life and liberty of the client that any sort of merely ordinary performance is not likely to be good enough. If the quality of performance is less than *excellent*, he is putting in jeopardy the satisfying existence of others; and he should not be in the position to exercise such power and influence over them.

This has implications for the importance of his work for his agency and for himself. The agency has been given the mission of providing rehabilitative and preventive services to criminal offenders in the community, and an ordinary level of services will not permit the complete fulfillment of its mission. The probation officer owes to his agency, from which he derives his basic position and authority, a level of performance which is above the usual standard. He also owes the same thing to himself. How can he live in peace with himself if he has in any way been responsible for the physical or mental suffering of a client or his family or the citizens of the community because his performance was not up to the very best of which he is capable? Can he ever feel pleased if he knows he is not doing as well as he can? And if he is not at peace with himself, is this not reflected in further hindrances to his performance? Can he really do a high level of work with the client if his opinion of himself is on a very low level because he knows he is not doing the best he can?

The importance of the probation officer's responsibilities demands excellence; but how can he attain and ensure the maintenance of that level of performance? The things which have already been said, or which may come later in these pages are all part of excellent performance. Some of these will be touched on below and others will not be repeated; but it is important to try to pull together at this point some of the major elements which contribute to excellent performance. They include involvement, optimism, responsibility, competition and commitment.

INVOLVEMENT

The degree of the probation officer's involvement with the client is crucial to the level of quality of his performance. He cannot be cooly clinical or standoffish or he will lose all possibility of establishing the sort of human relationship which may enable him to really accomplish something with the client. He must be human and friendly in order to avoid building barriers between the client and himself. He must be accepting and respectful of the dignity of the client in order to discover common ground of understanding upon which to build the relationship. He must be genuinely interested in the client as a person and warmly concerned about the resolution of the problems which contribute to his difficulties with life and the law.

But he must not go too far! He must not get so involved with the client that he takes on the client's problems as his own. Being human, he likely has all the personal problems he can handle. Getting over-involved with the client's problems will only decrease his ability to deal with his own, which in turn will decrease his ability to deal with those of the client. He must be able to *call a halt* to involvement so as not to be overwhelmed by an array of problem situations that are too great to analyze objectively and attack dispassionately.

The probation officer cannot afford to allow the client's problems to *get to him*. Overinvolvement is quite likely to lead to overindulgence with the client; a situation which will deprive him of the responsibility and the opportunity to participate in resolving his own problems. And his responsible participation is essential to success. There is also the corollary danger that the probation officer might overindulge in self-pity because he cannot seem to be able to cope with such a heavy load as that of his own and his client's problems.

Overinvolvement leads to loss of objectivity. In the relationship between the client and himself in trying to resolve client problems, it is the probation officer's responsibility to keep his head, to maintain his ability to think clearly about the problem and to not lose sight of the goals they have mutually set. If he loses this objectivity, it is unlikely that the client can maintain his; thus they both will wallow in uncertainty and empty activity, if indeed they are able to act at all. The confusion that results if the probation officer allows the client's problems to get him down will completely block even ordinary performance, to say nothing of excellence.

It is, admittedly, very difficult to strike the proper balance between concern and overinvolvement; but without it, all is lost. Alert response by the supervisor can help to keep things "on an even keel," as can a periodic review of his own work by the probation officer. Sound professional knowledge and practice as well as the exercise of good judgment are also helpful. There is no easy, ideal way to maintain this balance; it will take considerable alertness and effort on the part of the probation officer—and a little help from his friends. But, the level of performance depends on the proper balance of involvement. If the probation officer is dedicated to excellence, he will exert the effort.

OPTIMISM

There is always the danger that the probation officer may become cynical because of continued exposure to "unhealthy" social problems and people in trouble. When nearly all of his professional working time is given to close contact with situations and people which society usually defines as *bad*, he always runs the risk of beginning to consider his clients as problem people rather than people with problems; the distinction is more real than poetic!

If the probation officer loses sight of the dignity and human worth of his clients, the likely result of cynicism, he will begin to treat them as *problems* rather than trying to help them find some acceptable solution to the problems which beset them. It will not take long for this attitude to communicate itself to the client who will be totally rebuffed by it. The hostility toward authority that may already characterize his own attitudes will then be reinforced, completely destroying any possibility of a positive response to any services offered to him. In turn, this totally negates the probation officer's efforts toward excellence, if indeed such attitudes and efforts still exist at this point.

Here, too, the ideal remedy is hard to come by; but the one kind of activity which is probably most helpful is to attend some professional seminar or conference. Maintaining optimism requires refreshment; a refreshment of attitude, spirit and action. This can be provided by a period of time away from the job where one can begin to shed the daily pressure of responsibility for others, can relax his vigilance to "do his duty" and can be released from the necessity of professional alertness. He can socialize with others of his profession and learn informally that he is certainly not alone in his misery; he may even discover that he is better off than many of his colleagues. Such gatherings also provide the opportunity to learn new methods of dealing with old situations, the development of new trends with which he may later need to deal and new theories or ideas about what contributes to the very problem situations which may tend to make him cynical. This sort of rest, relaxation, refreshment and refilling are important antidotes for cynicism.

Another antidote is to get involved in activities in the community which expose the probation officer to "the other side"; that is, the positive and wholesome sorts of things that people do because they are beneficial and enjoyable. These may be hobbies in which one can participate to get his mind off his work and its problems, or they may be of a physically exhausting nature that relax both the body and the mind. Or the activity might be some sort of volunteer work with youth groups, such as scouts or church activities; senior citizens' programs; civic organization contributions to the community; or fostering his own education or contributing to that of others. There are scores of activities completely different from his daily work in which the probation officer can participate. Which he chooses is a matter of personal preference. The point is that this sort of *extracurricular* activity serves to help him see the more positive and acceptable side of people and thus help to avoid the buildup of cynicism.

RESPONSIBILITY

Excellence cannot exist apart from responsibility, because responsibility for action is the pathway to excellence of performance. Thus the probation officer must assume total responsibility for his actions because in no other way does he have control over the quality of his work. Of course, there are many things for which he must depend on others; information, reports, interpretation of data and a host of other things. But he must make the decisions that are his. He analyzes all the inputs according to the reliability of the source, but he is the synthesizer of this data and the one responsible for the output. He considers material from many sources, but the final decision as to his recommendations or course of action is his alone; and he must accept total responsibility for the outcome; good, bad, or indifferent.

To shirk his responsibility, or to run away from it, or to ignore it, is to destroy his self-respect. Without self-respect, he will not be concerned with nor dedicated to excellence. The result of this is not only the failure to perform at a level which can provide vital assistance to his clients, but is also likely to be as harmful as it can be helpful. There is simply no way in which the probation officer can do his job without a sense of responsibility for developing and maintaining positive and constructive attitudes about his work as well as for acquiring and updating the professional knowledge and expertise necessary to perform at a high level. There is simply no way that he can fulfill his functions with an *excellent* rating unless his actions every day, in all places under all circumstances, are carried out responsibly.

We have talked about possible remedies for overinvolvement on the one hand and cynicism on the other. There is but one remedy for irresponsibility; it is simply to be responsible. It is impossible to excel, surpass, or be of exceptional merit unless one acts to reach that level. The only remedy here is a simple one: do it!

COMPETITION

Competition provides the motivation to strive for a given goal in many aspects of our lives; it can also be at least part of the motivation for the probation officer to excel in his work. Yet, he is not competing against the other elements in the criminal justice system. Law enforcement, prosecution and defense attorneys and judges all have their own functions and need cooperation rather than competition. He is not competing against other helping agencies in the community; here, too, it is cooperation which enables each to do its job. He is not competing against fellow professionals, because there is sufficient work and recognition to go around to all. These are external factors, and not likely to be the competitive motivating force the probation officer needs to excel.

It is internal competition which can provide the motivation to go beyond the ordinarily expected standards. To excel, the probation officer must be in competition with his own best self. His aim should be that in every situation and action he will be the very best he can be. He must not make the mistake of measuring himself against what he knows others can do; he is not responsible for measuring up to them. He must measure himself against what he knows he can do, and always strive to better that performance by at least a little bit; he is responsible for measuring up to himself.

It is altogether possible that he will never realize his full potential. This is the case in most human endeavor; few people ever reach the highest level of which they are capable. The probation officer should not grow discouraged from the knowledge that he can improve his performance over its present level and, perhaps, still be far below his ultimate potential. The important point is that he continue his strivings to be better at his job; that he continue to be in competition with himself. If he does this daily, he will constantly be improving, constantly drawing nearer to his ultimate potential. Self-competition is the motivation for excellence.

COMMITMENT

This chapter is entitled "Commitment to Excellence"; and that is appropriate because excellence is not easily attained. There can be no excellence without solid commitment to get there. Commitment is not just an official statement of a belief, nor an intellectual idea about what one should do. Commitment is of a practical nature. It says about one, "I know where I should go and how to get there; I intend to keep trying no matter what happens; I will not give up." Commitment means there is a goal to be reached; it implies a basic attitude of deciding to work toward that goal; it implies striving, effort, work; and it implies perseverance in the face of adversity.

Commitment has its payoffs because it leads to step-by-step improvements, probably gradually over a period of time, which bring one closer and closer to excellence. As one sees improvements in his performance he is likely to be, at the same time, both pleased at the gains and inspired to continue striving for further gains. He will feel a genuine sense of professional worth and will know that his contributions to his clients and his community are above the ordinary. He will know that his work is excellent, even though he also knows that he has not yet reached the highest level of his potential. And he will keep working toward that end because he knows it is a worthwhile one, to be the very best he can be.

Part Four

TREATMENT

Chapter Fifteen

THE CONCEPT OF TREATMENT

IN MOVING FROM A PUNITIVE to a rehabilitative philosophy of dealing with the criminal offender, correctional leaders and writers have tried to use concepts and terms that suggest the newer philosophy. The concept of *treatment* is one such effort and was adopted from the field of medicine where the goal is to do something to the patient to cure the disease which has come upon him. Applying this idea to corrections has resulted in the use of the related ideas of diagnosis, social disability, and prognosis for recovery. Neither in the fields of social work nor corrections has the medical model been really satisfactory, because in looking at social behavior we are looking at "causes and cures" which are different from considerations of physical disabilities.

This illustrates our confusion over what we mean by *treatment* in the correctional setting. Current treatment philosophies and practices are explicitly or implicitly based on our concept of the nature of man, a confused conglomeration of beliefs; on our knowledge of behavioral causation, which is very limited; and on our understanding of the specific nature of the behavior which needs to be *cured,* a matter often difficult to determine. There is also great confusion about what we want *correctional treatment* to accomplish: revenge, retribution, reform, rehabilitation, resocialization, or something else.

The confusion of what we think we want is one of the greatest stumbling blocks to the idea of *correcting* the criminal offender. It is impossible to get the legislative, financial, or public support necessary to reach a goal when we cannot agree on just what is the goal. This is the basic dilemma of corrections! Over the years we have invested a lot of money, time and manpower in various experiments and programs which we hope will help us find the solutions to our many problems of crime and corrections; but we have invested very little in trying to arrive at general agreement about what it is we are trying to accomplish.

186

CORRECTIONAL TREATMENT

The most frequent general usages of the term *treatment* are either in a very broad sense which includes anything done to or for an individual, or in a medical sense which involves the systematic application of what is considered to be the remedy for the problem. Both of these usages are common to correctional thinking and language. In the broader sense, we seem to believe that anything the probation officer (or other correctional worker) does to, for, or about the client comprises part of the treatment program. If we are humane, kind, polite and nice to him, we are *treating* him; if we are concerned for his dignity and sense of self-worth, we are *treating* him; if we are aware of his rights and seek to avoid their violation, we are *treating* him; and if we say we are rehabilitating him we are *treating* him. To be sure, these things are all important aspects of the environment in which correctional treatment may take place, but in and of themselves they are treatment only in the very broadest sense, a sense so broad as to be almost without useful meaning. Just because we tell ourselves, the client and the public that what we are doing is "rehabilitative" does not mean that we are providing valid treatment for the client.

The implication of total cure of the disease as the result of the systematic and controlled application of the remedy is acceptable in medicine because many years of experimentation and experience, together with highly sophisticated equipment, has enabled doctors to be reasonably sure of the causes of the disease, or infection, or pain. They are also provided with considerable knowledge of the results of chemicals and drugs interacting with body chemistry and functions so that the outcome is fairly accurately predictable. There may be, in fact, a total cure of pain, infection or disease. However, these things are not true with social behavior and the adoption, by corrections, of the medical connotation of *treatment* has caused a great deal of needless difficulty and frustration through the years. This adoption has helped to create an atmosphere of unrealistic expectations of total *cure*, a situation which has been self-defeating.

It should be obvious that we do not know nearly as much

about causes of socially unacceptable behavior as we do about causes of diseases and illnesses; we know little about the deeper results of certain kinds of actions, *treatment,* on the behavior of individual human beings; we are nowhere near finding a *cure* for various forms of social maladjustment and misbehavior. Yet we continue to sing the praises of our rehabilitative facilities and programs as though they actually do cure. Perhaps it is this unreal expectation which has led us to grasp desperately at most anything positive, or good, or even new, and label it "rehabilitative treatment for the good of the criminal offender." If we cannot, in fact, expect total cure, then it is frustrating and self-defeating to try to function in an atmosphere where it is implied. We need to recognize the realities of our limitations and tailor our terminology so that it does not imply more than we can deliver, and thereby create an atmosphere of realistically attainable expectations. Until we do, we will not only be confused as to our goals, we will also be unable to develop effective methods to attain them and will eventually defeat our own efforts. On second thought, maybe this is what has already happened to corrections.

Rather than to think of correctional treatment in terms of a *cure,* we should consider it in terms of problem resolution which results in progress toward the goal of improved social adjustment. There are two levels toward which such treatment efforts can be directed. The first is to bring about sufficient problem resolution and understanding of himself and his situation that the client is able in daily living to avoid confrontation and conflict between himself and others and between himself and the expectations of the community. The second level is to bring about sufficient self-awareness to enable the client to develop personally, realize personal goals and reach self-fulfillment. Level one is basic and necessary for social survival; it is the focus of correctional treatment. Level two is secondary and needed to realize the greatest potential of the individual, but most people in society survive reasonably well without it; it is nice if correctional treatment can get around to it after first accomplishing its primary goals.

It is the responsibility of the probation officer to deal with the behavior and attitudes of the client; behavior, at least, if not attitudes, which has brought him into legal conflict with society. It is usually negative and unacceptable, if not destructive, behavior and attitudes that demand his attention. By their very nature they require confrontive action on the part of the probation officer; they require directive limit-setting and, on occasion, coercive reinforcing of the limits. The goal of all this is to bring about sufficient change of behavior by the client to enable him to live in the community without destructive conflict. In the process, attitudes may also be altered, but this is usually not necessary for the client to "get along" in the community. Few, if any, may be pleased with his negative attitudes (assuming they are, in fact, negative); but it is overt behavior which has caused the trouble. Attitudes are not in violation of the law, behavior may be; attitudes are not destructive for others, behavior may be. Of course, attitudes are important because they often trigger behavior. But the primary task of the probation officer is to deal with behavior; helping to change attitudes is a bonus, not always necessary or to be expected.

Based on this discussion it is appropriate to define *treatment* in the probation setting as the systematic application of resources to the resolution of client problems to the end that behavior is changed sufficiently to enable him to live in his community without destructive conflict. The application of resources may be very general in some circumstances and very specific in others; the behavioral change may be minor with one client and dramatic with another; the improved understanding and adjustment may be barely minimal for social survival or it may result in great self-fulfillment; and there may or may not be basic alteration of attitude. Hopefully, the probation officer and the resources he brings to bear will be the catalyst which sparks the change.

To avoid the unrealistic implications of the medical model, it would be helpful if we had a substitute term for *treatment*. Unfortunately, the synonyms also suggest the curative nature of the process. For lack of a better term which is concise and descriptive, we will use *treatment* but the reader should keep in mind the specific definition given above. Hopefully, in this manner we will be able to clearly communicate without getting tangled up in expectations or implications of a *cure* that is not realistically attainable.

THE NTN CONCEPT

Contrary to popular belief, it is not necessary to *do something* in every case of criminal behavior. This is a mistaken idea, prevalent even in correctional thinking, which is based on the belief that such behavior is a perverse, willful choice to do evil, so something must be done to show the offender that he cannot *get away with it*. Here we are not talking about detection of a crime, arrest, prosecution and conviction; if one violates the law he should be brought before the bar of justice. We refer, rather, to the treatment process which follows conviction. In many instances there is no treatment needed (NTN). That this is the case can be seen from the many thousands of people who go through the court process and are placed in probation caseloads where, for all practical purposes, they are left totally on their own, yet do not reoffend. They "learned their lesson" or, in the case of juveniles, simply matured into law-abiding adulthood without any assistance from the professional correctional worker.

Implicit in the probation officer's approach to treatment are assumptions regarding human behavior; what it is, what are its causes and what are the effective methods for changing it. One's view of the world, of the nature of man, of human behavior and of himself set the tone for his treatment philosophy and methods. If one assumes that all criminal offenders are pathological, *sick*, emotionally disturbed, or psychologically unbalanced, obviously his responses will be geared to restructuring of personality to correct, overcome, or at least to offset, the impact of these serious defects. Everyone has some psychological or emotional "hang-up"; no one is absolutely psychologically healthy and normal. Actually, we don't really know what that is, because it is an ideal construct without example in the real world. But this does not mean that all offenders are *sick* or disturbed or unbalanced; it means that they, like everyone else, have problems which need to be resolved. The problems are, perhaps, somewhat different from those of many of the middle-class probation officers who are making decisions about offenders, but they are different more in degree than in kind. Like the rest of us, some of the offenders' problems are very serious matters, with dire consequences if not resolved; some are moderately serious and could certainly do with a bit of solving for more comfortable social living; but many are so minor that even if they were totally resolved it would make little difference to the individual's ability to cope with his situation without destructive conflict.

It is grave error to assume that every offender has a seriously disturbed personality or is afflicted with some sort of pathological disorder. Such assumptions often bring about great frustration for both the probation officer and the client because they usually have no way of either verifying the assumptions or correcting the disorder if it does exist. Such assumptions also tend to send correctional workers off on useless, expensive and often harmful tangents, where no solutions are found but where delving into such things causes great suffering.

The idea of *no treatment needed* is particularly appropriate for those offenders who inadvertently violated the law or those whose attitudes are such that mere arrest and appearance in court constitutes all the deterrence that is needed. It is a useless waste to spend further time and resources on such individuals who need nothing more than what has already occurred to divert them from further illegal behavior. These offenders are better off without the help of correctional personnel; indeed, there is some evidence that contact with "defining agencies" actually contributes to the development of a delinquent or criminal self-image. In these cases, the less the contact, the better the self-image. With many who come to the attention of probation agencies it is sufficient to help support values and attitudes already geared toward a noncriminal orientation.

It should not be a blow to the probation officer's ego to admit that he is not needed by everyone; after all, no other professional is either. It should be enough that he can distinguish between those who can get along as well or better without him and those who can really benefit from his expertise. If he gives his time and effort to the latter, he will not be prone to fret about "losing" the former.

SOME PRINCIPLES OF CORRECTIONAL TREATMENT

Once it has been determined that treatment is necessary and feasible in a particular case, it is important to keep in mind some basic principles in the planning and implementation of a specific treatment program. These principles are discussed here in broad, rather than detailed, terms because they are part of the foundation on which a treatment program is built, not specific techniques of treatment. Mastering the specific techniques is a matter of lengthy study and practical experience; our purpose here is to lay a basis for the use of the techniques. As such, the principles discussed below are basic and vital to treatment but they are also the kinds of things we are often prone to forget or take for granted. We need to be reminded.

Principle One

No treatment program will be successful unless it is implemented with an attitude of positive acceptance and expectation.

Although the probation officer's position is one of enforcement of laws and rules, if his attitude is punitive and negative rather than constructive and positive, it is unlikely that behavior will be greatly affected for the better. As we will discuss later, when the probation officer conveys nonaccepting and negative attitudes to the client, the necessary effort and cooperation on his part to make a treatment program effective will not be forthcoming. This does not mean that the probation officer approves of the client's illegal and antisocial behavior and attitudes; it does mean that he treats the client with courteous consideration and dignity, recognizing that he is worthwhile even though his conduct may be offensive or destructive. The probation officer must remember that there are many reasons for a client to behave as he does and they do not all mean that he is inately *bad*.

The other part of this positive attitude is expectation. One of the basic tenets upon which correctional philosophy and concepts of treatment are built is the belief in the ability of people to change their behavior. This is, in fact, the goal of treatment as we have defined it. This is a basic concept of the helping professions and is rooted in knowledge of and experience with individuals who have made great changes in behavior. Without this belief in the ability of people to change and some expectation that change will occur, change is not likely to come about. The client probably has little, if any, initial expectation of changing his behavior; this is just not his line of thought until someone brings it to his attention. If the probation officer is not geared to belief in and expectation for change of behavior, he cannot be prepared to deal with the client's lack of expectations. If neither the client nor the probation officer believe in or expect change, there will be no goals set; if no goals are set, there will be no gearing up to work toward change of behavior; and if no one works toward it, change will not occur, at least not positive and constructive change.

Principle Two

No treatment program will be successful unless it deals with specific problems.

A great deal of illegal and antisocial behavior is merely symptomatic of underlying problems often not seen at first glance. Although part of the treatment program, perhaps one of the first steps, may be designed to alleviate acute and painful symptoms, the overall treatment process must deal with the problems which underlie the symptoms. Treatment activity must be appropriate to the specific problem, not merely to various problem areas in general. The scatter-gun approach is not sufficient; the probation officer must focus in on very concrete and specific considerations. Specific problems have potential solutions, but general problem areas can only be corrected by making changes usually far beyond the ability of either client or probation officer. Every attempt should be made to break problems down into components small enough to be solvable. If enough of the components are taken care of, the whole will pretty well take care of itself.

This stance implies that the probation officer must have a lot of practical knowledge about people, for by its very definition treatment implies an understanding of human behavior. It implies an ability to look beneath the surface, beyond the facades which people erect to protect themselves, to the basic reasons for behavior. It implies an ability to match solutions to problems without being drawn away from essential considerations by deliberate decoys or environmental distractions. With this kind of knowledge and ability the probation officer is in the position to assist the client to deal with specific problems in a positive manner. Without them, he will likely waste a lot of time and resources in useless pursuit of intangibles which are difficult if not impossible to resolve.

Principle Three

No treatment program will be successful if we fail to consider and treat the whole man.

Each individual is affected by many interrelated and sometimes conflicting areas of life: social, physical, psychological, economic, political, religious, family, work, associates, on and on. If the client has a problem in one of these areas and it is dealt with without consideration of how it is affected by other aspects of his life, the treatment will quite likely be negated. Of course, it is not always possible to be aware of all the interrelated webs of cause and effect in an individual's life, to say nothing of being able to deal with all of them at one time. But being aware that no aspect of the client's life is immune from the impact and influences of other, seemingly unrelated, aspects will help the probation officer to be on the alert for the many forces which can defeat his efforts. Being alert can help him be prepared to counteract these influences in the way best calculated to increase the effectiveness of the treatment program.

This calls for a kind of *systems approach* in the treatment program, not only from the viewpoint of treating the whole man, but also in coordinating all the community services and resources available for use in the treatment. Many probation clients are also clients of various other helping agencies in the community, and if their services are not coordinated there will be a wasteful duplication of efforts toward the client. Without coordination, some clients will try to play one agency against another in order to get what he wants with few controls. Worse yet, lack of coordination can be very defeating of a treatment program and destructive to the client if one agency is making demands on him which are in direct conflict with those of another agency.

Coordination is not a simple matter. Every agency has its own interests, programs and goals. Sometimes these are not compatible in a given situation and no agency outranks or has authority over another. Often, no one will take the initiative to coordinate various programs and services, a failure which results in duplication, conflict and sometimes disaster. Most agencies work with a highly varied clientele; the probation officer is responsible only for the probationer; therefore, it is logical that he assume the task of trying to coordinate the various community efforts directed at the probationer. This is, of course, one way in which he can make his own treatment efforts more effective as well as a way to expand the scope of treatment processes available to his client.

Principle Four

No treatment program will be successful unless the client is an active participant in its design and implementation.

One of the greatest mistakes correctional workers have made over the years in trying to implement their philosophy of rehabilitation is not involving the client in planning his own treatment program. In adapting casework processes from the field of social work we failed to accept and practice the idea of mutual planning for action, a concept which is very important to casework principles. The traditional correctional idea has been "we know what is best for you; you are not capable of contributing to your own treatment program, so we will do it for you." The result has been that correctional workers have done *to, for, in behalf of* and *about* the client, but seldom *with* him. This is one of the reasons we have been no more successful than we have in rehabilitating criminal offenders.

It would be difficult to overemphasize the importance of the client's participation in the planning of the treatment program. This is not to imply that he alone should make all the decisions; they are to be mutually made after joint discussions which explore the specific needs and the alternatives for meeting those needs. On occasion, the probation officer may have to make decisions and give directions that are not by mutual agreement; this is part of his function as a representative of the court. But he should never lose sight of the need to have the client's cooperation and active participation, rather than mere passive acceptance, in order to make the treatment program work. After all, the client is really the only one who can change his behavior, even temporarily, and this is the purpose and goal of treatment. Unless he is committed to the program designed to accomplish this end, the end will not be realized in fact. If he does not have a voice in what happens to him, and thereby feels a part of the process, he will not be committed to the program necessary to bring about the needed change.

Principle Five

No treatment program can be guaranteed to be successful, no matter how hard the probation officer tries nor how high is his level of expertise.

There are obviously many unforeseen results to any plan or process for modifying human behavior. With all the unknowns regarding causation, the general nature of the individual and the specific behavior to be changed, success can be counted on to be quite elusive. There is no way to be sure he will not make an error in judgment which will negate what has been done up to that point. There is no way that external forces, over which neither the client nor the probation officer have control, can be regulated in their influences on the whole treatment process. There are simply too many uncontrollable imponderables to guarantee the success of any treatment program; if everything meshes well it will likely be successful, at least in some appreciable measure, but one small and seemingly insignificant event can throw the entire process "off track" and cause it to fail.

Principle Six

We must continue to try!

Even though the possibilities of failure are great and the potential for merely marking time without progress are greater, the stakes are so high that the probation officer cannot afford to give up. Both the client and the community have so much to lose by failure and so much to gain by success that, even in the face of overwhelming odds or serious setbacks, we must continue our efforts. The probation officer should not become discouraged over failures or reverses. These he will have and, in some cases, after he has done all he can reasonably do, he will have to be instrumental in the incarceration of the client as a result of failure. If he has been faithful to his charge and has tried to humanly and professionally carry out his responsibilities, he can learn to accept some failures as part of his life without becoming discouraged about them. He must continue his efforts to change the behavior of the client so that it becomes more acceptable and constructive and his life becomes more satisfying and productive.

Chapter Sixteen

DEVELOPMENT OF A TREATMENT PLAN

A PLAN OF TREATMENT, whether it is extremely simple or elaborately complex, is important to the optimum use of time, facilities, personnel and other resources in dealing with the probation client. Unfortunately, along with corrections' failure to involve the client in planning for treatment, we have also failed to focus as closely as we should have on the idea of advance planning. Not only has our success been hindered by doing to and for the client instead of with him, our approach to treatment has often been of the *hit or miss* variety. We have not generally stressed the value and necessity of a well-thought-out plan of where we need to go prior to the time we get started. Current emphasis on local and regional planning, as a result of urban development in a haphazard fashion, should be an example to corrections of the chaos which can occur when there is no before-the-fact planning. Or perhaps we don't need to look outside our own field! If we simply took a good look at our own chaos due to failure to plan ahead, we might get the point.

It is not enough to merely *play-it-by-ear* in reaction to whatever situation arises while working with the client; and to our shame this is the way many probation officers approach their all important task of client treatment and control. Very, very few of us are sufficiently insightful, flexible, experienced, or have enough time to play that game. And it is a game; an exercise for the sake of doing something, without purpose or goal except to be amused. Perhaps even worse than a game because games usually have rules to follow, at least; but this hit or miss approach is totally without goals or regulations. In addition, we owe too much to the client, the community and ourselves to take a chance on *spur-of-the-moment* solutions to such vital concerns as the problems or situations of the client which might erupt into further illegal, antisocial, or even destructive behavior.

Proper correctional treatment is not just an *off the top of the head* response. Rather, it is a well-planned and organized attempt to help resolve those things which hinder the client from effectively coping with life and his environment. We are fully cognizant of the vital importance of developing a treatment plan which is tailor-made to the specific needs of a particular individual client, and are aware that this involves a great deal of personal human feelings and intangibles of human judgment. Yet, there is nothing inconsistent between this stance and a process of planning ahead as to what treatment is necessary. As a matter of fact, good planning helps to make more tangible the intangibles and to objectify subjective human feelings. In other words, there is no substitute for treatment planning on a rather detailed level in order to maximize the effectiveness of available resources to help reach the established goals.

We recognize that such planning is vitally important for the probation officer, but we also know that not everyone has the ability to carry it off. Is the ability to properly develop treatment plans which will be useful the result of some mysterious power that only certain elite people have? Is it an inherited ability? Is it somehow automatically invested in the probation officer when he takes the oath of office? Obviously, the answers are a resounding "No!" And it is fortunate that the answers are no, because so many good probation officers would be left out if such ability was mysterious, or limited, or inherited. Fortunately for the probation officer and the client the ability can be learned and cultivated. This is the thrust of this chapter, to set forth specific steps to be followed in the development of an appropriate treatment plan, in the hope that it will be beneficial to the learning process.

These specific steps are not to imply merely a mechanical approach to either learning the process or its operation. To learn and to develop appropriate treatment plans requires considerable intelligence, good judgment and insight on the part of the probation officer. The format used here is merely a useful vehicle for clearly setting forth the processes involved in developing a treatment plan. At first glance, the process may appear involved and complex. It really isn't; it applies to the development of the simplest treatment plan to meet the simplest of client needs. It also can be applied to a highly involved and complex situation where there must be extensive analysis of a multitude of factors and elaborate plans made to meet a variety of interwoven and difficult problems. The process is basic, but allows for expansion to cover complicated situations.

STEP ONE

Analyze the offender and what you know about him and his surroundings in order to determine the problem areas which may contribute to his illegal and/or anti-social behavior.

All criminal behavior is not alike; there are varying degrees and levels of motivation, personal involvement, intention, seriousness of results, mitigating circumstances and other factors. These differences are recognized in legal as well as in social analyses. There are many different kinds of offenses in the law and different factors to consider even in the same offense. We also recognize that all people are not alike and that behaviors are different even though they may all fit the same legal category. If the task of corrections is to deal with behavior, these differences must be recognized and dealt with differently.

There are reasons of some kind underlying all criminal behavior, even though it may not be possible in a given situation to fully determine what those reasons are. What appears to be the same sort of client problem may not result in the same sort of criminal behavior, and what appears to be similar behavior may not spring from the same kind of problems. Each individual is different, is subjected to differing kinds of influences within his environment and responds to those forces and events in ways unique to his own personality.

As we have already discussed, all criminal behavior does not arise from personality problems and deficiencies. Much of it is the result of the individual's inability to cope with the everyday problems of his life. Many probation clients are not basically criminally oriented; they are simply overwhelmed by the complexities and inequities of a society which does not seem to care for them or to be willing to give them a real chance to care for themselves. Many are the *born losers* who seem to have gotten off on the wrong foot and things are happening so rapidly that they never seem to be able to catch up.

The problems of the client which may be contributing factors to his unacceptable conduct must be clearly identified; the trouble spots must be plainly delineated. This is the beginning point; if the situation is not clearly understood here, that which comes after is quite likely to be inappropriate because it will be a random *hit-or-miss* reaction. This is like trying to erect a large building without laying a solid foundation for it. As we have already indicated, all people and all behavior are not alike; therefore one should not expect to achieve success by treating them all the same way. If we do not take the time to analyze the data available regarding a probation client to determine just what are the areas needing treatment attention, we might as well do the same thing with everyone because any success of random treatment will be a matter of luck.

STEP TWO

Establish a hierarchy according to the intensity of the problems.

Not only must the problems be identified, the probation officer must also determine just what impact they have on the client and what implications they pose for the treatment program. There should be a ranking of the problems according to their degree of seriousness in terms of what is necessary to resolve them. This has very important implications for the efficacy of the resources which are available. It may well be that the needed solution does not exist locally; then the question is whether or not it is feasible, or even possible, to go beyond local resources to find the solution. This is not to imply that the more difficult or the less difficult should receive first attention; it is merely an admonition to recognize what will likely be involved in the search for solutions and to be realistic about what can and what cannot be done.

Consideration must also be given to the intensity of problems in terms of their practical contributions to the client's unacceptable behavior. He may have all kinds of problems which really have little or nothing to do with his behavior either directly or indirectly. There may be only one thing (or a very few things) which has great effect on his conduct. The probation officer must be able to distinguish between these so that his problem-solving efforts are related to change of client behavior. He has too few resources and too many other demands to spend his time trying to help the client solve problems that have nothing to do with his illegal conduct. This does not mean that those areas are to be totally ignored, but rather that they are not to be the prime focus of attention. As we have indicated earlier, if the probation officer can help the client to resolve the problems which heavily contribute to his anti-social or illegal behavior, he may very well be able to cope with and resolve the remainder on his own.

The probation officer must always be aware that the very serious problems as he sees them may not be so defined by the client. We must never overlook or disregard the meaning of the problem and of his own behavior to him. And sometimes how the client sees his problems can determine their degree of seriousness, because if he believes it to be a major consideration when the probation officer sees it as minor, it will likely stand in the way of moving on to the resolution of other and perhaps more serious problems.

This sort of ranking of problems is not easy to do. Like so many other aspects of human existence and behavior, there are innumerable factors which influence the way both the probation officer and the client see the problems. Obviously, there will be mistakes made under such circumstances. Fortunately, these are usually not fatal and both can mutually examine the error and determine how to correct it and, perhaps, even make up for it. There is an element of trial and error in this process, but a careful analysis of everything the probation officer and the client mutually know of the situation can greatly reduce the margin of error and increase the probability of successful resolution of the problems.

STEP THREE

Determine what ends must be gained in order to resolve the problems which actually contribute to unacceptable client behavior.

Once the problem areas have been identified and their intensity of impact established, goals must be set, the attainment of which will be the practical resolution of the problem. Without specific goals to give direction to a treatment plan, the efforts of the probation officer are not likely to deal with specific problems in a way designed to bring about practical solutions. When one is working toward a set goal, as contrasted from aimless wandering or drifting with the tide, he is much more likely to put forth the sort of effort needed to get there. He will also be more confident of its eventual attainment because he can see how each step brings him closer to the goal. And the goals which are set must be relevant to the resolving of the problem. It is not enough to be doing something which is nice to do; the effort must be geared to the eventual solution of the problem.

There may very well be both short- and long-term goals, the former serving as stepping stones to the attainment of the latter. This is consistent with earlier comments about establishing a ranking of problems in terms of their impact on the client. Some problems are so pressing that they must be alleviated, if not resolved, at once; others can wait until one has the time, resources, or capability to get to them. Both the short- and the long-term goals must be integrated into a complete plan, however, or there may be unnecessary duplication or even contradictory actions in trying to separately and independently fulfill both. There is too much at stake to waste any motion.

The goals must be realistically attainable. When we set goals which are reachable, there is likely to be commitment to expend the efforts to get there; but when they are not reachable, there are likely to be rationalizations as to why we do not attain them, or even failure to try. The ideal solution to a problem may be unattainable for any number of valid reasons. In this case, we must be content to accept something less than ideal but something that will go as far as possible toward the resolution of the problem. There are times when the only goal one can hope to reach is a very modest one indeed. One should not be overly concerned about this because the successful attainment of a modest goal is more satisfying and commendable than the unsuccessful, though perhaps dramatic, attempt at attainment of the ideal.

This is a reality-oriented approach that is understandable and that makes practical sense to the client. He is not likely to be very interested in, let alone work toward, the ideal, especially if it is nebulous. It is as difficult for the probation client to work toward an abstract ideal as it is for the rest of us. We need to feel that we know where we are going, that we are moving in the right direction and that we are making progress. If, in addition, we believe that the end is worthwhile, we are usually willing to toil long and hard to get there. The probation client is not really different; he, too, will invest himself in ends which he considers to be worth his efforts.

STEP FOUR

Prioritize the goals which have been determined so that first things come first.

It is very important that the goals which need attention first are quickly addressed and, hopefully, resolved so that the problems do not stand in the way of working toward other goals. There are several ways to establish priorities depending on one's assessment of the situation. First priority may be given to the most pressing problem area in terms of the degree to which it contributes to illegal behavior. It may be that something is so off balance that there is no hope of establishing acceptable behavior patterns until it is set right. In such a case, this is obviously the first thing that has to be done.

Under other circumstances it may be that priorities will be determined on the basis of immediate physical or material needs, needs that are so basic to sheer survival that until they are satisfied everything else is considered relatively unimportant. Or priorities may be established because of the need for quick success experiences in order to build up the client's self-confidence or his trust in the probation officer. So many probation clients have experienced a continuing series of failures and now have no expectation of breaking the cycle. Some sort of quick positive action may be necessary to at least stir the beginnings of hope that things can be different.

These different bases for establishing priorities may exist side by side, with one or the other taking precedence at various times according to prevailing circumstances. Life is dynamic, with sometimes sudden changes. The problem that was a moment ago the most pressing may now have become secondary because of a sudden shift of circumstances. It has not been resolved, and doubtlessly will once again rise to the top of the list; but something else has dramatically been thrust to the fore. This is the way life is, and the probation officer must be alert to such changes and flexible enough to alter his emphasis and efforts to meet the new challenge. If he does not, the situation will likely deteriorate and he is left relatively helpless to be of assistance to the client when he is most needed.

STEP FIVE

Select specific courses of action designed to move step by step toward the goals which have been established.

As we have already indicated, many probation clients have great difficulty dealing with uncertainty and only understand the specific and concrete. Thus the probation officer must focus on very real, specific and often limited suggestions for actions to resolve the problems. If both he and the court have done their work well, in terms of establishing the framework of limitations and expectations within which treatment is to occur, the terms and conditions of probation will be a specific and readily understood part of this plan. One of the first things the probation officer will need to do is to make clear to the client the limits and expectations for his conduct. This should be done matter-of-factly, in simple language and with considerable tactfulness.

But it must be done in such a way that the client knows it is a *no nonsense* situation.

In the course of continuing personal contacts during the implementation of the treatment program, the probation officer can set specific tasks for each interview session. He should plan in advance the greater part of the interview, the issues to be addressed and the specifics to be accomplished; being alert to readjust the plans if the need arises. He should also see to it that specific tasks for things to be accomplished before the next interview session are mutually assigned. This should be something that the client has the ability to do; something that he can accomplish which will help him to see that he can make positive contributions to the resolution of his own problems; something that may help to build his self-confidence as it is done; something that is one more step toward the overall goals that have been established. Of course, the probation officer must be careful that such assignments can realistically be accomplished within the abilities of the client and the time available to work on them, or he is probably only setting the client up for one more defeat in a long line of defeats.

The basic principle underlying this idea of selecting concrete and very specific things to be done is a simple but often overlooked one: you cannot talk people out of their problems; something must be *done* about them. So often the people helping professions have seemed to rely solely on delving into the individual's past life as a means of helping him to understand his present predicament, as though understanding is all that is needed to solve problems. This approach has always been verbal; we *interview, counsel, talk to*, but we seem to be reluctant to *do* anything. The idea, perhaps, has been simply that the client will do for himself if he understands what it is he should do. This is, of course, an important element in the process; but there are often so many things that probation clients simply cannot do for themselves without a little help from the probation officer. Until we get away from the idea that talking about problems will somehow cause them to go away, and get down to the practical aspects of actually *doing* things with the clients, we will contin-

ue to have the same lack of success which has so often characterized correctional efforts in the past.

STEP SIX

*As various specific elements of the treatment program
begin, evaluate their impact on the resolution of the
whole range of problems, and if necessary, make modifications in both the goals to be attained and the specific
actions designed to attain them.*

The possibility of modification should not cause the probation
officer to be less diligent and thorough in the analysis of problems or developing plans for treatment. He must still do the very
best he can do in these areas within the limitations of resources,
facilities, time and expertise which are forced on him. Yet, he
must recognize that, no matter how good he is or how many resources are available to him he will make some errors. Evaluation and modification is a means to detect and correct such errors, hopefully, before they result in any real permanent damage to the client or the treatment process.

A little more freedom and confidence to try promising but
untested new approaches is another important function of this
evaluation and modification step. Many correctional people are
quite conservative in this area of trying new approaches, perhaps
because the criminal justice system of which they are a part is so
tradition-bound. But the complexities of our modern urban,
technologically oriented society and the client problems that go
along with it often demand a different sort of attack on the
problems. Being good enough for our fathers does not necessarily mean being good enough for the present-day situations. The
probation officer will likely feel more confident to try a new approach if he knows he can modify it in the event he discovers
it is not working out as hoped.

Following these steps will not guarantee a perfect treatment
plan for any client, but they will help the probation officer to
provide more thoughtfully organized, thorough and potentially
more effective treatment to all his clients because he is more likely to consider all the important variables involved for each.

Chapter Seventeen

THE HUMANITY OF PROBATION OFFICERS*

THE TITLE OF THIS CHAPTER is not intended to imply a discussion of the foibles and human failings of probation officers, although there doubtless are many which would make interesting reading. Rather, humanity is used here to denote the best qualities of humankind—kindness, considerateness, sympathy, mercy, compassion and understanding. In a complex society of computerized impersonality and identification by number, simple human concern is essential to a lessening of tension and turmoil. The probation officer must not grow hard and calloused in such a setting, but must maintain the *common touch* of basic human emotions.

To some this may seem to belabor the obvious and to others it may appear trite; but in an environment which creates inhumanity, it becomes necessary to remind ourselves that we, who are supposed to correct and rehabilitate, cannot allow our services to contribute to that creation through the exercise of inhumanity toward our probationers. The obvious and trite are most likely to be overlooked, especially in routine day-to-day activity. It is this very failing on a wide scale which makes it necessary to review the need for humanity on the part of the probation officer.

A HISTORY OF FAILURE

Many probation clients have long histories of failure in their families, schools, jobs, marriages and even in illegal activities. These people need successful experiences, even small and menial ones, to help them feel a part of the world. The probation of-

* Adapted from an article of the same title which appeared in *Federal Probation, Vol. XXXVI,* No. 2; June, 1972.

ficer can contribute to this success by treating the client with dignity and respect; not a difficult thing to do, but an action which helps him to feel that he is somebody.

We live in an environment which creates inhumanity. It has spawned poverty, violence and crime. It has brought about rootlessness, impersonality and noninvolvement. It has produced loneliness, restlessness and unconcern. As a result, we have no time for people as *people*. We have lost the sense of being a vital part of something important. Consequently, we feel little commitment to others or to the welfare of our communities.

This is particularly true of most correctional clients whose environment has been such that there is little they can do to influence, to say nothing of control, the forces and factors which are vital to their dignity, well-being, or even their lives. They are frequently the victims of social injustice, social rejection and social stigma. The insight and social skills necessary to deal with injustice, rejection and stigma are not characteristic of our clients. Such victimization may, indeed, convince them that they are "no good" and that they "can't make it." These feelings are quite likely, in turn, to lead to frustration, hostility and further illegal and/or antisocial behavior.

In his dealings with his clients, the probation officer must not further contribute to this demeaning and dehumanizing process through actions which deny their essential dignity and worth or which further isolate them from participation in the mainstream of social activity. This is a real possibility for probation officers because they work in an authoritative setting; and the occupancy of a position of authority often leads to arrogance; and arrogance generally results in a *put down* of others or arouses hostility in them. In either case, the probation officer loses the opportunity to be successful in his mission of rehabilitation because he ends up actually perpetuating the dehumanizing treatment to which the client has been so long subjected. The constructive use of authority is proper for probation officers; but arrogance is always destructive and has no place in a profession dedicated to serving others.

BE GENUINE IN RELATING TO PROBATIONERS

The probation officer must be real in relating to his clients. As we have already seen, it is easy to grow calloused toward the client when all one's time is taken up with trying to solve the problems of others and to enforce the regulations of the courts. But, if the probation officer becomes suspicious and cold, that attitude will reveal itself to the probationer. It cannot be successfully covered up by a "professional" facade—which is often disguised as being clinically objective, not getting over-involved, or merely performing one's duty. The result is that we "professionalize" ourselves out of meaningful contact with the very people we are charged with helping.

The probation officer must be sensitive to how he appears to his clients because they react according to how they see him, not according to the impression he thinks he conveys. It is difficult to long deceive people about how one really feels toward them.

A sensitive response to human needs will do away with the necessity to artificially project an *image*. Being genuine in relating to others makes its own profound impression, one on which it is probably impossible to improve. As trite as it may sound, there is nothing weak or unmanly or unprofessional in feelings of concern, compassion, understanding and warmth so long as these feelings are real and are not patronizing or condescending.

Awareness of the influences of cultural differences, desire for the protection of individual rights, respect for the integrity and dignity of the client; all these will result in treatment of clients as *people*, not as cases. Yet, they do not mean a disregard for the rights or welfare of the community. There is nothing necessarily incompatible between warmth and acceptance and firm enforcement of the law. The probation officer must take whatever corrective measures are necessary; but these must not allow him to demean the dignity of the individual. There must be a balance between compassion and control; between friendliness and firmness; between consideration and correction.

EFFECTIVE COMMUNICATION

As we have already indicated, the probation officer must talk *with* the client, not *to* him. This is the only way to effectively communicate. Trying to "treat" the probationer by issuing commands and directives, or giving friendly advice, or finding for him all the solutions to his problems will not be effective, because this approach is likely to arouse hostility and resistance or because what is being said makes no impression on him.

Like everyone else, the probation client is always interpreting what he hears from the probation officer, as well as the probation officer-client relationship itself, in terms of its specific meaning for him. This meaning is determined by what is traveling on what someone has called the "inner circuit." Such things as the client's unique past experiences, his cultural heritage, his immediate social environment and his pressing current concerns all condition the meaning for him of whatever the probation officer does or says.

Consequently, the client does not always hear what the probation officer intends to convey. And, to further complicate the situation, his response is based on his own interpretation of the event's meaning for him. It is no wonder that misunderstandings arise between probation officer and client. Such misunderstandings occur in everyday communication on all levels. The potential for such misunderstanding is, no doubt, much greater in the probation officer-client relationship with its overtones of "Establishment" vs. the rebels, authority vs. resistance, we vs. they.

So often in this situation, the probation officer may come to think that the client's reactions are deliberate defiance, or *he just doesn't care that I'm trying to help him*, or *he doesn't want to change his behavior*, or *we just can't seem to communicate*, or *he just won't learn*.

One of the ways in which the probation officer can help overcome these interferences to clear communication between himself and the client is to relate to and treat him with dignity, concern and awareness that he, too, is a worthwhile being. Of course, this will not solve all the communication problems, but it is an important step in the direction of reducing misunderstandings and of removing the barriers which frequently hinder effective treatment efforts.

CONTRIBUTION TO SUCCESS

There is a personal and professional "payoff" to treating people with dignity, respect, feeling; to relating to them as worthwhile and important. They will reciprocate the treatment and, thereby, contribute immeasurably to one's success as a probation officer. A fundamental treatment technique, long used by most probation officers, is a meaningful interpersonal relationship with the client; a relationship built on mutual trust and respect. If the client is not treated with concern, dignity and respect, this most important technique cannot possibly be effective.

In the long run, this is the only way for the probation officer to behave. All else; disrespect, contempt, unconcern, facade, distrust, will fail. Only the client can really be successful in changing his own behavior and attitudes; and his success is the probation officer's success. The probation officer has much less control over the client's behavior than he likes to think, especially if he gets "hung up" with his position of authority.

The most effective way to turn the client from his illegal ways is to treat him with dignity. He is less likely to recidivate if he believes he is *somebody* and if the probation officer reinforces this feeling through considerate treatment. Does he already have a sense of his own self-worth? If so, he will react with hostility to treatment by the probation officer which denies his worth. If he does not have a positive concept of himself, try to imagine what is done to him when one acts in such ways as to reinforce his negative self-concept. He is driven further and further away from any desire or motivation to conduct himself in a positive way.

Whatever he may have done in violating the law, he is a *man* and has the right to retain his dignity. This includes making his own decisions, within a framework of legally and socially acceptable behavior, of what he does and does not do. To strip him of all choice relative to his own conduct is to strip him of the human dignity which distinguishes man from lower orders of the animal kingdom.

There are, of course, some clients who will take advantage of this kind of treatment, partially because it is so different from the way they are usually treated and they do not really know how to respond to such expressions of acceptance. Some will be hostile because they will consider it to be a "put-on." Some will be passive because of confusion of not knowing what is the expected response. In every case the probation officer will have to start with the client where he is and patiently demonstrate genuine respect for him as an individual. The results will be most worthwhile as he sees clients grow as people. Whatever risk is involved in some clients taking advantage is minimal compared to the awareness that one has aided another to grow and to improve his relations with the community.

KNOW YOURSELF

For the probation officer to really know his client, he *must* know himself. To always treat others with dignity and respect, he must respect his own integrity. To be real in his relations with others, he must know who he is, what he is doing and why he behaves that way.

This kind of self-awareness is not always easy. Everyone has biases, prejudices and pet peeves, many of which were learned so early in life that one tends to regard them as part of his biological heritage. Self-discipline and control in relation to these do not come naturally. One must be aware of these feelings to be sure that they do not govern his actions. Biases can be unlearned; prejudices can be overcome; pet peeves can be tolerated. Self-discipline and rational control are necessary to guard against the problem of selective enforcement of probation conditions based on one's own biases.

One of the things with which most probation clients need to deal is their feelings; feelings about society, law, authority, themselves and a host of other things, without being shut off by the *helping agent*. Overt behavior is frequently the expression of feelings that can no longer be suppressed. The threat of punishment may have held behavior in check until the feelings were so explosive that nothing could stop the outburst. Society, in this circumstance, often deals with behavior but feeling is seldom considered; so it is usually only a matter of time until the outburst occurs again. For the probation officer to be the helping agent in dealing with the client's feelings, he must also be aware of, and able to deal with, his own feelings regarding, among other things, authority, acceptance, his clients, his job and himself. If he does not know where he is going in this regard, he will find it extremely difficult to help the client know where he is going.

The probation officer who does not know himself, his strengths and weaknesses, his virtues and faults, his potentials and limitations, will never really know his clients. Not knowing the client usually means insensitivity to his needs. Insensitivity to his needs means inability to help him meet those needs. Inability to meet those needs means social failure for him. Failure for the client means lack of success for the probation officer. To be successful, the probation officer must know himself and must discipline himself to always treat his clients with respect and dignity.

The probation officer must be aware of, concerned about and actively engaged in changing social conditions which contribute to the dehumanizing of individuals. He must be vitally concerned with social reform and with reform of the system for administration of criminal justice. But, in his concern for changing the system, he cannot afford to neglect his client. There is relatively little he can do as an individual to change the overall system; but he can determine that his treatment of the client will not be an extension of the brutality, callousness, unconcern and delay which so frequently characterize the system prior to his getting the client for correctional treatment.

If we can accept that crime flows from acts which demean the individual, then one way to prevent criminal and antisocial behavior is to treat law violators in a way that shows genuine respect for the dignity and worth of the individual.

Despite our traditional claims for the effectiveness of probation, treating the offender as a *second-class* citizen by denying him human dignity and worth is much worse than no probation service at all.

Chapter Eighteen

THE FUNCTION OF COERCIVE
CASEWORK IN PROBATION*

O NE HEARS A GREAT DEAL today about social permissiveness, individual freedom, right of free speech and allowing everyone to "do his thing." These ideas have been made the topics of books, magazine articles, newspaper editorials, protest demonstrations and political speeches; everyone seems to be getting into the act. On the one hand our courts are badgered for legal approval of more liberal expressions of individual freedom and on the other hand they are ridiculed for their lenient rulings which protect the criminal and tie the hands of law enforcement. There are alternating cries of anguish over the breakdown of law and order and of indignation over the development of a police state.

The writers, speakers and demonstrators cite the rising crime rates, campus disorders, police brutality, the generation gap, youthful disrespect for authority, authoritative disregard for the individual and a host of other themes to support their respective theses. They all imply, and often state, that it is a matter of unrealistic leniency or unconstitutional restriction, depending on which side the complainant finds himself, which is at the root of all our problems.

These are not tides of controversy which swirl outside the field of corrections. Indeed, some of the new recruits, especially those young people just out of college, may be particularly susceptible to being caught up in these controversies. They have been trained in times of less social restraint, exposed to the philosophy that every man should be free to "do his own thing" and, perhaps, influenced by the spirit of disrespect for law, order and

---

* Adapted from "The Function of Coercive Casework in Corrections," appearing in *Federal Probation, Vol. XXXV*, No. 1; March, 1971.

216

authority which infests society today. Yet, they are coming into a field specifically assigned the responsibility of protecting society through the exercise of restraints, the enforcement of law and order and the use of authority. It is little wonder that some of the young enforcers of society's regulations may have conflicts of identification between society and the violators of society's laws.

In this setting, it seems important, indeed imperative, to draw the attention of the newcomer and the veteran alike to these conflicts and to explore some ideas which may help to orient one to a resolution of them.

WHAT IS COERCIVE CASEWORK?

At the heart of the philosophy of probation work is the two-fold concept of social control and social treatment. They are not mutually exclusive or separate entities, but intertwined; the one impinging on the other, modifying and shaping, being modified and shaped in turn. Ideally, of course, we attain the goal of control through the means of treatment. However, this statement taken alone is easily misconstrued; therefore, it needs some explanation and analysis.

There is, in the minds of many practitioners of the helping professions, an irreconcilable conflict between the use of casework techniques and the use of authority. This apparent dichotomy has been the topic of many debates and journal articles and need not be belabored here. The conflict remains unresolved and will probably continue so for a long time to come. We do not expect to resolve it here; only to try to approach it from a slightly different perspective.

The definitions of social casework are almost as numerous as are the numbers of persons defining it. However, they all generally are focused on the processes by which the individual is helped to more effectively function within his social environment. The emphasis is on the individual in the recognition that no matter how similar one's situation may appear to be to that of another, each problem, and each attempt and method to resolve it, has its own unique meaning to each individual. The method which works for one person may not work with another. One of the basic and most important tasks of the caseworker is to fit his treatment methods and techniques to the unique needs of his client.

To *coerce* is to restrain or constrain by force, especially by the use of legal authority. *Restrain* carries the idea of holding in check, controlling, curbing. *Constrain* gives the idea of forcing into, compelling, obliging to action.

By *coercive casework*, then, we mean the use of restraining and constraining legal authority in the processes of helping the offender to function in his social environment without resorting to illegal or antisocial behavior.

This is, ideally, the underlying philosophy of establishing and enforcing specific conditions of probation because those conditions are to be used for guidance of the client's behavior. He is placed under restraints when instructed not to associate with certain kinds of people, not to leave the jurisdiction without permission, or not to possess a weapon. He is constrained when instructed to report regularly to the probation officer, to maintain gainful employment, or to make restitution to the victim of his offense.

Perhaps a graphic example of this approach is the condition of probation which requires the probationer to participate in a program of psychotherapy. Despite some objections that such an order violates the basic need for client motivation for such therapy to be effective, most veteran probation officers know of specific instances where the proper motivation has developed *after* the therapy program has begun.

There are many who hold that the foundation of effective casework is the belief that motivation to improve or to resolve problems must come from within; that casework is not effective unless it is desired and voluntarily requested by the client. Somehow, the client must engage himself in grappling with his own problems if they are to be resolved. They believe that every man has the right of choice and it is wrong to impose on him official values or solutions to problems from without.

We do not deny the innate dignity of man, nor his right to freedom to make choices. We do not deny the validity of the above-noted ideas, nor of the basic responsibility of the individual to deal with his own problems, with his own resources; but, neither can be deny the necessity of the orderly functioning of society, nor of all citizens to behave so as not to disturb that orderly functioning. Neither can we deny the importance of client and probation officer alike recognizing that the exercise of the right of choice carries with it the necessity of accepting the consequences of that choice.

It is essential to recognize that underlying our highly developed society are orderly behavior and relationships, without which society could not exist. When individuals act so as to disrupt this order, some action must be taken to restore it. In the case of the criminal offender (and many others, for that matter) this action may be through coercion, for his own and society's welfare.

THE FUNCTION OF COERCIVE CASEWORK

While it is true that effective casework is not something done *to* or *for* the client, but *with* him, it is also true that sometimes it is a matter of some action which *gets his attention* or *holds him still* long enough for him to recognize that there *is* motivation from within; he may only need to make way for it to begin to function. Or, it may be necessary, through restraint and constraint, to structure action until the validity of it can be understood and accepted for itself as a way of life.

In this initial stage of the probation treatment process, one need not necessarily be complicated in the design of his casework methods and techniques. He may need only to set, and enforce, some behavioral limits to inform his client, "You can go this far, but no further"; to say, "No! You cannot do that."

If it is true that "nothing succeeds like success," it is also true that nothing fails like failure. In direct proportion to his lack of success, the individual is likely to feel ineffectual, then powerless, then useless, then helpless. At this point he also ceases to care; and that is when he is the most disruptive and dangerous.

The offender, often habitually unsuccessful in his attempts to adjust to the pressures and demands of society, needs to have successful experiences, even if they are at first coerced. A definite "shall and shall not" approach is often necessary until the client reaches the point where he can be comfortable with the restraints and constraints imposed on his conduct; until the motivation for lawful and acceptable behavior comes from within himself, from the knowledge of the benefit to be derived from avoiding the kind of disruptive behavior which subjects him to social sanctions.

The aim of providing success experiences is to persuade the offender of the validity of society's ideals and to have him internalize them as his own. He must come to view his behavior in the light of its impingement on others and learn to regulate it accordingly. To reach this goal requires not only casework treatment but behavior control as well.

There is a common misconception that delinquent and criminal groups have their own set of values, so will not accept and live by the values of the larger community. However, making the values of society meaningful and relevant to these groups can provide the motivation for them to modify their own value systems and to incorporate society's values into their own codes of conduct.

This will entail the application of realistic values that are relevant to present conditions, not merely harping on traditional concepts based on outmoded social codes. To sharp and inquiring youth, it will also require pertinent explanations of the *why* of these values.

It is imperative, in this regard, for society to propagate its value of the necessity to behave in accordance with law. Various subgroups, including the criminal and delinquent subcultures, actively propagate their value codes. It is no less acceptable for society to vigorously engage in such activity, despite current criticisms of such practice. The probation officer needs occasionally to remind himself and others, including his clients, that society also has rights and needs.

A POSITIVE APPROACH

We readily recognize the necessity of forcible restraint of those who represent a violent threat to society; and, for the protection of others, we put these persons behind bars. This is a negative action. There is a positive side to this same action, however, especially in regard to those offenders who are not placed behind bars, but are allowed to remain in the community on probation.

This positive action, what we have termed *coercive casework*, is that restraint and constraint on the individual's behavior designed to help persuade him of both the short- and long-run validity of accepting society's values and regulating his conduct accordingly. The goal, of course, is to have him internalize these values, making coercion unnecessary. It is the same kind of discipline we enforce with our children as we try to instill within them acceptable standards of conduct. These standards are at first enforced through various restraints and constraints. As the child matures and restraint becomes self-discipline, the enforced standards become clear through understanding and habitual through regular observance.

It is behavior, illegal and antisocial, which brings the individual into the correctional system. It is both behavior and the attitudes leading to it which we must help to change. While the techniques for accomplishing this goal may be varied and require individual application according to need and circumstances as well as an explanation of *why*, the underlying philosophy is as simple as "thou shalt not" and "thou shalt." This is not a new concept, certainly; but it is a basic and necessary one both in terms of individual benefit and the ongoing and orderly· functioning of society.

Chapter Nineteen

THE PROBLEM OF NONCOMPLIANCE

ONE OF THE CARDINAL COMPONENTS of the concept of probation is the establishment of specified conditions according to which the lawbreaker is expected to conduct his life. In exchange for not imposing the full penalty provided by law, the court granting probation sets forth the conditions by which the offender is to live, under threat of the imposition of the penalty for any noncompliance on his part. Thus, in practically every case in which an individual is granted probation, there are some behavioral conditions imposed on him.

These conditions may vary from a simple requirement to refrain from any further violation of law to very extensive and inclusive requirements covering everything from behavior, associates and residence to finances, restitution and employment. They may vary from one jurisdiction to another or at different times in the same jurisdiction. They usually vary according to the nature of the offense and often according to the individual offender. Some of the conditions involve the offender's civil rights, such as restrictions on certain licenses, residence requirements or his submission to searches, while others may be more or less for agency convenience in keeping track of him. Other conditions may be designed to gain reparation for victims or to protect the public from further depredations by the offender. Still others may *specify* certain *implied* conditions, such as that requiring the offender to violate no law, an act which by definition would constitute noncompliance with the probation grant.

Although some of the typical conditions of probation require certain legally defined behavior, most are of a technical nature. By this we mean that the breach of these conditions would not ordinarily be a violation of law; they have become behavioral restrictions only because the offender has been placed on probationary status and is, therefore, required to give a stricter accounting of conduct than is the nonoffender. Since most probation conditions are technical, it follows that most violations of probation conditions will also be of a technical nature. This is not to imply that the probationary status is rescinded and he is incarcerated for technical violations more often than for violations of law; the opposite is actually the case. It is simply an observation that most client behavior which is unacceptable is contrary to the technical conditions rather than statutorily illegal.

This area of *negative* behavior by the probation client constitutes a problem in that there is so much of it that it occupies a great deal of the probation officer's time. It is also very frustrating because he is often dealing with relatively minor situations which become nuisances, even if they do not become serious impediments to the probation program. This chapter deals with the problem of technical noncompliance precisely because it does take so much of the probation officer's time and because it is not an easy thing for most probation officers to handle without becoming frustrated and/or overreacting to the situation.

THE IMPORTANCE OF PROBATION CONDITIONS

All the conditions of probation are serious behavioral requirements, even the technical ones. They form the foundation upon which the court expects the client to build his future conduct and become the framework within which both the probation officer and the client find guidance as to the actions which will and will not be found acceptable. Ideally, the conditions of probation set forth by the court provide clear direction as to what the offender must do to redeem himself in the eyes of the community. For every violation of the law a penalty is prescribed which represents the community's assessment of the seriousness of the conduct. If, for whatever the reasons, the penalty is not imposed by the courts, the community expects some kind of compensatory behavior on the part of the offender. When he is placed under probation conditions, they become the guidelines for this compensatory behavior. Therefore, from both legal and social points of view, the conditions of probation take on serious importance.

The conditions of probation are also important for treatment considerations. Despite valid criticisms of the routine and indiscriminate use of blanket conditions to cover all cases, practitioners generally agree that well-chosen conditions of probation can be helpful tools in planning, implementing and following through with the treatment program. As we have already seen, it is the probation officer's responsibility to carry out the needed treatment plan within the framework of legal and judicial constraints on both himself and his client. He may be hindered in working with the client by these restrictions, but he has no choice other than to abide by them. Even so, experienced counselors recognize the therapeutic value of setting and enforcing limits on behavior and of requiring the acceptance of responsibility for one's behavior. Both of these can be reflected in carefully imposed conditions of probation.

These considerations, the legal and social expectations of behavior and the treatment implications, underscore the importance of setting the conditions of probation only after very careful and thoughtful attention by both the probation officer making recommendations to the court and the court itself. The conditions of probation have sufficient consequences for the offender and the community that the decision-makers would be derelict in duty if they approached this task in a haphazard or nonchalant manner. In this context, it should be observed that the conditions of probation must be therapeutic in design and tailor-made to the situation and the client. A vital principle of the concept and philosophy of probation is the individualized application of processes designed to assist the offender to take advantage of the opportunity provided him to readjust his life style enough to avoid further illegal behavior and, perhaps, even increase his satisfaction with life. Any sort of automatic or blanket imposition of conditions of probation does violence to this concept and will quite likely seriously hinder rehabilitative efforts.

CONSEQUENCES OF NONCOMPLIANCE

As we have already noted, most breaches of the conditions of probation are of the technical rather than the illegal variety. This in itself often makes for problems. Violations of law are usually much more clear-cut and generally easier to handle. In fact, the probation officer may have no discretion at all here if he is by law or by judicial or administrative policy required to report all such violations to the court for decision and action. He usually has some discretion, however, regarding technical violations; but this does not necessarily make them easier to handle. No matter how diligently the probation officer tries to prevent such breaches of these conditions, they will occur. The client may even project the blame for them onto the probation officer for being "too strict and legalistic!"

Many of the violations may be so minor as to seem to be inconsequential or they may be nuisance behavior. They may be frustrating and disconcerting to the treatment plan, or they may be signs of forthcoming problems, especially if they grow worse over a period of time. In any case, the probation officer must deal with every such violation in some manner; they must not simply be ignored, no matter how small and seemingly inconsequential they may be. The "dealing with" may be only to inform the client of the probation officer's awareness of the breach and a warning against further such actions. Most technical violations usually call for some sort of adjustment in behavior rather than return to court; but the adjustment must be made.

The probation officer cannot allow himself or the client to grow lax as to the importance of complying with the conditions of probation. This is what will happen if there is noncompliance and the probation officer is aware of it, but nothing is done about it. Such action will inevitably lead to a breakdown of the relationship between the probation officer and the client because it fosters a sense of distrust between them, an atmosphere of unreality and game-playing and an implied approval of deception for one's own benefit. One of the basic tools the probation officer has at his disposal is the personal relationship with the client based on mutual respect, trust and a sense of personal responsibility. When noncompliance occurs, both client and probation officer are aware of it and it is ignored, the relationship is destroyed and the positive good it could have produced is then negated.

Another consequence of noncompliance which is ignored is the dilution of the meaning and importance of law in general and probation in particular. Probation is a legal status imposed by the court on some individual lawbreakers. For it to be effective, the principals must recognize that this involves a respect for and compliance with the requirements and restrictions which are a part of that status. The same reasoning applies to the system of law generally. Ignored noncompliance is, then, an attack on the validity of legal processes and statuses. Even if the attack is not a conscious undermining of the legal structure, its continuance will subtly bring about the same result.

A consequence of ignored noncompliance which is, perhaps, more commonly recognized is the cumulative effect of "getting away with it" again and again. When the client sees that there are no negative sanctions for noncompliance, he is likely to feel safe and insulated from legal action. He may then expand his negative behavior to include more serious or even illegal actions. The probation officer is being unfair to the community and the client when he allows this to occur and then takes drastic action after things get beyond his control. If the client is lulled to sleep by the probation officer's inaction, then "pounced upon" when he "goes a little too far," the probation officer is not responsibly performing his functions in terms of treatment of the client or protection of the community. He should deal with each breach of conduct as it occurs and thereby, hopefully, keep the behavior from becoming more serious, illegal, or harmful.

STRATEGY FOR GAINING COMPLIANCE

This heading does not imply a "soft-headed cop-out" in terms of deception of the client or lowering of the standards of behavior. Rather, it has to do with well-planned good sense. We have already noted that technical violations of the conditions of probation are inevitable and that such action can have serious consequences. It makes good sense, then, to try to plan and act in ways calculated to minimize noncompliance. This is a question which must be considered at the time of setting forth the conditions of probation, not after they have been breached. The probation officer can play a very crucial role here, especially in his recommendations of these conditions for the court's determination.

This leads us to make one other necessary observation at this point; the conditions of probation must be legal in every sense of the term. There are statutory and case law foundations for this statement, but it should be obvious that no condition of probation should compel the client to break the law and no condition should require something of him which is outside the jurisdiction of the court to order. To do so, of course, undermines both the legal system and the rehabilitative philosophy. In this regard, the conditions of probation should always be specified by the court, not the probation officer. This is not to give him an easy out by placing the responsibility elsewhere; rather, it serves to strengthen the hand of the probation officer in enforcing those conditions.

The comments in this section are based on a simple hypothesis: the probation officer can expect client noncompliance in direct proportion to the degree that the conditions of probation are complex, ambiguous, irrelevant, negative and unrealistic. Stated more positively, the client is much more likely to comply with the conditions of probation if they are simple, clear, meaningful, positive and realistic. Let us briefly examine each of these necessary components of the strategy to gain compliance.

The more simple the conditions, the easier it will be to gain compliance. We have already discussed the difficulty many probation clients have in coping with the complexity of their lives and the need for the probation officer to help them simplify the issues. The same principle holds true here. The greater the impact the condition of probation is likely to have on the life style of the client, the harder it will be for him to comply. This is not to imply that requirements are to be watered down to minimize their impact; they should be as strong as is needed. However, as we will discuss shortly, they must also be realistic and not require more of the client than the situation demands. Unfortunately, some conditions of probation are imposed as a punitive measure rather than because they can contribute to a program of readjustment. Such situations are very difficult for the client to handle, increase already frustrating tensions and often set him up for immediate failure. The conditions of probation should be as simple as can be and still set the appropriate framework for the implementation of needed treatment processes.

The clearer the conditions, the easier it will be to gain compliance. Here, again, we refer back to some of our previous discussion where we pointed out the problem anyone has trying to measure up to standards which are unknown or confusing to him. There *should* be behavioral expectations imposed on the client in those areas where his conduct has been illegal or where certain actions are necessary to help him better cope with social requirements. However, the expectations must not be ambiguous or he will never be able to comply. The client should never be put in a situation where he has to *guess* what the court or the treatment plan requires of him. All expectations should be clearly specified so that neither he nor the probation officer will have questions as to their meaning.

The more meaningful the conditions are to the client, the easier it will be to gain his compliance with them. This meaning relates to individualized considerations, especially as he views them. If he is not convinced that the conditions of probation are relevant to his offense, his personality and his needs, they will have little meaning for him. If they have little meaning for him, he will not be inclined to accept them; therefore, he will be far less willing to comply with them, and the compliance that there is will be superficial, not getting to the roots of his problems. This is not to imply that he must agree with every condition set down or it should be abandoned. As discussed in a previous chapter, it may be necessary for the client to be forced to observe some conditions until he is convinced that they are valid.

The point here is that, in the final analysis, only the client himself can comply with the conditions of probation. If he sees them as irrelevant, it will be difficult for him to comply no matter how he is threatened. One way to help gain his acceptance, support and commitment is to involve him as much as possible in the planning of the conditions.

The more positive the conditions, the easier it will be to gain client compliance. Very few people respond positively to negative proscriptions because we do not seem to want someone to tell us what *not* to do. A *do not* statement seems to stir us to test the limits, whether we are children or adults. Conditions of probation are typically given as a series of "thou shalt not's." This series of negatives often stirs negative reactions in the client. As we have already noted, it is necessary to set and clearly state the limits of behavior expected of the client. But these can be just as well couched in positive as negative terms. This will help to establish a climate of expectation of success rather than failure, because the focus of attention is on areas of client strength rather than weakness. Such a positively oriented approach will help the client to feel he is respected, is being *assisted* rather than dictated to or treated as a child. In turn, this will contribute to his feelings of self-worth and self-confidence and will most likely result in more willing compliance with the conditions of probation.

The more realistic the conditions, the easier it will be to gain compliance. Realistic, as used here, means that the conditions of probation are reasonable in light of what the client has done and how much of a risk he represents. It also means the conditions should be feasible in terms of whether they can be accomplished and whether the facilities and resources needed for their realization are available. There is an implication of enforceability here, too. No term which cannot be enforced should be included in the conditions of probation because unenforceable conditions of probation, like noncompliance which is ignored, tend to dilute the force and undermine the system of justice. This kind of realistic approach may not constitute the ideal in any theoretical sense, but it most closely approximates it when the practical constraints are considered. In reality, when we can reach this, we have done all that can be expected and have probably done that which is realistically effective.

The problem of noncompliance, especially if it grows out of complex, ambiguous, irrelevant, negative or unrealistic conditions of probation, is of more importance and concern now than ever before because of the current trend in legal processes governing actions taken as a result of violation of these conditions. The suggestions given here should help to resolve the problem of noncompliance. It will also be helpful if the probation officer approaches his task with the awareness that the conditions of probation should be specific enough to be clear but flexible enough to be workable, and stringent enough to be felt but not so burdensome as to be discouraging or harmful. He should also remember that those conditions represent a social contract with two-way expectations—the client is expected to comply with the conditions and the probation officer is expected to use his expertise to assist the client in his efforts to live up to expectations.

Chapter Twenty

SHORT-TERM TREATMENT IN PROBATION

THE CENTRAL CONCERN of correctional treatment is the question of how to provide the most effective treatment programs for an individual law breaker within the limitations imposed by legal, economic, political and social restraints. This is at once the major dilemma in corrections and the reality of the situation. Much effort and expertise have been directed toward solving this problem through the years, but no ideal solution has been found. This failure is due to many factors including our lack of knowledge about human behavior, lack of resources to explore potentially effective processes, lack of precise experimental efforts on a coordinated basis and several philosophical differences about how to deal with the criminal offenders.

One of these philosophical problems, as we have already discussed, is that of assuming all criminal behavior is the result of a *sick* personality which needs to be mended if not completely cured. This restructuring of an abnormal personality takes a long time; it can not be rushed because the personality must be rebuilt little by little, in the same way that it becomes warped. Therefore, we place the offender in the hands of correctional workers, both inside and outside of penal institutions, for long periods of time. The rationale here, it seems, is that the longer the "rehabilitation" period, the more likely it is to be permanently successful. Whenever corrections has examined the question of length of sentences, or "treatment periods," the results have usually been to increase the time or, at least, not to decrease it.

In recent years, various types of private social service agencies and some individual psychotherapists have begun to experiment with short-term, or brief, treatment approaches. These efforts have been motivated by such things as high workloads, the dull-

231

ing effects of extended treatment periods, simple lack of time to devote to each client due to the transient nature of the population and the desire to experiment with an approach different from the traditional concepts. There has apparently been little application of these concepts in corrections, especially with adult probationers; most correctional efforts along these lines have been with juveniles or in institutions.

It is the thesis of this chapter that short-term treatment of probation clients is feasible and has potential for considerable success, especially if applied within the concepts of treatment as discussed in this section of this book. In this perspective, short-term treatment is defined as intensive treatment of probation clients for a brief period of time in which specific problems are identified which can be resolved relatively quickly, goals are set within a realistic framework to attain this resolution and plans are carefully laid out as to the steps necessary to reach the goals toward which all treatment is directed. In other words, it is time-limited, problem-identification, goal-directed and well-planned activity with the client in the probation setting. This concept will be expanded and each element discussed in detail.

THE PROBLEM IN PROBATION

Almost everywhere around the country there has been a steady increase in probation caseloads. This is due to many factors including increasing population, a rising crime rate with more offenders processed through the criminal justice system, an expanding acceptance of the use of probation in lieu of incarceration and a growing emphasis on local level correctional efforts as opposed to state level efforts. At least in the foreseeable future these caseloads will not likely diminish, but will continue to grow. Yet, nowhere have probation staffs increased in the same proportions as have caseloads. This situation has led to further dilution of the level of treatment services provided to probation clients; we have attempted to provide "patch-work" treatment to too many clients with too few practitioners.

Increased staff to meet the increasing demands for service, however, is not the answer; it is far too costly and unwieldly, if there were no other reasons. More importantly, there is no solid evidence to support the often repeated assertion that smaller caseloads are the ultimate necessity. What evidence is available tends to show that the emphasis on numbers, per se, is sadly misplaced; because it appears that the basic emphasis in the caseload, client needs, as opposed to size of caseload, and the quality of the relationship which developes between practitioner and client are the factors which make for successful treatment.

This leads one to question the effectiveness of the conventional approach to probation treatment. In most areas, the present imbalance of practitioner-client ratio results in the probation officer providing *crisis supervision;* that is, giving attention to "putting out fires" on the "hot" cases which simply cannot be ignored any longer. The result of this state of affairs is irregular and unplanned contact with the client, a situation which degenerates into total neglect and frequently ends in the client returning to court for a new criminal offense. Where this happens because the probation officer has not been able to adequately perform his function, it represents a failure to fulfill the basic intent of probation philosophy. Critics then point to the "inherent ineffectiveness of such lenient treatment of the offender in granting probation in the first place." Caught up in this spirit of "we knew it wouldn't work" are the public, the police, the courts, the prosecutors and even some probation personnel. Obviously, when no one has confidence in the system and no one really tries to make it effective, it *doesn't* work.

The tradition in all correctional settings, including probation, has been long-term sentences for *treatment* and it has generally been difficult to get legislators, courts and correctional officials to go along with short-term treatment, early release on parole, or short-term probation periods. The length of this *treatment* is related to our traditional philosophy of punishment, because the longer sentence (even probation) is seen as a larger dose of the same good medicine. Besides, crime and criminals are so bad that it takes a long time to deal with the behavior and cure the offender. Such a philosophy loses sight of some of the basic principles of human behavior and of the idea that not every offender needs our brand of *treatment* to restore him to the straight and narrow path of acceptable behavior.

All this means that it is necessary for us to find some effective alternatives to the conventional way of providing treatment to the offender in our probation caseloads. We can not afford the "flying by the seat of one's pants" approach of the past which makes for extreme susceptibility to aimless drifting in the treatment process. We must find better ways of dealing with the client than *crisis supervision* and "putting out the fires." We cannot tolerate deterioration of noble intentions into total neglect. We must focus on the needs of the client and find ways to help him resolve his problems so that he can get on with the business of living a law-abiding and, hopefully, a more productive and satisfying life. The question is, "How can we do it?"

THE PROPOSED TREATMENT PROGRAM

The short-term treatment approach, which has been demonstrated as effective in private social service settings, should be adopted in the probation setting, within certain limitations to be described below, as a means of meeting the challenge to provide effective probation treatment services to an increasing number of clients. The basic concept is to provide realistic, problem identification, goal-directed treatment to probation clients for an intensive but short period of time, followed by a "tapering-off" period in minimum service caseloads.

There will be some modifications of the concept of short-term treatment as it is adapted to the probation setting from that of private social service agencies because there are some basic differences in both the clients and the settings alike. Unlike private social service agency clients, the probation client does not come asking for assistance with his problems; it is not a voluntary treatment situation. This means that there will be considerably more hostility and resistance to treatment which must be overcome, or at least counteracted, before voluntary cooperation can begin. Although this is sometimes difficult to accomplish, it can be done, as we have already discussed. Usually it is a time consuming activity, but may be counterbalanced by the skillful use of another difference between the private social service and the probation settings, namely, the authority position of the probation officer. His counsel and advice are more than merely friendly suggestions, even though he may endeavor to create that impression. Whether he and the client like it or not, his advice is really direction against a backdrop of awesome legal power over the life of the client. If the client does not perform in required ways and make designated modifications in his behavior, the stakes are much greater than merely not getting problems resolved; he is also in danger of losing his freedom. If the probation officer uses his position of legal authority with understanding for the dignity of the individual and in a nonpersonal and firm manner, it can be a very strong positive bond between himself and the client as well as a supportive force for problem solving.

Another important difference between private social service and probation settings is that of general attitudes about the respective clients. As a rule, people feel sympathy for the individual who has had a run of unfortunate and debilitating experiences and support the idea of some agency providing counsel and assistance to help him "get back on his feet." Public attitudes are somewhat different regarding the criminal offender; the prevailing philosophy, even in legal statutes, is that something must be done about the offender, not because he needs assistance to "get back on his feet," but because society needs to be protected from him. This philosophy establishes a different frame of reference for the probation officer dealing with his client. One of the results of this situation, as we have already seen, is the traditional length of the probation period. This is a practice apparently based on the reasoning that the longer the probation period, the greater the punishment; and the greater the punishment, the greater the eventual rehabilitation. Although this is false reasoning, it does have tremendous influence on how offenders are handled in the legal process. The probation officer must contend with this situation and find means to negate its influence and its hindering of the rehabilitative process.

The client of the private social service agency usually has serious problems with which he needs assistance and often has an extensive history of such problems. Many of these clients, however, have considerable strengths with which to work, thereby offering considerably more potential for successful resolving of the specific problem areas. On the contrary, a large proportion of probation clients are found to have fewer basic strengths or other supportive factors, a circumstance which is greatly compounded by his illegal behavior which results in adding to his array of problems. Very often, especially with juveniles, the probation officer gets involved with the client only after other community agencies have given up on him and, as a last resort, "turned him over to the juvenile authorities." Yet all these agencies, parents, schools, youth counseling organizations and even law enforcement, after they have "washed their hands of the matter," expect the probation officer to work overnight miracles with the juvenile. Although no such miracles can be expected, the probation officer must still work with the client; he has no choice of who will be accepted as does the worker of the private social service agency.

This leads to another major difference between such agencies and the probation officer; the limitations and constraints of legal requirements and technicalities. These include such things as no choice over acceptance of clients, others usually make the decision for the probation officer and he must take what he gets, and the problems and consequences inherent in the protection of the client's legal rights from abuse by the "authorities" who, in the thinking of many citizens and appellate judges, want to browbeat him and deprive him of his constitutional rights. The responsibility to protect the public from the client is also a factor here. If a client of a private social agency subsequently injures the community it is not usually reflective of the agency's responsibility or *failure* to rehabilitate him. Indeed, most of the time, no one knows he has even been a client of the agency. On the other hand, if a probationer injures the community, the press usually reports that the offender was on probation and the implication is that the probation officer did not do his job or the new offense would not have occurred. Sometimes this may very well be the case, but the public so often blames the probation officer rather than the probationer. This is true in some instances long after the probation period has been terminated, and the implication is "if you had cured him like you were supposed to do, he would not have gotten sick again." Medical people or workers in private social agencies are not saddled with such unreasonable responsibility. Because the probation officer works in a public agency and is supposed to be a protector of society, he is blamed and the effectiveness of his endeavors is called into question whenever the offender, or former offender, reoffends. Obviously, this creates a much different setting for the probation officer than is true of the private social service worker.

Regardless of the differences in clients and settings, the concept of short-term treatment does offer an effective alternative to the conventional modes of treatment for probation clients. At this point, we must discuss the basic components of the program in some detail. These are tied into the philosophy of probation and the principles of treatment discussed in previous chapters. There will be some overlapping and repetition because of the necessity to discuss the components in sufficient detail to make them clear.

Problem-focused

To be effective, this program must focus on practical problem-solving; not on character rebuilding or personality restructuring, but on behavior change through the resolution of problems which give rise to illegal and/or antisocial conduct. Corrections has for too long been encumbered with the impossible goal of achieving a total *cure* for criminal behavior and bringing the offender to some state of near perfection. This is an illusory and unrealistic goal which has hindered the development of other approaches which are far less idealistic but far more practical and effective in actually changing behavior.

We need to remind ourselves that all criminal behavior is not the same and does not all arise from personality deficiencies which require extensive psychotherapy aimed at restructuring the individual's personality in more "normal" terms. Many criminal behavior problems result from the individual's inability to cope with the very practical problems of everyday existence; an inability often brought on as the result of lack of financial resources, lack of clear understanding of expectations for behavior, lack of intellectual capacity to deal with sophisticated and complex social requirements, lack of personality development and strength to adequately deal with a "world that is too much with us." Instead of striving for a total and permanent cure, corrections should focus on developing methods by which the client is assisted to learn to cope with his situation in more socially accepted, legal and effective ways.

One of the basic elements of this short-term treatment approach is the identification and separation of the client's problems into components small enough for him to handle. This is very important, because society is so complex that no one can cope with its impact unless he routinizes some of its demands, counteracts its influences and simplifies his reactions to it. This reduces the number of complex areas and releases more energy and time to deal with them. Consequently, the client's ability to cope with his situation will be enhanced and the potential for success will be greatly increased.

Living organisms, including the human body, can heal themselves to a remarkable degree when given the opportunity, without stress, to learn to cope with their environment. The real impact of tranquilizers is not to make the professional healer more effective, but to lower the stress and tension level to the point where the body can cope with its environment and, over time, natural restorative processes can complete the task of healing. The human psyche also has restorative powers, and most people are capable of coping with their environment if it is not overwhelming but is of a scope small enough for them to handle. The purpose of helping the probation client to resolve some of his problems is to relieve him of the stress and tension of trying to take on something which is too much for him. It is to reduce the problem areas to manageable proportions so that he is able to cope with them through his own strengths and resources without external assistance.

The problems must, however, be clearly identified, the trouble spots plainly delineated and the real meaning of the problems to the probationer explicitly determined if the probation officer would ever hope to make progress in helping the client learn to cope with his situation. Although some of these problems will be internal and psychological, most will be external and environmental. It is the latter which are of greatest concern to the client, are the most readily recognizable and are usually the simplest to resolve. The probation officer must restrict the focus of treatment to the problems which can be dealt with within the framework of the time, agency facilities, worker abilities and client capabilities which are available to be used as problem-solving resources. He must be sure not to overextend his resources or "bite off more than he can chew," and he must make sure that the client clearly understands what are and what are not the realistic expectations of accomplishment within the limitations imposed by both internal and external considerations.

Goal-directed

Once the problems are identified, goals must be set as to what must be done to result in resolution of the problems. As we have already indicated, these goals must be limited and reachable; limited achievements revolving around the specific problem areas and realistically attainable ends which get to the core of the problems. If the goals are appropriately limited in their scope, the short-term treatment approach can be very effective; if they are grandiose and expansive they will only result in greater frustrations. If the goals are understandable and attainable to the client, this approach can assist him in their realization; if they are beyond his capabilities they will result in disinterest and lack of commitment.

This is a reality-oriented stance in which every effort of both the client and the probation officer is directed toward clearly ascertained ends which are attainable in the foreseeable future, rather than some high-sounding and idealistic but nebulous goals "out there somewhere." This approach is grounded in life as it is, not as one might wish it were. It is the recognition of limitations and influential variables beyond one's control which is counterbalanced by the realization that dealing with one item at a time is not only possible but also gives additional strength and resources to then move on to the next item. It is the piece by piece, block by block, layer by layer method of steadily building a strong structure which will be able to withstand the elements. It is the only way to be sure one eventually arrives at his goal even if he is detoured from time to time on the way.

Whatever happens, neither the probation officer nor the client should lose sight of the goal; and it will probably be necessary for the former to remind the latter of just where they are supposed to be going. Every action, especially major ones, should be viewed in light of the question, "Will it help us toward the goal?" If so, pursue it vigorously; if not, be reluctant to take the action unless it is absolutely necessary. Perhaps the best way to do all this is to write down the objectives in the beginning as they are mutually determined. This will not only help to clearly specify just what the goals are so that everyone understands them, it will also serve to keep them in focus when things get clouded over with disappointments, frustrations, or setbacks.

All this effort toward set goals presupposes that the goals have been carefully determined after analysis of the problems and what is necessary for their resolution. We have already spent some time in discussing this process, so it is sufficient here to simply remind us that without a carefully considered analysis of the problems any goal set will be haphazard, uncertain and not too apt to be reached; or if it is reached, not likely to contribute very much to the resolution of the basic problems.

Planned

In this area, too, we have already commented on the tasks of the probation officer and the client, so we will not belabor the point. In order to fit this element into the overall perspective, however, it must be observed that many probation clients come from a background which gives them a *here-and-now* orientation that is often quite different from the experiences of the probation officer. Most of them are not accustomed to foregoing present needs, pleasures, desires, or opportunities in order to gain greater benefits in the future, an orientation likely to be basic in the probation officer's attitudes. Many of the offenses committed by probation clients are impulsive and geared to immediate self-gratification; therefore when they do find themselves in a position to seek assistance, their concern is likely to be for immediate relief, even though temporary, from the acute pressures of the situation.

This setting demands that the probation officer direct his and the client's attention to very specific and concrete *here-and-now* actions which can contribute to the resolution of basic problems. When it is necessary to get this specific, there must be careful planning of each step that will be taken because slight deviation now will eventually lead one far wide of the goal. This kind of planning really constitutes a diagram of the specific steps to be taken, one by one and in sequence, to reach the goals established to resolve the problems identified. It is the development of a plan of action which enables one to steadfastly remain on course no matter what happens.

This sort of planning is necessary to prevent the principals involved in the treatment programs from wandering in all directions, rather than moving step by step toward a goal. It will help to prevent a useless going around in circles which expends a lot of time and energy but which gets nowhere. Yet, for all the specific planning he may do, the probation officer must also remain flexible in his thinking so that he can make quick adjustments of plans and actions if needed. Plans should be based on careful analysis of problems and determination of goals, and should be laid out in reasonable detail before the treatment program is implemented. Yet, enough flexible contingency should be built in to allow for adjustments demanded by the *up and down* nature of life.

This emphasis on the present, on limited but attainable goals, on specific and concrete plans and actions, all of which are familiar and understandable to the probation client, are necessary to gaining his commitment in working toward the goals. He is not likely to be enticed or even threatened into efforts whose purpose and ends he does not fully comprehend as somehow being to his advantage. Like most of us, he wants to know where he is going, or where someone is leading him, before he exerts great effort to get there. He also wants to know that getting there will result in benefits to him. The problem-focused, goal-directed, and planned approach outlined here will provide this understanding to him and will come closer to gaining his cooperation in the attainment of the goals.

Timely

Considerable experience and some research have shown that the most crucial period for the probationer is that immediately following his appearance in court at the time he is placed on probation. This is a difficult time for him and if he can make it "over the hump" of the first several months adjustment period, the prognosis for success is greatly enhanced. The impact of his recent court appearance, the relief of not losing his freedom, an awareness of either strained or supportive family relationships, embarrassment over his circumstances, perhaps a new sense of shortcoming and other situational factors all contribute to the creation of an atmosphere in which the community often has its most favorable opportunity for the rehabilitation of the offender.

The kinds of changes in one's life which may occur in the crisis of arrest, trial and sentencing can be the trigger for the motivation to try new ways of dealing with life. At this time of susceptibility to influences heretofore ignored, the individual going through the crisis can often be assisted toward resocialization because his motivation to change his life style may be at a peak. Not to begin immediately to work with such an individual toward the resolution of the problems contributing to his crisis situation is to miss the possible golden opportunity to get through to him. Thus the probation officer should make every effort to begin his work with his client the moment he leaves the courtroom in order to make the most of the opportunity. This immediate involvement in setting goals and working toward the resolution of problems is an essential component of the short-term treatment concept. Since the time is short, there is no time to be wasted.

Time-limited

Limiting the span of time over which treatment is carried on is, by definition, an intrinsic part of the short-term treatment concept for a very simple reason: it is not the length but the quality and ultimate effectiveness of treatment which are crucial. Quality and effectiveness are not necessarily equated with length. The general consensus among experienced correctional workers is that the problems of many correctional clients can be resolved in relatively short periods of time because those problems are situational and do not require lengthy psychotherapy. Thus, short-term treatment is not second rate treatment. So long as quality is maintained, it can be very effective; if quality deteriorates, treatment of any length of time is useless.

The idea of time-limited treatment is not to merely reduce the period of time treatment is provided, but to make the time limits an intrinsic part of the treatment process. The time limits put pressure on both the probation officer and the client to get moving and keep moving in efforts to resolve problems: "We only have a brief period of time to do this job, so let's get down to business now, cut through all the unnecessary folderol and focus on problem-solving actions." This is consistent with the philosophy of probation and the principles of treatment already discussed; and because it is treatment under the pressure of a limited amount of time, there is less "playing it by ear" and more solid dealing with problems in a realistic way. This sort of specific and planned dealing with concrete situations in recognition that the time allowed is brief makes goal-setting and goal-directed activity all the more crucial. The process is designed to more quickly mobilize both the probation officer and the client to intensively work toward the goals set, thus resulting in more positive and permanent results.

Another advantage of the time-limited treatment approach is that neither the probation officer nor the client are as likely to be drawn away from the goals to deal with problems or issues which do not really interfere with the client's ability to cope with his situation. Besides, these side issues may be of a sort beyond the expertise of the probation officer to handle and may result in stirring up other issues which are better left alone. The concentration on a few of the most basic, influential and realistic problems will avoid the kind of dilution of effort which renders such activity ineffective. Sometimes extended treatment of this sort results in loss of previous gains because of *overkill*.

Much of correctional treatment is based on an interpersonal relationship between the probation officer and the client which should lend dignity, stability and reality to the problem-solving attempt. It doesn't always work this way because sometimes two people just cannot seem to work together. Because they both have human failings and feelings, extended treatment may result in negative relations simply because they get tired of one another. This destroys the relationship in terms of positive future contributions to problem solving and may even nullify what has already been gained.

Short-term treatment helps to avoid fostering the kind of dependency which often characterizes extended treatment efforts. This is a particular danger where the philosophy of the worker is to do *for, to,* or *on behalf* of the client, an all too common attitude in correctional processes. Over an extended period of contacts with the worker and reliance on him and his resources in this frame of reference, it is difficult for any but the strongest clients not to become dependent. Such dependency defeats the aim of probation philosophy, which is to help the client learn to cope with life's problems and resolve them without being overly dependent on someone else to do for him or resorting to illegal behavior.

The "other side of the coin" is the situation in which the probation officer meets his own personal psychological needs by having others dependent on him. This gives him a sense of power because someone cannot get along without the good things he has to offer. Such a situation is just as harmful, perhaps even more so, than having the client dependent on the worker because it demeans and weakens what should be one of the client's strongest links to the world of reality and independent action. Nothing but tragedy can result from the situation where the probation officer tries to manipulate the client to fit his own personal requirements rather than to discipline himself to respond to the needs of the client.

The time-limited concept is well suited to the basic casework principle of taking the client where he is and moving at a pace he can handle toward the goals. The directive framework, the sense of urgency and the participation of the client can make the brief treatment approach effective if both the probation officer and the client decide to make time work for, not against, them. Much of its value is a matter of attitude; an attitude which recognizes that "there isn't much time, there is a lot to be done, so we must get moving on it."

Observations on Method

It is crucial, as we have already discussed, that the client be actively involved in the identification of problems, the setting of goals and the activity necessary to gain the goals. This kind of participation will help him to feel that he has not lost all control over his life. Consequently, he will be much more likely to quickly mobilize his own resources to resolve his problems, especially if he is conscious of the limited amount of time available.

Of necessity, due to time-limitations, the approach will be structured in the sense of being well-planned and directive, involving setting of limits of behavior, dealing confrontively with situations as they arise and constantly keeping the goals in mind. At the same time, it is a supportive process which reassures the client in the validity of his efforts, encourages him to action and advises him about technicalities with which he is not familiar. This approach takes note of and respects the strengths which the client possesses and builds on them as natural foundation for development. It should quickly cut through superficial facades and get to the solid assets of the client as the most logical and effective beginning point.

Continuous appraisal of the progress toward the goals set will be necessary to avoid being led off on tangents, getting mired down in detail, or getting lost in the maze of treatment possibilities; all of which lead to *dead-end treatment*. This appraisal should be accompanied by an air of optimism and expectancy, which is contagious and serves to increase the determination and effort of both the client and the probation officer in bringing all their combined resources to bear on resolving the problems involved.

THE PARTICIPANTS

The short-term treatment approach as outlined here will not be the ultimate answer for all probation clients nor for all probation officers. Yet its simple and practical processes are easily understood, can be implemented without great complications and offer potential success for a large proportion of both clients and officers. The important question, then, is just what kind of probation client is best suited to this treatment modality and just what sort of probation officer can make best use of it?

The Probationers

Research studies in short-term treatment in private social service agencies demonstrate that proper selection of clients is an essential element in the effectiveness of the approach. The selection was related both to the projected goals of treatment and characteristics of the clients. We have already discussed the projection of goals in terms of their relation to the problems to be solved, the understanding and agreement of the client that the goal is appropriate and the realities of setting goals that are reachable. Let us limit our present discussion to the selection of appropriate clients.

The short-term treatment approach is best suited to and most likely to be effective with clients who will admit that they do have problems which contributed to their illegal behavior. Many probation clients tend to project their troubles to others and to blame other people, events and legal processes for their ills. Of course, these things may make the situation worse for him, but the problems of his behavior basically lie within himself. In short-term treatment the limited time available demands immediate recognition of and responsibility for one's own problem behavior. It also requires a willingness to deal with those problems. The client must be motivated to accept the assistance offered by the probation officer and to exert his own effort to bring about change of behavior which is necessary to help him avoid further conflict in his community. This motivation must come from within the client, although it may be the result of the application of *coercive casework* by the probation officer.

Another client characteristic which is essential is some degree of intelligent insight into his own situation. He must at least be able to see and understand the consequences of his behavior in terms of how the community reacts to his violations of the law and how his behavior got him into his current circumstances. There are many people who are aware that things are not going well for them, but they do not seem to be able to see that their own conduct and other basic problems are the causes of such difficult living. The client who can best take advantage of short-term treatment is one who can look at himself and his situation and understand the relationship between what he has done and the consequences of that action. The corollary characteristic is to take responsibility for one's behavior and to grasp the necessity of change in that behavior so as to avoid further social and legal conflict because of it.

The client also needs to have some reasonable degree of environmental support. Unless he is strong enough to overcome the lack of such support, a circumstance which is quite unlikely for many probation clients, the limited-time span will probably not contribute to successful treatment. It usually takes a lot of time to bring about serious changes in one's environment or to develop sufficient change in the individual to enable him to cope with an environment which offers no real support for his efforts. Unfortunately, most people, lawbreakers and otherwise, cannot make it entirely on their own in our complex and rootless modern society; all of us need the help and support of others. In many respects, the probation client, often merely because he occupies that particular status, has even more working against him; therefore he probably needs assistance that many others do not need. Failure to recognize this and to account for environmental support in the selection of clients for short-term treatment is to invite frustration and failure which not only negates treatment efforts but may also hinder any other attempt at learning to cope with his life.

The Practitioner

Not all probation officers will feel comfortable with the short-term approach to treatment because their philosophy of what probation is all about is not in agreement with the philosophy of probation suggested in this book. Some probation officers are psychologically oriented in their belief that probation casework should focus on bringing about sufficient personality change to enable the client to ideally cope with the world around him; this would obviously require extended periods of psychotherapy. The stand taken in this book is that such extensive psychotherapy is not the job of the probation officer. His function is to work with the client to bring about change in behavior; after all, it is behavior that is illegal, not personality structure. The practitioner who subscribes to the extensive personality change position would not see the value in a time-limited approach to practical problem-solving.

He would also be likely to have to contend with stumbling blocks created by his assessment of the nature of the client's needs as being rooted in a *disturbed personality*. His fear would then naturally be that the time-limited approach would be grossly inadequate to meet these needs of the client. In this case he would not only be uncommitted to the concept, he would also be reluctant to even give it a try. If he does not believe the approach will work, it won't, because he will not really be trying to make it work. It is easy enough to find needs in almost any client that will require extended treatment, if that is what the practitioner wants to find. When he makes such an analysis and suggests it to the client, and the client passively agrees that this is an acceptable plan, the practitioner is likely to take the client's acceptance as an overt expression of the needs. It may be, however, that the client is only accepting what the *expert* tells him and does not see his needs in the same light, but is too timid to disagree. Of course, this gets the entire treatment process off to a very unproductive start and it is the logical consequence of the "I know what is best for you" philosophy.

The time-limited treatment approach is not easy on the probation officer; it requires a great deal of concentrated planning, it takes a lot of energy and it creates a lot of pressure. Yet, it is a very challenging alternative because it is an opportunity to quickly see the practical results of one's efforts, something that *people helping* does not often provide. The approach is challenging also because it concentrates a lot of effort in one circumstance, causing the practitioner to call on all his ingenuity and resources to bring about realization of the goals which have been established. It thus offers job satisfaction which one finds quite different from the frustrations of long, drawn-out treatment processes where the frustrations and failures seem to be far more numerous than the rewards and successes. In turn, this sort of satisfaction should spur one on to greater efforts, help to intensify the contagious atmosphere of enthusiasm and expectation and contribute to future successes. But, of course, the probation officer would never experience this aspect of short-term treatment if he never tries it.

The practitioner who engages in time-limited treatment needs special skills in order to be effective because events are moving so rapidly. He needs self-discipline, personal restraint, mature personal adjustment, sound professional knowledge and sensitivity to the needs and feelings of others; traits which should be characteristic of any good probation officer. In addition, he needs the ability to quickly recognize positive strengths on which to build, to readily focus on conflict areas and to make instantaneous but sound judgments and decisions. He must be able to readily establish rapport with the client, be flexible to adapt to rapid change and fast movement and have the courage to act on intuitive understanding.

Fortunately, one does not have to be born with all these important characteristics; if so, most of us would come up lacking. They can be developed to the point where they are integral parts of the overall ability of the practitioner which are applied to a situation almost without conscious thought. It takes patient striving to get to this point, but the possibilities which are then opened up are exciting and rewarding.

THE PAYOFFS

The short-term treatment approach is not a magic formula to solve all the problems of probation officers and their clients. It is but one alternative among many which can be adapted by some practitioners to some situations. But it does have some important payoffs for the client, the probation officer and the agency. Some of these payoffs are psychic, some are practical, and some are economic; they are all very worthwhile.

The time-limited approach provides the client and the probation officer an opportunity to quickly see the results of particular actions, allowing for immediate corrections if mistakes have been made. This permits adjustments which can bring about successful experiences quickly, enabling the client to build self-confidence and a sense of responsible accomplishment. These attitudes, in turn, create an atmosphere in which to bring about more successes. The "other side of the coin" is seen in some studies of short-term treatment which indicate that when it does not immediately achieve its goals, there is less feeling of failure than in extended treatment. Apparently, both client and practitioner feel that not as much has been invested, so not as much has been lost.

Another payoff is of the "ever widening circle" variety. A small success or bit of progress in a specific area, especially in a brief period of time, can set in motion a chain reaction which may move from one problem area to another, bringing about change which was not contemplated in the initial goal setting or treatment planning. The client may discover resources and strengths that he did not realize he possessed; the probation officer may find effective techniques where least expected. As one problem area is brought under control or resolved it will likely release client energies and attention to focus on the resolution of other problem areas. Once positive change begins to occur, there is no predicting where it might lead.

A very practical payoff, especially from the viewpoint of agency administrators, is that through the short-term treatment approach, more intensive treatment can be provided to more clients over the long-run than can conventional extended treatment processes. When this thought is coupled with that of proper selection of clients to whom time-limited treatment is provided, it has important implications for the effective delivery of quality probation services to a growing clientele. This gets at the very heart of a major problem in the field, namely, how to provide the most effective service to the greatest number of people with the limited resources available.

There is also a payoff in cost-effectiveness. This is not to imply that we can put a price tag on solutions to human problems, but rather to show the practical values of short-term treatment. Such a consideration is necessary in order to rationally allocate available resources to best advantage. Evidence has shown that short-term treatment is just as effective (usually more effective) than extended treatment. Assuming even equal effectiveness, the cost in time and money is much less. Whatever is saved can be utilized elsewhere in agency programs or, if short-term treatment is expanded, intensive services can be provided to more clients with no increase in costs or staff.

The short-term treatment approach offers sufficient potential for success for enough clients that every probation agency should implement it on as wide a scale as is feasible within the framework of staff resources and client needs.

Chapter Twenty-One

HOW TO EXTEND YOURSELF

I_T SEEMS THERE IS NEVER_ a dearth of clients for probation officers. No matter what new approaches are developed or what
practices are changed, there are more than enough clients to go
around. The probation officer usually has so much to do that he
never gets it all done; things, and people, and clients, and events
keep piling in on him so that "daylight" is always a long way off.
This can get to be a very frustrating burden which sometimes
leads to both physical and mental exhaustion from overwork,
loss of enthusiasm for the task and subsequent mediocrity of
work, or simply giving up and moving on to some other career.

Typically, the probation officer has times when he feels overwhelmed by the size of his workload, the complexity of his
duties and/or the vital importance of his task. He needs to find
effective ways of doing more or covering a greater portion of his
responsibilities in the same amount of time. Since he cannot usually hope to do everything, he must establish priorities for *first
things first* and be well organized in the use of his time, energy
and other resources. Short-term treatment has already been presented as one method by which the probation officer can extend
himself to more adequately cover a larger proportion of the
workload. There are also other ways in which he can accomplish
the same end, but they require the use of good judgment to
know where to draw the line between what he must do himself
and what he can share with others. This chapter addresses itself
to some of the ways in which the probation officer can extend
the reach of his activity in providing services for his clients.

USE OF THE GROUP-WORK APPROACH

Group-work has been an integral part of correctional practice
for a long time, especially in institutional settings where it
seemed to reach its peak several years ago. Although the traditional one-to-one counseling relationship has been the preferred

technique in probation activity, group work has been used very successfully in many situations in different parts of the country. Unfortunately, it has been seen by some as the panacea for corrections and has thus been used indiscriminately by many untrained probation officers and with any and all types of clients. One result has been that irreparable damage has been done to some clients who were not ready for the experience or should never have been subjected to it. Consequently, group work has gained an unfavorable image in some quarters and is thus downgraded as a correctional counseling tool.

The truth is somewhere between the *panacea* and the *tarnished image* poles. Group counseling can be a most useful technique if employed by a skilled leader and if the clients who participate are properly selected. These two factors are crucial and deserve some further explanation as does the concept and purpose of group work in corrections. The discussion will not be intensive because there are many books on the subject which can be consulted for detailed study. Here, we will only highlight some of the more important general considerations for probation officers in becoming oriented to the use of group work as a method to extend his activity.

Group work, as used in the probation setting, is not a substitute for the individual counseling relationship between the probation officer and the client. Rather, it is a supplement to the one-to-one approach for two reasons: not every client should be included in a group; and the group is not likely to be able to deal with every client problem, some can only be resolved by the probation officer and the client working together outside any group situation. The group process can, however, complement individual counseling because some clients and problems can best be dealt with in a broader setting.

The purpose of group counseling, as envisioned here, is to help the offender learn to satisfactorily adjust to his social environment by beginning on a small scale in an accepting atmosphere. This process is not to deal with serious emotional problems of clients; that should be left to experienced psychotherapists and probably to individual therapy. The group should deal with the here-and-now problems of behavior and attitude of the client as revealed in the group meeting itself as well as in the everyday life of the individual. This is best done through an exploratory discussion process as the group deals with those topics which arise out of its interaction or which are placed on the agenda because they are important to social adjustment. The topics may deal with individual value systems, standards of conduct, attitudes toward others and toward oneself, feelings of frustration when facing an unaccepting world, daily events and various problems of social adjustment, or many other themes applicable to the needs of the group and the individual participants.

The basic idea of group work is to help the individual more clearly see himself and his world and to give him some practice in dealing with both in an atmosphere which is accepting of trial and error efforts in the learning process. When he has learned new ways of behaving in the group, he can then begin to transfer these into the larger world where he has had problems. Because of his group success experiences, he can be more confident and effective in coping with and adjusting to the larger world.

The group approach offers some important advantages in providing effective treatment for probation clients in addition to the economic consideration of reaching more people in the same period of time and with the same staff resources. One of these advantages has to do with capitalizing on the individual's need for group identity as part of his self-concept, and channeling this need toward positive and wholesome relationships in a setting designed to support lawful behavior. The probation officer can thus help the individual to build on the group experience to strengthen his self-concept as well as his ability to cope with his surroundings in the larger society.

The *we* feeling and the positive impact it can have on the participant's self-concept is further enhanced by his recognition, through group processes, that he is not so different from others, but that they share many of his own problems. He learns that others have similar feelings, expectations and frustrations concerning life in general and their legal problems in particular. Under skilled leadership, the entire group can explore these commonalities and begin to work through problem areas while building on present strengths. This is done in a mutually accepting, supportive and *trying-it-out* atmosphere which is often less threatening than the traditional one-to-one authority relationship between probation officer and client.

In this regard, it may be noted that many probation clients have a background of conflict with authority figures which tends to deter, if not negate, some of the efforts of the probation officer, himself an authority figure. The group setting may provide the atmosphere where the expression of different opinions by group members can be tolerated and understood in contrast to the traditional probation officer-client situation where the authority relationship may hinder communication and acceptance. Many probation clients will more willingly accept confrontation and correction from a group of peers than from the probation officer who represents the authority of the establishment against which they have so long rebelled.

Another advantage of the group approach is that it gives each participant numerous opportunities to contribute to the resolution of others' problems as well as gain their contributions to the resolution of his own. Many times the knowledge that he has been able to provide help to someone else can strengthen an individual's feeling of self-worth and his ability to help himself. The group experience provides this possibility in a way that cannot be done by the one-to-one counseling approach.

There are some disadvantages in group work against which the probation officer must guard. Some of the more important include the possibility that group counseling often may be very shallow in content, a situation which can create additional frustrations. In some cases in which group members are well acquainted with one another, they may not participate honestly and thereby defeat the very purpose of the group. This leads to another disadvantage to group work, namely, the impossibility of guaranteeing confidentiality, without which group members will be unlikely to participate at all. The group leader must also guard against stronger and more aggressive group members attacking and destroying weaker members. It is this situation which has been the most important factor in making group work suspect as a valid and effective correctional counseling tool.

Selection of group participants is a very crucial consideration, both to the effectiveness of the group process generally and to the impact the group has on the specific individual. Not every probation client can handle the stresses of group participation; some are so nonverbal that a problem discussion approach would be meaningless to them because they would not be able to participate. These may prefer the quieter, less stressful and more private one-to-one method of trying to discover and resolve problems. On the other hand, some clients would feel very awkward dealing with the probation officer directly where it's just "him and me." These clients may come to life in the more impersonal group setting and thus be able to handle the authority relationship more successfully.

The individual with fairly strong tendencies toward group identification will be able to speak more freely than the *lone wolf* who is content to go his own way. The outgoing and gregarious client is more likely to respond to group processes than is the withdrawn individual, although including him in the group may be the best way to draw him out of himself. The person who likes to get involved with others in working on projects or solving problems will likely fit more easily into a group than will the person who feels uncomfortable around others.

It is important to remember that there are no hard and fast rules for who should be included in a group. The client who may, on the surface, appear to have the traits which would make group participation difficult, may very well be the one most helped by the group experience if handled properly. The probation officer must be very careful to select only those group participants who will not be damaged by the experience. There really are no other guidelines which are unchanging.

Just as we can observe that not every client is suitable for inclusion in a group, so we can observe that not every probation officer can easily function as a group leader. To be sure, he can be trained and he can learn group work techniques enough to get by; but if he does not possess certain characteristics and is not sold on the idea of the group approach, he will not likely be very successful. Among these necessary characteristics are the following: understanding the dynamics of the group process, which are different from individual one-to-one dynamics; knowledge of the principles of behavior change in the group setting; power of observation of several persons and events at the same time; ability to verbally communicate simply and clearly; ability to maintain control over the group and its activity, including protection of weak members; and ability to lead the group and move with it rather than to authoritatively order its movement. Other characteristics not so directly related to group work but which are important include: sincerity, integrity, openness, genuine liking for people, ability to listen, patience, stamina and personal emotional control.

Before he initiates a group counseling project, the probation officer should give careful consideration to such things as his own ability to lead a group, choice of clients to include, purposes of the group, its size and how long it will run, the time and place of meetings, rules governing the sessions, questions of confidentiality of discussions, whether participation will be voluntary and whether he will have a co-leader. Perhaps the best way to properly consider all of the ramifications of the group work approach is to read some of the practical and simple works from group counseling authorities and to discuss the proposal in detail with one's supervisor.

USE OF COMMUNITY RESOURCES

Various noncorrectional resources available in almost any community, regardless of its size, can be creatively used by the probation officer to extend the effective scope of services provided to his clients. This, however, requires interest and concern on his part for the broader needs of his clients and a thorough knowledge of what resources are available to be tapped or can be created. This is a responsibility that the probation officer must assume; he cannot expect his clients to be aware that these resources exist, let alone know how to take advantage of them. Yet, because of his position and the contacts it affords, the probation officer should be familiar with community resources and how to utilize them.

The probation officer's ability to provide extended services to his clients will be in direct proportion to the scope of his knowledge of available resources in his community. If he is just starting out, it will take some time and a lot of work to become thoroughly familiar with the various resources and what they have to offer to his clients. If he is not a novice and already knows many of these resources, he will still need to keep alert to learn about new services being developed and about modifications of services of those resources he has been using. Only in this way can he have at his fingertips the information necessary to match client need with available services. There is no excuse for the probation officer not to thoroughly know all the services in his community. This is his responsibility, his duty, because he never knows just when a client will be in need of usual or unusual services which can be provided by some agency or other resource in the community.

In order to make most effective use of these resources the probation officer must do more than simply be aware that they exist. He must also establish a personal liaison with key persons in the various agencies. In this way he can best be kept informed of program changes, has a direct link for referral purposes and is often able to speed up the implementation of service when rapid response is critical. This is not to imply that the probation officer makes personal connections in order to bypass regular agency referral or service procedures. Rather, it is to demonstrate that personal knowledge of these procedures and acquaintance with one or more of the persons responsible for them can provide a ready entree to these services when needed. A contact, perhaps by telephone, between friends or known professional colleagues can be very beneficial for paving the way for a client who usually feels lost when making application for such services. The probation officer, knowing what services are available and what are the referral criteria, can provide information which is helpful, whereas the client, not having the same advantage of knowledge, may not give a complete picture and thereby miss out on the service. In short, there is no substitute for the personal touch when the probation officer has a client who needs the help of some other community resource.

The provision of the best services possible to meet client needs requires the ability on the part of the probation officer to strike a proper balance between the services he can provide and those which other resources make available. In this regard, and as we have already discussed, the probation officer must be realistically aware of his own limitations in terms of expertise, resources and time. He must know what he can expect to be able to provide and what he cannot provide. He must understand that he is to do all he can and, if more is needed to provide adequate service to the client, he must then ask for help from other sources. Striking this proper balance requires that he know when he has reached the point where he must refer his client to some other resource; and this point, of course, varies with each client according to his needs and with each probation officer according to his ability and resources.

The idea is for the probation officer to make use of available community resources to provide the services that he cannot provide due to expertise, specialization, facilities, or time. Thus he might refer a youngster to the Big Brothers or Big Sisters organizations when he is in need of companionship and guidance which are so time consuming that the probation officer cannot possibly meet the youngster's needs. A youth might be referred to the Scouts in order to help provide needed exposure to wholesome youth activities which has been lacking. A young probation client might be referred to some other community resource which can provide meaningful adult contact and influence in his life. An emotionally disturbed adult might be referred to a community resource with facilities to provide psychotherapy to deal with his problems. The list of possibilities is endless because the list of client needs is endless and because it often takes only a simple action, if it is the right one at the right time, to meet many of these needs. The probation officer with a little imagination can often find the necessary resource in unlikely places if he is knowledgeable of both client need and community resources and he is ever alert to make use of all the help he can get.

Sometimes the probation officer finds himself unable to meet a particular client need and unable to locate any community resource to help. In such a situation, as we have already discussed, he will have to work with other interested parties to create new and needed services in the community. This is not always an easy or quick accomplishment; but it is part of his overall responsibility to assist the offender in the resolution of his problems, especially those which brought him into conflict with the legal behavioral norms of the community.

USE OF PARAPROFESSIONALS AND VOLUNTEERS

Although there are differences between paraprofessional and volunteer aides, they are similar in many ways, especially in that they both can provide very valuable assistance to the probation officer in extending his efforts on behalf of meeting clients' needs; therefore, the two groups of aides are considered in conjunction. A great deal has been written in the last few years about the services which can be provided by both paraprofessionals and volunteers. Neither are new ideas in our society but both have gained new prominence in the field of corrections in recent years and are in active service in many parts of the country. Our discussion here will be brief; only enough to show how they may be helpful to the probation officer in extending services to his clients. For additional and more detailed discussions, the reader is urged to peruse some of the books and articles on the subject elsewhere.

There are some distinctions between paraprofessionals and volunteers which often make a difference in the way they are perceived by the probation officer and the client. The paraprofessional does get paid for his work and is, therefore, able to provide more time on a regular basis to assist the professional probation officer. In addition, the position is sometimes a training ground for a future professional career. The volunteer, on the other hand, does not get paid, often works full time at another career job and so has limited time to give to his volunteer tasks. Consequently, the two groups have been used differently in correctional agencies and have often been blended into the work of the professional staff in such a way as to greatly enhance and expand the level and scope of services provided to correctional clients.

The paraprofessional aide can work with and under the direction of the probation officer who is responsible for the client to accomplish some of the important functions which do not require the same level of training and expertise as do some of the counseling functions. This is not to imply that the tasks assigned to the aide are only the routine, unrewarding, or unsatisfying ones. If this is the case, his performance will eventually become practically useless because the work is not meaningful to him. Yet there are many daily tasks that do not require extensive training and experience which are responsible and can be fulfilling. Some of the activity involved in gathering data for the pre-sentence report can be of this sort, as can some of the record-keeping functions of the probation officer's task. The aide can assist in some of the interviewing, especially to provide a different perspective for evaluation of the client, and can even do some of the preliminary interviewing alone.

Paraprofessional aides can be very helpful in the development of contacts with prospective employers to whom probation clients may be referred for jobs. The aide can follow through on the referral and do a lot of job coaching for the client to help him improve his skills at job seeking. These tasks do not require extensive counseling expertise and their performance by a paraprofessional aide frees the probation officer to give more time to other pressing professional responsibilities.

Although the paraprofessional aide does a lot of the "leg work" involved in many of the duties of the probation officer, he should not be considered as a second-class worker. Within the scope of his assigned functions, which should be satisfying to him and meaningful to the overall client-helping process, he should be considered as a responsible assistant whose time and effort are vital to the total work of the probation officer.

Sometimes, these paraprofessional aides are themselves probation clients or ex-clients. If this is the case, they must be selected with great care and wisdom to avoid possible conflicts of responsibility as a probationer and as an aide. These are quite distinct roles and areas of responsibility and can cause a great deal of trouble if they are not kept separate. But even where the idea of paraprofessional is not involved, the probation officer can often make use of one probationer in his caseload to assist another. For example, employment is often a problem and many clients are in need of jobs. The probation officer might be able to have one client, who is employed and may have the necessary contacts and influence, to help another client get a job. Many probation officers have found that excellent therapy for one client is to get involved in helping someone else. This enables the probation officer to extend the range and scope of services provided his clients.

One of the best and least costly ways for the probation officer to extend himself is through the use of volunteers. Citizen volunteers are probably the most underdeveloped, and potentially the most powerful, resource available in corrections today. Of course, there is little, if any, scientific data to prove the effectiveness of volunteers as a correctional strategy, but a long history of volunteerism in this country attests to the ability of the citizenry to get the job done when such energy can be tapped. Because of the way in which our culture has developed, especially the professional correctional practitioner's position, many probation clients seem to be able to relate easier to a volunteer, one who is not being paid to work, than to the probation officer whose job it is to deal with the client. There seems to be an added attraction to the arguments of someone who is there because he wants to be over those of the person who is there because it is his job, no matter how sincere the latter is. The history of success of religious groups, Scouts, Big Brother/Sister, senior citizens groups, and many others demonstrate that the volunteer can be an effective and potent force in a wide variety of activities.

Working with and under the direction of the probation officer, the volunteer can relieve him of some of his routine duties so that he is able to give more time and energy to professional duties that he alone can perform. Thus, in the long run, all his clients benefit from the volunteer's efforts either directly or indirectly. Like the paraprofessional, however, the tasks assigned to the volunteer must be meaningful and challenging to him or he is likely to become bored, lose interest and drop out of the effort. It might be more difficult to provide these meaningful challenges for the volunteer than for the paraprofessional aide because of the difference in amount of time to invest and mere availability at the right moment. However, the imaginative probation officer who appreciates the service of the volunteer and who works closely with him in developing programs will have little difficulty providing a challenge, if for no other reason, simply because there are so many different people needing help at various times.

Perhaps one of the greatest services the volunteer can provide is to engage in the time-consuming supportive relationships which many probation clients need, and with which the probation officer is frequently overburdened. He can also be of great assistance in informally monitoring the behavior and performance of the client in the community. In this process, however, there is always the danger of complicating the flow of communications between the probation officer and the client because a "middleman" is added. This is particularly crucial because the probation officer alone has the ultimate responsibility for the outcome of the case and is the only one who must answer to the community for his effectiveness. If the "middleman" would avoid the creation of communication problems between client and probation officer, he must be careful to keep the probation officer informed of what goes on with the client.

In addition to providing immense assistance to the probation officer in his work, use of volunteers has an even greater overall benefit: it gets more private citizens involved in the correctional process, thereby creating greater understanding for the problems and needs of corrections. In turn, this is likely to result in more intensive and broader based community support for corrections generally and probation specifically.

Conclusion

EQUAL TO THE CHALLENGE

THE INTENT OF THIS BOOK, as noted in the Preface, was to be of some practical help to the probation officer in his everyday work. It is hoped that this objective has been attained and that the comments have also been challenging to the practitioner, whether he is a newcomer or a veteran. If this is the case, even with a few readers, the effort will have been worthwhile.

The tone of the comments is not meant to imply that the probation officer as described herein is the perfect embodiment of the ideal practitioner. The description of professional probation practice of the preceding pages is not unanimously accepted by everyone in the field; in fact, some would probably take very strong exception to some of the thoughts presented here. The author has no quarrel with this; he does not expect everyone to agree with him. And, by this time, the reader should have become aware that we do not believe it is possible to attain such an ideal; yet the ideal must in some way be envisioned and every practitioner should be striving to reach it. This book does make it clear that this striving is not an easy task. It requires a sincere dedication to the concept and use of probation as a viable means of dealing with law violators. It calls for professional integrity and alertness to make the most of every opportunity to improve one's ability to do his job as nearly like the ideal as is humanly possible for him.

Part of the backdrop against which the issues in this book have been developed is the basic question of individual accountability of performance. The legal, social, professional and moral overtones of this question have arisen and have been addressed at various points throughout the preceding pages. There is one other thought to which we now turn our attention for it ties together individual accountability and the challenge to strive for the ideal. It has to do with establishing responsibility for probation clients who are not "successful" throughout the probation process.

The usual question asked when probation clients "do not make it" and are subsequently reprocessed through the criminal justice system is, "What did he do (or not do) to cause the failure?" The probation officer should be asking, instead, "What did I do (or not do) to contribute to the failure?" Of course, client failure is not all or always the fault of the probation officer, but we must never overlook the possibility that his failure to do his job properly may very well contribute to client failure. We have not traditionally considered this aspect of success-failure rates in probation, but we should do so regularly. This approach is consistent with the thrust of this book dealing with the professional responsibility of the probation officer to give his very best to his task. Asking the question will also be an important factor in the probation officer's efforts to hold himself accountable for the quality of his performance.

Throughout this book there has been an emphasis on this quality of performance and the professional practitioner's accountability for it. The challenge presented here is not an easy one by any means, but meeting that challenge has possibilities of helpful contributions to one's community and personal job satisfaction, the depths of which we have not even begun to explore.

The challenge is there! Are we equal to it?

BIBLIOGRAPHY

PART ONE: PHILOSOPHY

General

American Bar Association: *Standards Relating to Probation*. New York, ABA, 1970.

Annals of American Academy of Political and Social Science, *381: The Future of Corrections*. Philadelphia, The Academy, 1969.

Chute, Charles L., Bell, Marjorie: *Crime, Courts, and Probation*. New York, Macmillan, 1956.

Clegg, Reed K.: *Probation and Parole: Principles and Practices*. Springfield, Thomas, 1964.

Commission on Law Enforcement and Administration of Justice: *Task Force Report: Corrections*. Washington, U.S. Government, 1967.

Cooper, H. H. A.: Toward a rational doctrine of rehabilitation. *Crime and Delinquency, 19:*228, 1973.

Dressler, David: *Practice and Theory of Probation and Parole, 2nd ed.* New York, Columbia, 1969.

Goldberg, W. A.: *Adult Probation in the United States, 1968.* New York, NCCD, 1968.

Johnston, Norman, Savitz, Leonard, and Wolfgang, Marvin E. (Eds.): *The Sociology of Punishment and Correction.* New York, Wiley, 1970.

Kay, Barbara, and Vedder, Clyde B.: *Probation and Parole.* Springfield, Thomas, 1963.

National Council on Crime and Delinquency: *Standards and Guides for Adult Probation.* New York, NCCD, 1962.

Newman, Charles L.: *Sourcebook on Probation, Parole and Pardons.* Springfield, Thomas, 1964.

Philosophy of Probation

Bates, Sanford: When is probation not probation? *Federal Probation, 24:*13, 1960.

Bixby, F. Lowell: Probation is not freedom. *Federal Probation, 26:*47, 1962.

Chandler, Henry P.: Probation and parole officers: the importance of their work. *Federal Probation, 20:*9, 1956.

Czajkoski, Eugene H.: The need for philosophical direction in probation and parole. *Federal Probation, 29:*24, 1965.

Raeburn, Walter: Probation was made for man. *Federal Probation, 22*:16, 1958.

Scarpitti, Frank R., and Stephenson, Richard M.: A study of probation effectiveness. *Journal of Criminal Law, Criminology, and Police Science, 59*:361, 1968.

Functions of the Probation Officer

Gronewold, David H.: The probation officer as a helping person. *Federal Probation, 20*:5, 1956.

Hardman, Dale G.: Functions of the probation officer. *Federal Probation, 24*:3, 1960.

Ives, Jane K.: The essential task of probation-parole officers. *Federal Probation, 26*:38, 1962.

Miles, Arthur P.: The reality of the probation officer's dilemma. *Federal Probation, 29*:18, 1965.

Probation Law

Chappel, Richard A.: Due process of law as it relates to corrections. *Federal Probation, 29*:3, 1965.

Cozart, Reed: Civil rights and the criminal offender. *Federal Probation, 30*:10, 1966.

Fisher, H. Raymond: Parole and probation revocation procedures after Morrissey and Gagnon. *Journal of Criminal Law and Criminology, 65*: 46, 1974.

Holtzoff, Alexander: Duties and rights of probations. *Federal Probation, 21*: 3, 1957.

Holtzoff, Alexander: Criminal law and the probation officer. *Federal Probation, 23*:3, 1959.

Price, William: Due process in corrections. *California Youth Authority Quarterly, 26*:5, 1973.

Rubin, Sol: Legal framework in which probation functions. In *Techniques of Probation*. Boston, Law-Medicine Institute, 1965.

Rubin, Sol: Probation and due process of law. *Crime and Delinquency, 11*: 30, 1965.

PART TWO: PROFESSIONALISM

Probation Officer as a Professional

California Probation, Parole and Correctional Association: *The Practitioner in Corrections*. Sacramento, CPPCA, 1965.

McHugh, Thomas J.: How professional are probation and parole? *Federal Probation, 21*:7, 1957.

Mangrum, Claude T.: In search of professional identity. *California Youth Authority Quarterly, 23*:3, 1970.

Mangrum, Claude T.: The probation department, a client-centered agency. *California Youth Authority Quarterly*, 25:26, 1972.
Stein, Philip: Are probation officers really professionals? *Crime and Delinquency*, 17:296, 1971.

Professional Relationships

Allenstein, Morton B.: The attorney-probation officer relationship. *CPPCA Journal*, 7:25, 1970.
Cayton, Charles E.: Relationship of the probation officer and the defense attorney after Gault. *Federal Probation*, 34:8, 1970. ffi
DeVore, Lloyd L.: Police/probation reciprocal training. *California Youth Authority Quarterly*, 25:36, 1972.
Portman, Sheldon: The defense lawyer's new role in the sentencing process. *Federal Probation*, 34:3, 1970.

Training for Probation Work

Ives, Jane K.: Basic training for probation officers. *Social Casework*, 54:7, 1963.
Ives, Jane K.: The learner in probation work. *Crime and Delinquency*, 11:239, 1965.
Johnson, Kenneth D.: The role of social work education in preparing personnel for the corrections field. *Federal Probation*, 20:54, 1956.
Leeds, Clarence M.: Probation work requires special training. *Federal Probation*, 15:31, 1951.

PART THREE: PERFORMANCE

Investigation and Report Writing

Administrative Office of the United States Courts: *The Presentence Investigation Report*. Washington, U.S. Government, 1965.
Bartoo, Chester H.: Hidden factors in the probation officer's recommendation. *Crime and Delinquency* 9:276, 1963.
Bartoo, Chester H.: Setting forth the adult defendant's previous arrest history in the probation report. *CPPCA Journal*, 1:16, 1964.
California Youth Authority: *Guide for Court Investigations and Reports*. Sacramento, CYA, 1955.
Carter, Robert M.: It is respectfully recommended. *Federal Probation*, 30:38, 1966.
Gunning, Robert: *The Technique of Clear Writing*. New York, McGraw-Hill, 1952.
Keve, Paul W.: *The Probation Officer Investigates*. Minneapolis, U. of Minnesota, 1960.
Keve, Paul W.: Professional character of the presentence report. *Federal Probation*, 26:51, 1962.

Keve, Paul W.: Art of the presentence report. In *Techniques of Probation.* Boston, Law-Medicine Institute, 1965.

Kohut, Nester C.: *The Probation Officer Reports in Court.* Chicago, Family Law Research and Publications, 1966.

Stump, Lawrence M.: Court investigations and reports. *Federal Probation,* 21:9, 1957.

Treger, Harvey: The presentence investigation. *Crime and Delinquency,* 17:316, 1971.

Venezia, Peter S., and Cohn, Alvin W.: *Uniform Probation Reports: A Feasibility Study.* New York, NCCD, 1968.

Zoellner, David: Writing the evaluative section of probation court reports. *CPPCA Journal,* 2:20, 1965.

Interviewing

Bartoo, Chester H.: Interviewing candidates for probation. *Federal Probation,* 25:19, 1961.

Cohn, Yona: Channeling the probation interview. *Crime and Delinquency,* 14:226, 1968.

Garrett, Annette: *Interviewing: Its Principles and Methods, 2nd Edition.* New York, FSAA, 1972.

Halleck, Seymour L.: Initial interview with the offender. *Federal Probation,* 25:23, 1961.

Hartman, Henry L.: Interviewing techniques in probation and parole: Part I. *Federal Probation* 27:(1)14, 1963; Part II, 27:(2)15, 1963; Part III, 27:(3)8, 1963; Part IV, 27:(4)17, 1963.

Treger, Harvey: Meaningful inquiry into lives of offenders. *Crime and Delinquency, 11:249,* 1965.

Wiggins, James W.: Some considerations in interviewing. *Federal Probation,* 23:36, 1959.

Caseload Management

Larson, Lawrence C.: Standards for chronological case recording. *NPPA Journal,* 5:256, 1959.

Miles, Arthur P.: The utility of case records in probation and parole. *Journal of Criminal Law, Criminology, and Police Science,* 56:285, 1965.

Nicholson, Richard C.: Use of prediction in caseload management. *Federal Probation,* 32:54, 1968.

Sumner, Helen: The probation officer and case recording. *NPPA Journal,* 4:139, 1958.

PART FOUR: TREATMENT

General

Gibbons, Don C.: *Changing the Lawbreaker: The Treatment of Delinquents and Criminals.* Englewood Cliffs, Prentice-Hall, 1965.

Glasser, William: *Mental Health or Mental Illness?* New York, Harper & Row, 1960.

Glasser, William: *Reality Therapy.* New York, Harper & Row, 1965.

Klockaro, Carl B. Jr.: A theory of probation supervision. *Journal of Criminal Law, Criminology and Police Science, 63:*550, 1972.

Lehman, Paul E.: The medical model of treatment. *Crime and Delinquency, 18:*204, 1972.

Lytle, Milford B.: The unpromising client. *Crime and Delinquency, 10:* 130, 1964.

McIntosh, John W.: Achieving adjustment through altered attitudes. *Federal Probation, 24:*21, 1960.

Menninger, Karl: *The Crime of Punishment.* New York, Viking, 1968.

Menninger, William C.: The therapy of friendship. *Federal Probation, 21:* 41, 1957.

Newman, Charles L.: Concepts of treatment in probation and parole. *Federal Probation, 25:*11, 1961.

Paludon-Muller, B.: Modern methods of treatment of offenders. *Federal Probation, 36:*36, 1972.

Payak, Bertha J.: Understanding the female offender. *Federal Probation, 27:*7, 1963.

Perlman, Helen Harris: *Social Casework: A Problem Solving Process.* Chicago, U of C, 1957.

Shah, Saleen A.: Changing attitudes and behavior of offenders. *Federal Probation, 27:*20, 1963.

Shah, Saleen A.: Treatment of offenders: some behavioral concepts, principles, approaches. *Federal Probation, 30:*29, 1966.

Sims, Leon J.: Supervision: an opportunity for rehabilitation. *Federal Probation, 26:*37, 1962.

Sygert, Luther M.: Individualized treatment in probation. *Federal Probation, 20:*18, 1956.

Zalba, Serapio R.: A look at correctional treatment. *Federal Probation, 25:* 40, 1961.

Casework in Probation

Arcaya, Jose: The multiple realities inherent in probation counseling. *Federal Probation, 37:*58, 1973.

Berman, Nathan, Purvis, Jack, and Cole, Dorothy: Casework with law violators. *Crime and Delinquency, 7:*137, 1961.

Fike, David F.: Family-focused counseling. *Crime and Delinquency, 14:* 322, 1968.

Glasser, William: Reality therapy. *Crime and Delinquency, 10:*135, 1964.

McCormick, Paul: Transactional analysis: a promising treatment method for corrections. *CPPCA Journal, 1:*18, 1964.

Marcus, Eric H.: The probation officer and Gestalt theory techniques. *CPPCA Journal, 7:*3, 1970.

Overton, Alice: Establishing the relationship. *Crime and Delinquency, 11:* 229, 1965.

Rachin, Richard L.: Reality therapy: helping people help themselves. *Crime and Delinquency, 20:*45, 1974.

Shireman, Charles H.: Casework in probation and parole: some considerations in diagnosis and treatment. *Federal Probation, 27:*51, 1963.

Thorne, Gaylord, Tharp, Roland G., and Wetzel, Ralph J.: Behavior modification techniques: new tools for probation officers. *Federal Probation, 31:*21, 1967.

Constructive Use of Authority

Carter, Robert M.: The "authority problem" revisited. *Federal Probation,* 25:52, 1961.

Fink, Arthur E.: Authority in the correctional process. *Federal Probation* 25:34, 1961.

Hardman, Dale G.: Authority is my job. *NPPA Journal,* 3:215, 1957.

Hardman, Dale G.: Authority in casework—a bread and butter theory. *NPPA Journal,* 5:249, 1959.

Hardman, Dale G.: The constructive use of authority. *Crime and Delinquency,* 6:245, 1960.

Yelaja, Shankar A. (Ed.): *Authority and Socialwork: Concept and Use.* Toronto, U of Toronto, 1971.

Short-Term Treatment

Kerns, Elizabeth: Planned short-term treatment, a new service to adolescents. *Social Casework,* 51:340, 1970.

Krimmel, Herman E., and Falkey, D. Bruce: Short-term treatment of alcoholics. *Social Work,* 7:102, 1962.

Middleman, Ruth, and Seever, Frank: Short-term camping for boys with behavior problems. *Social Work,* 8:88, 1963.

Nebe, Nikolous: Essential elements in short-term treatment. *Social Casework,* 52:377, 1971.

Reid, William J., and Shyne, Ann W.: *Brief and Extended Casework.* New York, Columbia, 1969.

Townsend, Gladys E.: Short-term casework with clients under stress. *Social Casework,* 34:392, 1953.

Williams, Lorraine O'Donnell: Short-term treatment of women: an experiment. *Federal Probation,* 21:42, 1957.

Groupwork in Probation

Crites, M. Mark: Group counseling for probationers and staff. *Crime and Delinquency,* 11:355, 1965.

Elliott, Mabel A.: Group therapy in dealing with juvenile and adult offenders. *Federal Probation* 27:48, 1963.

Geertsma, Robert H.: Group therapy with juvenile probationers and their parents. *Federal Probation, 24:46*, 1960.

Irwin, Olive T.: Group therapy with juvenile probationers. *Federal Probation, 31:57*, 1967.

Mandel, Nathan G., and Parsonage, William H.: An experiment in adult group supervision. *Crime and Delinquency, 11:313*, 1965.

Smith, Alexander B., Berlin, Lavis, and Barsin, Alexander: Group therapy with adult probationers. *Federal Probation, 24:15*, 1960.

Vogt, Herbert: Group counseling in probation. *Federal Probation, 25:49*, 1961.

Vogt, Herbert: An invitation to group counseling. *Federal Probation, 35: 30*, 1971.

Walker, Glenn J.: Group counseling in juvenile probation. *Federal Probation, 23:31*, 1959.

Wall, John Jr., and Ellis, June: Group treatment of adolescent males in a Juvenile Court setting. *Federal Probation, 23:64*, 1959.

Use of Community Resources

Gardner, Eugene J.: Community resources—tools for the correctional agent. *Crime and Delinquency, 19:54*, 1973.

Moeller, H. G.: Corrections and the community: new dimensions. *Federal Probation, 32:25*, 1968.

Para-professionals and Volunteers

Biless, Donald W., Pilcher, William S., and Ryan, Ellen Jo: Use of indigenous nonprofessionals in probation and parole. *Federal Probation, 36:10*, 1972.

Hall, Harvey, and DiGregoro, Beverly: Recruiting professionals as volunteers. *CYA Quarterly, 26:29*, 1973.

Harejsi, Charles R.: Training for the direct-service volunteer in probation. *Federal Probation 37:38*, 1973.

Lee, Robert J.: Volunteer case aid program. *Crime and Delinquency, 14: 331*, 1968.

Leenhouts, Keith J.: Royal Oak's experience with professionals and volunteers in probation. *Federal Probation, 34:45*, 1970.

Schier, Ivan H.: The professional and the volunteer in probation: perspectives on an emerging relationship. *Federal Probation, 34:12*, 1970.

Schwartz, Ira M.: Volunteers and professionals: a team in the correctional process. *Federal Probation, 35:46*, 1971.

Segurdson, Herbert R.: Expanding the role of the nonprofessional. *Crime and Delinquency, 15:420*, 1969.

Terwilliger, Carl: The nonprofessional in corrections. *Crime and Delinquency, 12:277*, 1966.

Unkovic, Charles E., and Davis, Jean Reiman: Volunteers in probation and parole. *Federal Probation, 33:41*, 1969.